Praise for *The Big Book on Borderline*

"Shehrina Rooney has written a deeply c⟨                    ⟩ncour-
aging book about borderline personality disord⟨  ⟩(BPD). This complete
guide will help many individuals diagnosed with BPD and their families.
I'm exceptionally proud to recommend this book to my clients."

—AMANDA L. SMITH, LCSW, author of *The Borderline Personality
Disorder Wellness Planner for Families* and *The Dialectical Behavior Therapy Wellness
Planner*

"A lively and informative book about an often-confusing topic, by
someone who's really been there. Borderline personality disorder is a wide-
spread mental health problem affecting millions of people and their close
family and friends. Everyone needs this information. Shehrina Rooney
presents it in a very personal and yet highly-educational way, including
taking you inside the thinking of someone with BPD and what she had
to learn on the road to recovery. Her story shows that self-management
skills CAN be learned and that there IS hope, despite all the frustrations
and set-backs. Now she's helping others with this disorder, those around
them, and even professionals, to learn what it takes to succeed."

—BILL EDDY, therapist, lawyer and mediator; co-founder High Conflict
Institute; developer of the New Ways for Families skills-training program; author
of *It's All Your Fault! 12 Tips for Managing People Who Blame Others for Everything*

This is the book that the world has been waiting for—a guide that
people with borderline personality disorder have desperately needed, and
this is the book that I feel can save lives, create understanding, and help us
in the fight against stigmatizing this complicated and poorly understood
illness. I tip my hat to Shehrina for being an inspiring trailblazer by
writing an easy-to-read book full of 'aha' moments for people with BPD,
for their loved ones, and for professionals alike. It really is a complete
A-Z guide for all. I'm so excited to promote this book and much a much-
needed change for BPD!

—CORY HANNA, YouTube Channel *The Borderline Life*

"Whether you have borderline personality disorder yourself or have someone in your life who struggles with it, Shehrina Rooney's *Big Book on Borderline Personality Disorder* provides a consumer to consumer comprehensive guide to understanding and coping with a wide range of situations in life created by the disorder. Follow these principles and help yourself or your loved one regulate emotions and take back your life!"

—**JEFF RIGGENBACH**, PhD, President of CBT Institute of OK; author of *The BPD Toolbox: A Practical, Evidence Based Guide to Regulating Intense Emotions*

"I found *The Big Book on Borderline Personality Disorder* accessible, informative and realistic. For a long time now I have thought there should be a book written for people with lived experience that explains BPD in an honest, simple, clear manner. This is the book."

—**KAREN BAILEY,** BPD Carer Advocate, Australia

"*The Big Book on Borderline Personality Disorder* is a good mixture of personal experience and self-help. It is full of information on borderline personality disorder (BPD), aimed at people with the disorder, or those wanting to find out about it. It is easy-to-read and offers useful self-help techniques and advice for both sufferers and loved ones. People with traits of BPD might recognize many things about themselves that they had not previously understood. This book is a one-stop-shop for education and inspiration for those living with BPD and those who love them. Shehrina insightfully explains her diagnosis and the diagnosis of many, making the behaviors of the disorder understandable, and goes a step further providing practical applications of daily skills for recovering, even creating her own 10 steps of recovery."

—**FREDERIC BIEN,** President, Personality Disorder Awareness Network, www.pdan.org

# THE BIG BOOK ON
# BORDERLINE PERSONALITY DISORDER

## SHEHRINA ROONEY

UNHOOKED BOOKS
An Imprint of High Conflict Institute Press
Scottsdale, Arizona

Copyright © 2018 by Shehrina Rooney
Unhooked Books, LLC
7701 E. Indian School Rd., Ste. F
Scottsdale, AZ 85251
www.unhookedbooks.com

ISBN: 978-1-936268-61-0
eISBN: 978-1-950057-00-9
Library of Congress Control Number: 2018961768

Cover design by Julian Leon, The Missive
Interior layout by Jeffrey Fuller

*Printed in the United States of America*

# A NOTE OF CAUTION TO THE READER

This book provides information about a serious mental health disorder. The information provided is intended to help you be more educated and aware of borderline personality disorder. Knowledge is power. However, this information can also be misused. Therefore, we caution you not to publicly label people who may or may not be diagnosed with this disorder, nor to use this information as a weapon. Before you go further, we ask that you make a commitment to use this information with caution, compassion, and respect. You are advised to seek the advice of a professional like a therapist or other mental health professional when warranted. The author and publisher are not responsible for any decisions or actions you take as a result of reading this book.

• • • • •

Throughout this book I have chosen to reference the DSM-IV-TR (the Diagnostic and Statistical Manual of Mental Disorders, Fourth Edition) instead of the more recent DSM-5. I have nothing against the DSM-5, but when I was first diagnosed, and throughout my recovery, it was the DSM-IV-TR that I turned to when trying to understand my disorder. I found its structure easy to understand, and it helped me make sense of why I was the way that I was. (My YouTube videos are also based on the DSM-IV-TR.)

# DEDICATION

*I dedicate this book to my Mum, the most amazing woman I know, and to my children who fill my heart with love, joy and gratitude every single day.*

# CONTENTS

# INTRODUCTION

*"The butterfly goes through a period of darkness
before it grows its wings and flies."*
*—Deborah Stamp*


Chances are, you bought this book for one of the following reasons:
A. You have borderline personality disorder, think you may
have BPD, or believe that you have some of the BPD traits
but not enough for a diagnosis.
B. You have a loved one or know someone who suffers with BPD.
C. You are a medical professional or student in the field of mental
health.

If you are in category A, I hope that while reading this you have
plenty of aha moments. I want you to:
* Gain a better understanding of yourself
* Become more self-aware and learn to recognize the BPD
symptoms in day-to-day life
* Know that it is not your fault
* Finally start to see some light at the end of the tunnel
* Learn some helpful skills that you can put into practice today
* Start to take back control of your life

If you are in category B, I hope you will:
* Gain a better understanding of your loved one
* Understand that it is neither their fault nor yours
* Understand how to cope in times of crisis
* Learn some skills that can help *you*

If you are in category C, I want to:
- Give you an insight into someone living with BPD rather than just a textbook version
- Help you to understand that people with BPD can be very different from one another
- Present you with living proof that this disorder can be managed with the right treatment

If you happen to be someone who doesn't fall into any of the categories above, I thank you for buying this book simply to educate yourself about something that is greatly misunderstood by the masses. It is with enormous thanks to people like yourself that, together, we can help smash the stigma.

So who am I and why did I write this book?

My story begins on a cold and miserable day in November 2015. As I sit in front of my laptop, I contemplate abandoning my idea all together. Am I really willing to disclose my deepest, darkest secrets to the world? What will people say? What will people think? As far back as I can remember, I have concealed my true self with a mask that I unconsciously wear. Am I truly prepared to drop the facade and reveal the real me? The good, the bad, and the downright ugly? There is a lot of ugly.

I sit staring at the screen in front of me, my heart pounding, my stomach in my throat, conjuring every excuse I can imagine to justify discarding my plan. This could benefit so many people...or it might go so terribly wrong. Am I being brave? Or am I being incredibly stupid? Only time will tell. I take a deep breath in, breathe out slowly, and, with my hand trembling, I hit the button. My video goes public.

For those of you who know me, I want to thank you for buying my book. For those of you who don't know me, I thank you also—and may I introduce myself to you?

My name is Shehrina and my YouTube channel is Recovery Mum. I consider it important to inform you that I am not a qualified or trained medical professional in the field of mental health. I do believe, however, that I am more than qualified to write this book for you, for I am experienced up to the eyeballs—and then some.

I have spent many harrowing years of my life wanting to die. I refer to this time as the Dark Years. Unfortunately, the Dark Years spanned more than half my lifetime—an awfully long time for someone to wish they were dead. Those who knew me as a child would have considered me to be happy and confident, while inside I was anything but. From an incredibly early age, I struggled with anxiety and a compelling fear that those I loved most would abandon me. When my teenage years hit, I transformed from a seemingly cheerful but cheeky child into an intolerable and angry monster, regularly throwing tantrums that would put any two-year-old to shame.

I was not your typical grumpy teenager merely overloaded with hormones, but one with an intense self-hate and a penetrating anger toward those closest to me. That deep-seated anger soon turned inward, and I began self-harming. My insecurities continued to grow, and by age sixteen I was caught in the grips of an eating disorder and regularly turning to alcohol to help solve my problems. When the alcohol stopped doing the trick, I turned to drugs. By the time I was twenty, I was both a drug addict and an alcoholic, and my mental health was deteriorating at a rapid speed.

I was diagnosed with anxiety and depression and subscribed pills, none of which helped. Eventually I hit my first rock bottom, no longer wanting to go on living this painful life. I attempted suicide, the first of many attempts, some of which were very nearly successful. At twenty-one I went to live as an inpatient on a mental health ward. I can't even express how utterly terrified I was, but by spending time on the ward and being observed, I was finally given the diagnosis of BPD. This was my first milestone on the road to recovery, although it would be many years before I would be anywhere near recovered.

I was twenty-five when I had the opportunity to start a dialectical behavior therapy (DBT) course. DBT helped me in so many ways, and I saw some major improvements in my life. But the drug and alcohol abuse, bulimia, and self-harming continued.

Pregnant with my first child in 2008, I was taken off a lot of my medications. I quickly fell into a deep depression—one that sunk even deeper after the birth.

Two years later and with my second child only a couple of months old, I discovered that the person I had trusted most in the world—my husband—had betrayed my trust. For people with BPD, this is one of our biggest fears. When it happened to me, I felt my world had ended. I turned to drink and drugs to numb my pain. The following two years are a blur—they were spent in a drug-induced haze and alcoholic stupor, crying uncontrollably daily.

I had two beautiful children and my wonderful stepson who lived with us, yet I still attempted suicide in order to shut down my uncontrollable emotions. These were the most painful years of my life, the Dark-Dark Years. I look back in amazement and wonder how I got through them in one piece. Someone once said to me that their biggest success had been that their suicide attempt was unsuccessful. This echoes exactly how I feel today.

It was these Dark-Dark Years that led me to begin a stint in rehab that lasted seven long months. Relapse unfortunately followed, as well as a divorce, relocation, a pregnancy that involved social services, my children coming back to live with me, and learning to become a mum all over again, only this time to three children. Emotionally I was in tatters, yet for the first time in my life I could see some light at the end of the tunnel. I was attending 12-step meetings for my addiction and was back under a superb mental health team.

By attending 12-step meetings and watching the power of one addict helping another, a seed was sown. What if I could achieve the same result within the world of BPD?

Which brings me to that day in 2015 when I first posted a video on YouTube. I could never ever have anticipated the overwhelming response that I received. I never envisaged that I would have my eyes so widely opened to this disorder. For many years I had felt so different and so alone—I had no idea that there is a whole world of people out there just like myself. It has taken me more than thirty years to find my tribe, but we have found each other and for that I am forever thankful.

Since that first video went public I have had my fourth (and final) child, and I've continued posting videos weekly. Today, I am happy and free from the shackles of my emotions. Today, I can be a wonderful mum, daughter, sister, partner, and friend. So why did little old me decide to put pen to paper? As I have just mentioned, the response I have had on YouTube has been amazing, and yet there is a bitter-sweetness to it. I am overjoyed that I have managed to reach and engage so many people all over the world, and yet I feel a deep sadness that I can no longer reply to everyone's messages. And then I had an epiphany. I *could* answer everyone's questions—within a book. I know the burning questions that you have, because they've already been asked. I know what interests you, because they've already been shared with me. Communication between myself and my wonderful and loyal subscribers has led me to feel confident that I can write a book that contains everything you need and want to know about BPD, no matter who you are or what your circumstances.

Now, my lovelies, let us begin our journey of acceptance, understanding, and hope, for with these three things you are equipped with the primary tools to get you on the road toward the light at the end of the tunnel—where knowledge, healing, and freedom await you in abundance.

With all my love,
Shehrina
a.k.a. Recovery Mum

PART I

# THE BASICS

Chapter 1

# FOR THE
# NEWLY DIAGNOSED

*"Stars can't shine without darkness."*
D. H. Sidebottom

The day that we get the diagnosis of borderline personality disorder is a day filled with contradicting feelings, from relief to fear, anxiety to hope. We feel relief because up until this point, we usually think of ourselves as bad people, not knowing why we behave the way we do. We finally have a name for what causes our suffering and realize that there isn't something fundamentally wrong with us—we have an actual illness.

Getting our diagnosis is crucial because it is a step on our road to recovery. Once we know what is wrong with us we can then look into treatment options; we can learn about the disorder and become self-aware. As daunting as it first feels, getting diagnosed is actually a good thing. We are not evil people with no morals; we are people suffering with illness that is beyond our control at this point.

What usually follows getting a diagnosis of BPD is a need for understanding. What exactly is borderline personality disorder? We go online in an attempt to learn about the disorder, taking in as much information as we can, trying to digest it all. Fear, anger, and hopelessness may swiftly follow; we read that our behaviors push people away and we wreak havoc in relationships, we are manipulative and evil, we make terrible parents and there is no cure. The sheer volume of both inaccurate and highly stigmatized and misleading information out there is astounding. It is therefore no surprise that we are often left feeling even more helpless than we had been prior to our diagnosis.

While looking for information on BPD we must be wary of the sites that we visit and understand that, although people have opinions on BPD, their opinions are simply that: an opinion that does not equate to fact. When newly diagnosed, we are vulnerable, so it is imperative that we protect ourselves as much as possible. This includes being careful when seeking out information about this disorder. If we come across a site that speaks negatively about BPD, our best bet is to turn away from it. We already know that our behaviors hurt others; we do not need reminders of that as soon as we are diagnosed. Now is the time to understand *why* we behave in the way that we do and the reasons behind our actions.

It is important to know that while there is no cure for BPD, this disorder *can* be managed. It is *not* a life sentence. We can learn to manage the symptoms so well that if we were to go for a diagnosis at a later date, we would not get diagnosed with BPD, as we wouldn't meet the criteria. There are more treatments available for BPD now than there ever have been, and we are living in a time when it is more understood than ever before.

Once diagnosed, we can finally move forward and start focusing on our recovery and the amazing life that lies ahead of us. Within this book you have a wealth of information on BPD, including the ten steps of recovery. So sit back and get reading. Your journey has begun.

Chapter 2

# PERSONALITY AND THE BRAIN

*"I think, therefore I am."*
—Descartes

This is an extremely important chapter for me to include in my book. I am somebody who needs to know the what, why, where, and how of everything. It was never enough for me to just accept that I have this debilitating disorder without questioning everything about it. The problem with mental health is that it centers in the mind—in other words, people who have a personality disorder tend to either forget they have it or outright disbelieve it is even a thing. But the mind, the brain, is a real thing. It's our very own control center, determining how we behave, think, and feel—the very things that make up our personalities. There are numerous definitions of what makes a personality, but for the sake of this book I am going to keep things as simple as possible.

In order for us to understand what a personality disorder is, we must first look at what constitutes a healthy personality. Why do some people manage to think, feel, and behave in a socially appropriate way and others do not? Why do we even have a personality? What is its purpose?

I am going to take us back 200,000 years when the first Homo sapiens (that's you and I) appeared. Life here on Earth was unrecognizable to the Earth that we know today. Imagine yourself and a handful of others being picked up and placed in the middle of a jungle, with no clothes, no home, no car, no phone—with absolutely nothing—just your body, your brain, and your fellow people. How would you survive? This is exactly what our very first ancestors had to do: live in the wild, hunted by predators while also hunting for their own survival—and they did survive, for if they hadn't, you and I would not be here today.

Back when our prehistoric ancestors lived, it was imperative for the survival of the human race that we stick together in "packs." A single human out on their own did not stand much of a chance against a hungry predator. Working together as a "tribe" enabled us to defend ourselves from attack, thus ensuring our survival. And this is where our personalities came in.

In order to survive, we needed personalities that enabled us to build intimate relationships with others (for reproduction purposes) and to work well as part of a team (for protection, among other things).

Human beings have always been social creatures. We want to feel included, we want to feel part of. Rejection and exclusion do not feel good—and they are not supposed to. Rejection and exclusion are the very things that risk our demise (at least 200,000 years ago they did). A person with a healthy personality is able to socialize with others, to build close relationships and seek companionship. Somebody with a healthy personality may not always see eye to eye with everybody, but they are able to navigate their way through life and overcome social obstacles. Not every single person thinks, feels, and behaves the same—even those with healthy personalities. Human beings are all unique, and culturally we can differ immensely, but people with healthy personalities are able to build relationships with others within their culture and generally get on with those around them.

Unfortunately, this is not the case for those of us with personality disorders. Our personality—the very thing that is supposed to help us connect well with others—seems to work against us and do the exact opposite of its intended purpose. It is as if our personality is malfunctioning. We feel and think in such a way that causes us to behave in a manner that alienates us from our fellows and that causes destruction in both our lives and the lives of those around us.

To understand why and how we think, feel, and behave the way we do, we need to delve into the three-pound jelly-like blob that is our brain. I am not a neuroscientist (as you can probably guess from my brain description); in fact, I am not medically trained in any capacity. But my thirst for knowledge has allowed me to gain a basic insight into how this entity that resides in our skull works. I am going to share with you the information that I have learned over the years, from reading books to watching videos on this subject. The brain is a truly magnificent mechanism, and the human brain in particular is pretty remarkable. In this chapter I will discuss the workings of a typical brain; in the next chapter I will focus on the brain of somebody with borderline personality disorder.

Let's start by discussing two brain structures: the limbic system and the prefrontal cortex. I'll also go over neural pathways and neural plasticity (no, it does not mean our brain is made of plastic!).

### The Limbic System

The limbic system, one of the most primitive parts of our brain, is a set of structures (we have two, one on each side) that are responsible for our emotions and our motivations, which are there for our survival.

The limbic system can itself be broken down into different parts. I will focus on three parts of the limbic system: the amygdala, the hippocampus, and the hypothalamus.

### The Amygdala

The amygdala is like an emotion processor. Sensory data goes in, the amygdala processes it, decides what needs to happen next, and outputs the information to a different part of our brain to initiate the relevant behavioral response. In simple terms, the amygdala detects a threat and sounds the alarm. It is most commonly associated with fear, as well as anxiety, anger, and violence. It is the most primitive part of our brain, and it works without us even being conscious of it doing so. When we are born, our amygdala is fully formed.

### The Hippocampus

The hippocampus (which is shaped like a seahorse) is mainly responsible for converting short-term memories into long-term memories. While creating the long-term memories, the hippocampus will combine the memory with an emotional response before transferring it to the long-term memory "box."

So imagine back to when you were a small child. A song is played and your mother and father are dancing happily while listening to the song. You feel happy and content while watching your parents laughing and smiling. Your hippocampus takes that short-term memory and stores it alongside your positive emotion, then transfers it to your long-term memory. When that same song is played years or decades later, a positive feeling is triggered.

Now imagine a different scenario: You are a child sitting in a car and a song comes on the radio. Your mother and father are screaming at one another while you are watching from the back seat gripped with fear. The memory of this song and the emotion of fear are then stored together in your long-term memory. If you hear that song as an adult, the amygdala will respond accordingly, with fear.

### The Hypothalamus

This structure is responsible for regulating our autonomic nervous system (ANS). The ANS controls things such as our blood pressure, heart rate, respiratory rate (breathing), digestion, urination, and sexual arousal in response to emotional stimuli. For example, if the emotion of fear is triggered in us, it is our hypothalamus that sets off our fight-or-flight response. Our blood starts pumping harder, our heart rate increases, digestion slows down—all preparing our body to respond to the threat. Our ANS will release hormones such as adrenaline (the fight-or-flight hormone), which will in turn lead to cortisol (the stress hormone) being released into our bloodstream.

### The Prefrontal Cortex

This is the part of our brain that differentiates us from other animals. Humans have the largest cerebral cortex of all animals, and it is this area of our brain that is responsible for thinking, reasoning, and logic. It is also the newest part of our brain in the evolution of mankind, and it is not fully developed until early adulthood. Our prefrontal cortex has the power to override our basic instincts—in other words, our limbic system. If we feel a strong emotion, it is our prefrontal cortex that will jump in and stop us from acting impulsively on it.

### Brain Plasticity

Brain plasticity, known as neuroplasticity to the professionals, simply means that brains can change. There was a time when it was believed that brains, once wired up, stay that way—a fixed entity. The thinking was that a personality someone developed by the time they were twenty would be the personality that they would have for the rest of their lives. It is now known that this is not the case. Brain plasticity is the brain's ability to transform throughout our life. It is ever changing—no matter how old or young you may be. Every day of our life, new connections are made in our brain, new neural pathways can be formed or older ones can be made stronger. Likewise, neural pathways can also be weakened or disappear entirely. Our brain literally never stops changing. For a disorder like borderline personality disorder, this is an extremely important point, especially in regard to recovery. Why? Because BPD is a brain disorder.

### Neural Pathways

These are basically pathways or "roads" that transfer information from one part of the brain to another. Every time we try something new we create a new neural pathway. Habits are formed when those regular pathways are transformed into "super pathways." So, for example, you are feeling bad and you eat some chocolate—a pathway is built. In the future, when you feel bad you know that you can eat chocolate to make yourself feel better. The more you do this, the more "super" that pathway becomes. It eventually becomes an unconscious choice to take this path—you just take it. Obviously there are other, healthier things that can also make you feel good—but the pathway to feel good via chocolate is the pathway with least resistance, since you've done it so many times—so you automatically do it again.

Imagine walking in a forest where nobody has ever walked before. You walk left through the overgrown undergrowth. The route you have taken now has a small but obvious pathway. If you were to turn around and walk back over that same pathway it would become even more obvious. If you carried on walking up and down this same path it would become a path that is very easy to walk down. This is exactly what happens in our brain. The more we do something, the easier it becomes to do it. Likewise, if we were to stop using that path in the forest and start taking a new route, the old path would eventually become overgrown again and the path would disappear, making it harder to walk down.

The brain is so much more complex than I could even begin to explain to you (not because you wouldn't understand it but because I don't!), but hopefully understanding a few of the basic structures and how they work will enable you to comprehend my next chapter.

Chapter 3

# BORDERLINE PERSONALITY DISORDER

*"Nature loads the gun, environment pulls the trigger."*
—Unknown

B orderline personality disorder is a severe mental health condition. The term "borderline personality disorder" was first coined when it was widely believed that those with this disorder sat on the edge between neurosis and psychosis. Huge leaps have been made in recent years that have replaced outdated myths with factual evidence. I have hope that one day the old and dated term "BPD" will be renamed with the more realistic and true-to-form title of "emotion dysregulation disorder."

Borderline personality disorder is characterized by the inability to regulate emotions. Inability. It is not a choice. People with this disorder are unable to control the intensity of their moods, therefore causing the sufferer to experience extreme and fast-changing moods, along with volatile relationships, to name just a couple of the symptoms. This inability to regulate emotions resides in the brain.

So, again, we are going to look at the workings of the brain—this time the brain of those with BPD. Someone with this disorder has a brain that differs from that of the general population, a fact that medical science has now proven with the use of brain scans. While research is still in its infancy, clear differences in some of the structures proves that borderline personality disorder is a brain disorder.

### The Amygdala

The most primitive part of our brain, the amygdala is responsible for detecting threats and regulating emotions and behaviors such as fear and aggression (which 200,000 years ago was vital for our survival). Brain scans have shown that those with borderline personality disorder have a considerably smaller amygdala than the rest of the general population. It is unknown why the amygdala is smaller and whether it was like this from birth or has undergone atrophy (deteriorated). The smaller the amygdala is, the more overactive it is. Those with BPD experience extremely intense emotions, meaning that our amygdala has taken over and the emotions we are experiencing are out of our control.

### The Hippocampus

Brain scans have shown that the hippocampus in those with BPD is dysfunctional. It misinterprets threats and it sends flawed messages back to the amygdala.

### The Hypothalamus

In those of us with BPD, the hypothalamus is in a constant state of hyperarousal. Studies have shown that those suffering with BPD have abnormally high levels of cortisol (the stress hormone) in their bloodstream (Jogems-Kosterman et al. 2008). High levels of cortisol literally eat away at different parts of the brain, eroding them. Parts affected by this include the amygdala, hippocampus, and prefrontal cortex (Redmayne 2015). This could also suggest why many people with BPD also suffer with their memory—the hippocampus, one of the parts that is eroded by cortisol, has the main responsibility of converting short-term memories into long-term memories.

### The Prefrontal Cortex

As we know from chapter 2, this is the part of our brain that is responsible for reason, logic, and thinking. It is the prefrontal cortex that can prevent us from getting ourselves into trouble. Imagine you are at work and have just spent the past week working tirelessly on a really important document. You have finally completed it and are extremely proud of your work. You hand it to your boss, who takes one look at it, tells you it's awful, and throws it in the bin. What do you do? Your limbic system (emotional brain) is screaming out for you to punch your boss or throw something hard across the room. *But* your prefrontal cortex steps in and stops this from happening. The voice of reason tells you that there will be consequences if you punch your boss. It makes you stop and think before you act.

Brain scans have shown that the prefrontal cortex of those of us with BPD is both inactive and inefficient (Ruocco, A. C., S. Amirthavasagam, L. W. Choi-Kain, S. F. McMain. 2013). This would explain the impulsiveness commonly displayed in this disorder, resulting in us repeatedly acting without any thought of the consequences and the inability to think rationally.

Now I am not sharing this information with you to use as a get-out clause for this disorder. I do not want anyone to think, "Well, it's not my fault, so I don't need to do anything about it." The fact is, although living with borderline personality disorder is extremely painful and soul destroying, and it is not our fault that we have it, this does not mean that we cannot do something about it. Remember brain plasticity? We have the power to change our brain.

**What Is Borderline Personality Disorder?**

This disorder can be summed up as the inability to regulate our emotions, although this does not in any way express the true severity of it.

For many years those in the mental health profession feared working with BPD patients due to the seriousness of the disorder. We were extremely difficult patients to treat, with a suicide rate of 10 percent and a very poor recovery rate. But that was then and this is now. It is now proven that this is a disorder that *can* be managed with the right treatment.

So what *exactly* is this disorder and how does it present itself in people? This is a difficult question to answer, as there is no one definitive answer. There are nine symptoms listed in the DSM-IV-TR (*Diag-*

*nostic and Statistical Manual of Mental Health Disorders, Fourth Edition,* produced by the American Psychiatric Association and used by professionals to diagnose mental health disorders). The DSM-V lists them a little differently. For somebody to receive a diagnosis of BPD they must display at least five out of the nine traits to meet the diagnostic criteria. That means there are 256 possible combinations of traits or symptoms, which is a huge number. Yet, in spite of this, there is still a typical BPD stereotype, which I will discuss later in this chapter.

Let us first take a look at the nine symptoms in the DSM-IV-TR:
1. Frantic efforts to avoid real or imagined abandonment
2. Unstable personal relationships
3. Distorted and unstable self-image
4. Impulsive behavior
5. Self-harming behavior including suicidal attempts
6. Extreme mood swings
7. Chronic feelings of emptiness
8. Explosive anger
9. Feeling suspicious, out of touch with reality

It is important to know that the same traits can also present differently in different people. As an example, take two people with BPD who both present with the fear of abandonment. Person A may hold on to a relationship for dear life, becoming jealous and obsessive. Person B, on the other hand, may avoid intimacy and close relationships, coming across as quite cold and uncaring.

The main characteristics of borderline personality disorder displayed externally tend to be: unstable relationships, extreme mood shifts, impulsive behaviors (including self-harm), and intense anger. That said, there are people with BPD who do not exhibit symptoms to the outside world.

## Quiet BPD and the BPD Spectrum

There are those of us with BPD who either manage to function quite well in day-to-day life, seem to function well but are in fact not coping at all, or cannot function at all.

People on the lowest part of the BPD spectrum are unable to live life day by day and struggle with every area in their life. At the top of the spectrum are those who are "high functioning." These people may be able to hold down a job but struggle with intimate relationships. They are unlikely to get a diagnosis of BPD due to the fact that the traits are not causing them enough problems for them to seek help. Due to this some medical professionals and members of the general public argue that there is no spectrum, for if someone is high functioning they can't possibly have BPD.

Most of us with BPD agree that there are times in our life—sometimes days, sometimes weeks or months—when we are able to function fairly well. During these times we often question whether the BPD has disappeared—only for it to resurface with a bang and relegate us to the very bottom of the spectrum. I therefore believe that those of us with BPD can move up and down the spectrum rather than remain at the same fixed point all of the time.

There are also those of us with BPD who do not suffer from violent rages and unstable relationships. Instead, we may internalize our anger. When we feel angry we are far more likely to retreat to our room, isolate, and self-harm than have a full-blown eruption in front of our loved ones. Those of us who tend to internalize things can be referred to as having "quiet BPD." The traits are still the same but rather than being externalized they are internalized. Rather than turning the anger on others, we turn it on ourselves. Those of us who internalize our BPD are harder to diagnose due to the fact that BPD is often associated with huge external displays. The loved ones of those with quiet BPD do not truly see what is going on, as it is often kept private. Work colleagues may have no idea that we are struggling on a day-to-day basis. Family members may only have an inkling.

We also find that many BPD symptoms can interweave with one another. As an example, here is the thought process of one person with BPD:

*I hate myself and do not even know who I am (trait 3), so I don't know why anybody would want to stay with me (trait 1). I become obsessive over my partner (trait 2) and start acting out by doing things like using drugs (trait 4). I start thinking my partner is cheating on me and have intrusive thoughts about all the things he has done behind my back (trait 9). When I next see him I explode over the tiniest thing (trait 8), and when he walks out I turn the anger on myself (trait 5).*

It is almost as if one symptom can trigger another and so on.

## The BPD Stereotype

BPD might just be the most stigmatized mental health condition. The popular stereotype of someone with BPD is just one of the contributions to the huge stigma. When people hear the words "borderline personality disorder" a couple of things may happen:

- They stare vacantly, as they have never heard of it (ridiculous considering this disorder affects more people than schizophrenia and bipolar!)
- The stereotypical image pops into their mind and their expression is a mixture of disgust and dread

So what does this stereotype look like? Why do we have a stereotype and how does this contribute to the stigma that already envelopes BPD?

The typical BPD stereotype tends to be female even though this disorder also affects men. She is seen an attention seeker, a manipulator and due to her dishonesty, must not be trusted. Some may describe her as a black widow who lures men in with her overtly sexual nature, only to attack and cause harms once she is done with them. She is often described as a drama queen, violent, psychopathic, anti-social, crazy and an unlikeable trouble-maker. In order to explain the stereotype further, I want to paint a couple of pictures. Both stories include the same female, but the first is an external representation—how the outside world perceives her. The second portrayal is from the woman's point of view.

### Story 1—An Outsider's Perspective

*Mia is a 21-twenty-one-year-old female. She is outgoing and confident, and some would even say overtly sexual, always on the lookout for a new man. One Saturday night she meets Toby. They are both smitten with each other and the relationship moves at an alarming rate. It is not long before they are living together. Mia seems to change, though. She becomes very controlling, and if Toby doesn't do as she wishes she will stop at nothing to force him to listen to her. Manipulation, attention seeking, even violence start becoming the norm. Toby loves her but cannot deal with her intense rage. He tries to leave a few times, but she blackmails him to stay with her, threatening to kill herself if he leaves. He feels trapped. His friends call her a "psycho" and tell him to get out while he can. One day he returns home and finds she has left, disappeared without even a goodbye. He hears through the grapevine that Mia has met somebody else and is really happy. He doesn't understand how a girl who had told him repeatedly that she loved him so much could do this. His friends think she did him a favor and that he had a lucky escape. "That is the problem with these sorts of girls," they say, "They will chew you up and spit you out as if you mean nothing to them. They are cold and callous and do not care about the damage and destruction they leave in their path. If anyone comes across someone with this disorder, run!"*

The problem with this portrayal is that it only looks at the behaviors of the person with BPD. Their thoughts and feelings do not come into it—and why should they? The outside world cannot read minds or understand how somebody else is feeling. Yet, it is this omission that leads to the negative stereotype that is prevalent in the general population. This misunderstanding, or seeing only part of the picture, can be very damaging. To stamp out this portrayal, educating people on this subject is key.

Let's now look at the story from Mia's point of view.

### Story 2—An Insider's Perspective

*My name is Mia and I am twenty-one. To my friends I come across as confident, but that is because I have gotten in the habit of wearing a mask, not a real mask, an imaginary one that I can put on and then be-come whoever I want to be. For I want to be anyone but me. I don't even really know who I am anymore, let alone like myself. Then I met Toby. He was everything I could have ever dreamed of and was so nice to me. When I was with him I felt as if I was whole for the first time in my life. We were so in love. We decided to move in together and it was wonderful. Life seemed perfect for a short time—until Toby wanted to start seeing his friends more often. I don't understand why he would want to see them when we are so happy when it is just the two of us. One night he said he was going out and we had a huge row. The panic I felt inside at the thought of him leaving me to see his friends was excruciating. I know what men are like when they go out. He would probably meet someone else and never come home. I screamed at him and threatened to leave him if he went out. He tried to calm me down and I attacked him, hitting and scratching his face. He stayed in with me that night. I felt bad but I just don't know what I would have done if he had gone. I literally can't deal with the pain I feel. The following Friday he called me after work to say he was going for drinks after work with his colleagues. I felt as if I had been punched in the stomach, I wanted to throw up. I hung up the phone, and when I tried to call him back he wouldn't answer. I know that something is going on between him and that slut in his office. I started swigging out of the vodka bottle and smashing up the flat. How could he do this to me? When the vodka stopped numbing my pain, I cut my arms for some kind of relief from my emotional pain. When Toby came home he said that I cut myself to spite him, and he walked out. I over-dosed and ended up in hospital. When I got home everything went back to normal between us—except I am now living with constant thoughts of Toby cheating on me. I try calling him multiple times a day, and if he doesn't pick up the phone I feel so helpless and desperate. I feel as if he hates me and is just biding his time before he leaves. One day it all becomes too much. I pack my bags and leave before he comes home from work. I have decided I cannot live like this anymore, with us constantly hurting one another. I don't tell him where I am going and I change my phone number. I feel such anger toward him and never want to set eyes on him again, because just looking at him causes me pain.*

From this story we start to get a more truthful representation of BPD. This disorder is so much more complex than just our behaviors. It is not simply a case of violence, manipulation, and jealousy—it is about survival. Our behaviors, although often self-destructive, are our way of coping with the chaos going on in our head. They are our way of surviving in a world that seems determined to destroy us.

Various factors contribute to the stigma of BPD besides our behaviors. Possibly the chief culprit is the label "borderline personality disorder." Borderline. As mentioned previously, this name was first created due to the belief that the disorder lay on the border between neurosis (anxiety, obsession, etc.) and psychosis (losing touch with reality). Over the years the word "borderline" has come to suggest that this is a disorder *bordering* on being a mental health disorder. Considering the devastation this disorder causes not only to the sufferer but also to those around them, it seems implausible that even the mere suggestion that it is not quite a mental health disorder is absurd. I personally believe the term "borderline" stemmed from the fact that our emotions sat on the borderline between "okay" and "I want to die." The name has so many different connotations, and for this reason the disorder is extremely misunderstood.

Another factor that influences the way people view us is, unfortunately, the mental health professionals themselves. Obviously there are many professionals who bend over backward to help us; some even make it their life's ambition to understand and treat those with BPD. Sadly, however, there are the minority who continue to add fuel to the stigma. I have often sat there open-mouthed while reading messages from my subscribers.

"My psychologist says there is nothing they can do for me."

"My psychologist said I am too old for therapy." (This comment was made by someone in their thirties.)

"My doctor said it would be pointless to refer me for therapy."

These are just a few of the messages I have been sent. Pretty shocking. It comes as no surprise then that when we get a diagnosis of BPD we can be left feeling as if we have been handed a life sentence. How can we possibly be expected to feel otherwise when those who are supposed to help us believe that we are past the point of help?

So how do we help smash this stigma? Education is key. This disorder affects up to 2 percent of the U.S. population alone—that is nearly 6.5 million Americans. Not a small number, to say the least. Of those affected, 8-10 percent go on to commit suicide (Gunderson JG, 2001). Some in the BPD community cite figures as high as 6% of the U.S. population. So why are so many people completely unaware of this disorder? If we ask someone if they have heard of Alzheimer's disease, I bet my bottom dollar that most people would say yes. BPD affects 50 percent *more* people than Alzheimer's. It is more common than schizophrenia, more common than bipolar, yet these disorders are far more recognized and accepted than BPD.

It is my goal to destroy this unjust and undeserved stigma. Yes, we can be difficult people to live with. Yes, our behaviors can cause a lot of hurt. I am certainly not denying these things. But if this disorder were more understood, and those with it were less judged and criticized, I believe we would be closer to eliminating the myths that surround it and be one step closer to a cure.

## Living with Borderline Personality Disorder

I have touched upon what constitutes BPD, but this alone can never truly describe the feeling of living with it on a day-to-day basis. I will try and explain in detail how it *feels* to live with this disorder rather than focusing on external behaviors. Here are snapshots from my own personal experiences:

> *Have you ever ridden a roller coaster? A really fast one with sharp bends and sudden drops (perhaps in the dark)? I suppose this is the best analogy for what living with BPD feels like. I spend my days on an emotional roller coaster, one moment speeding toward a great height and believing momentarily that I am free and happy, only seconds later rushing*

*toward the ground, destroying everything in my path as I do so. I do not choose to ride this roller coaster. In fact I would do anything in my power to get off, but it is out of my control. I am strapped into my seat with no means of escape. Those who I love and care about are also fastened into their seats beside me. They wrongly assume that I am the conductor of the ride—I am the one at the controls. The difference between the other passengers and myself is that they have the choice to get off, and so often they do, for why would they stay? I certainly wouldn't if I were given half the chance...*

*Some days I wake up and I feel different. Not good, not bad, just... calm. I like these mornings. I start to believe that, actually, I am normal, I have somehow managed to step off the roller coaster that is my life. I am okay, I am free, and all is well. I go about my day and even start to walk with an ever-so-slight spring in my step. For the first time in months I can start to envisage a happy future ahead, one free from the chains that bind me. Those close to me observe this change and share my joy, for my freedom equals their freedom. I begin making plans, a new college course, a new hobby, the world is my oyster, and all the while my loved ones are pushing me on, encouraging me, not wanting me to lose momentum. I don't want to lose momentum either because I am enjoying the calm. Life is good. And then, without warning, my world comes crashing down. I am heading straight toward the ground and I am terrified. I never saw this coming, I had no time to prepare. And then I grasp the reality of what has happened. I had never actually stepped off the roller coaster at all. The slow uphill incline had deceived me and everyone else into thinking I had both feet on the ground, when really all the while I was heading straight toward the point of no return...*

*I have always felt different from those around me, almost as if we are the same species on the outside and yet worlds apart inside—if men are from Mars and women are from Venus, then I must be from Pluto. I fear other people and yet I hold on to them, thinking that they may in some way complete me, for I do not feel whole, I often feel as if I am nothing, barely alive. I have a hollow deep within me that nothing seems to fill. A* void, a nothingness. I try desperately to fill this empty space but to no avail. External things only seem to help temporarily. I am detached from those around me, and the more I try to attach the more I seem to disconnect…

I question daily if I am a bad person. I believe I must be, for why else would I hurt those closest to me? The more love I feel toward someone the more I seem to punish them. The truth is, I do more than just hurt them, I absolutely destroy them, and then externally I move on. Except I do not really move on, I hold on to all the hurts that I have caused. I internalize them and then I use them to torture myself. I hate who I am. I hate what I do. I have a deep-seated anger at myself and at the world around me. Why am I the way that I am? Why do the smallest, most insignificant things in life absolutely floor me? "Sensitive" is too minimal a word for what I feel. One meaningless look can cut me to the bone. Like a wounded animal, injured and distressed, I attack anyone who approaches. The void within continues to grow vaster, and it is not long before pure desperation forces me to seek something to fill it. Have you ever tried to fill a bottomless pit before? It's a pointless and tiring task that only heightens the feeling of longing…

I want so desperately to be happy and content, often believing a relationship is the one thing that will fulfill me, but my world is full of contradictions and opposites. When I love someone, I hurt them. When I want someone, I push them away. I can come across as confident while inside I am dying. Like an armadillo—tough on the outside but soft and vulnerable inside. To the outside world I am a she-devil who is to be avoided at all costs. I do not blame people for feeling this way about me. How are they to know that no matter how much they hate who I am, I hate myself more? I have a beast that lives within me, one that I have no control over and one that is so formidable it has the power to destroy anything I hold dear to me. I never know when my beast will rear its ugly head, instead I live with the knowledge that it is there and it is only time before it does…

My whole world is one of confusion. All or nothing. Black or white. Good or bad, except the times that I think are good, I now know are just *times when the roller coaster is on the painful incline toward further de-struction. There are those who say this is not an illness, those who believe I am simply immoral and cruel. Who am I to argue when my behaviors in-dicate that they are correct? All I know is that I have had enough. I have had enough of the pain I see etched in the faces of those I love, knowing that it is I who has caused such agony. I am tired, tired of fighting, tired of fighting others, and tired of fighting myself. I wish with all my might I could destroy the beast inside of me, I just don't know how…*

So there you have it: a glimpse into my world. It's not pretty—but as we'll see in this book, it is possible to smooth out the ups and downs of the roller coaster and live a happier, more stable life.

## What Causes BPD?

There is no definitive answer to this question, as the exact cause is still unknown. It is believed that a combination of factors can trigger this disorder.

### Biology

There is strong evidence to suggest that heredity plays a part in this disorder. If we have a family member with this disorder, we are at a greater risk of developing it. There is the argument, however, that this may be due to us "learning" the family member's behaviors as opposed to it having been passed down genetically. I personally believe that I was born with this disorder.

### Brain Abnormalities

As discussed at the beginning of the chapter, brain scans have shown that those of us with BPD have a brain that differs from that of non-sufferers. It is unknown if the brain is like this from birth or if it has undergone atrophy due to environmental factors.

### Environment

Growing up in an unstable environment seems to be a trigger. Many people (but not all) with BPD have suffered abuse (either sexual, physical, or mental), neglect, or trauma in their childhood. If a child experiences loss at a young age, either through death or divorce, they also have a higher risk of developing this disorder.

I must point out that I never suffered at the hands of abusive parents. In fact, I had extremely loving parents. My parents divorced when I was five years old, and while this may have affected me, I am sure that I already had this disorder by then. I feel it is important to share this because I am aware that parents of those with BPD can often have a hard time with it. They can be made to feel as if it is all their fault that their child has this disorder. Unfortunately, there are some instances when the parents did play a part in it, but in other cases the parents are left asking themselves "Where did I go wrong?" and the simple answer is this: They probably didn't.

## My Own Childhood

I grew up in a semidetached home with my mum, dad, and baby brother, Carl. Looking back, I can see that we were actually quite poor, although this never occurred to me growing up. My dad, an Irishman, worked for the airlines while my mum stayed at home and raised us kids. I wish I could remember more from my childhood. The few memories I do have tend to be happy ones: my mum reading us stories, my dad buying us ice cream, that kind of thing. My parents did not have the best relationship, mainly due to the fact that my dad liked a drink and my mum did not. When I was five, my dad moved back to Dublin, Ireland. During the main school holidays, summer, Christmas, and Easter, my brother and I would board a plane to go and see him. My dad lived with his parents, my dear Nana and Grandad Rooney (Granda, as I called him). Our holidays were pretty idyllic; my grandparents owned a farm (agricultural—not with goats and pigs), and I don't think I could ever truly explain the pure fun and excitement that we had when we stayed there. Our holidays were spent playing on the beach, going to the local fair, visiting old castles, or spending time with my uncles, auntie, and cousins. I was incredibly close to my grandparents, and having to leave them and my dad at the end of the holidays was sheer torture—not because I didn't want to go home toMum, but because I wished I could take them home with me.

Christmas Day was always spent with my mum at her parents' house. My Nan always cooked the most wonderful dinners, and Grandpa always ensured the house was done up like Santa's Grotto. All of my aunts and uncles would be there with my cousins for a day of pure fun.

I did not have a particularly hard life. Yes, I can remember some arguments that my parents had; yes, my dad enjoyed a drink. But abuse? No. As I mentioned earlier, I believe I was born with this disorder. One of my reasons is this: From an incredibly young age (about fifteen months old) I would have extremely intense reactions to certain songs or stories. Whenever my mum would sing "Rock-a-Bye Baby" from a book of nursery rhymes, I would get really upset and cry when she got to the part "and down will come baby." I could not bear the thought of baby falling. It is bizarre to have so many gaps in my memory, yet still remember the hurt I felt when she would sing this to me. It was the same with the story "The Ugly Duckling." I couldn't bear the thought that the other birds were mean to the duckling.

I can remember being three years old and sitting on the windowsill and crying because my daddy had just left. I can remember waving to him while tears streamed down my face. It felt like I had lost my dad forever. Yet he was just on his way to a work function and would be gone for a few days. That fear of abandonment was there within me even though I had never been abandoned before. I sometimes wonder if this was one of my "traumatic events." The outside world would hardly classify it as trauma, but, to me, a highly sensitive child, it was. Perhaps this is where my genetics met my environment and the trigger was pulled, perhaps the trigger was pulled at a later date, who knows?

The fact remains, we cannot find all the answers as to why we developed this disorder. Neither can we change the past. But we have the power within us to make sure we have a hell of a good future. And that power lies right here in the present moment.

Chapter 4

# MYTHS

*"Myths are a waste of time. They prevent progression."*
—Barbra Streisand

**B**orderline personality disorder is a disorder that is shrouded in myths, another factor adding to the stigma. Before we jump into the rest of the book, which focuses on the truths and facts regarding this disorder, I wish to dispel as many of the myths as I can. I do not want them hampering recovery by taking up valuable space in our mind, and I certainly do not want us to be reading this book while having a nagging doubt at the back of our mind that stems from one of the many myths.

*Borderline personality disorder only affects women.*

BPD is not choosy when it comes to who develops it. It affects both males and females, old and young, rich and poor, and people all over the world. It is true, however, that more females than males get a diagnosis of BPD. Nobody knows for sure if this is because it is generally more common in females or if it is because men are less likely to get diagnosed, even if they are also sufferers. I discuss the reasons why this might happen in the chapter 20, "BPD and Men."

*There is no treatment for BPD.*

If we were to go back a number of years, then this "myth" would be fact. For a long time, there was no proven treatment for BPD. Today, however, there are a number of treatments that have been proven to help manage BPD symptoms. This myth might also stem from the fact that there is no cure for BPD. While this sounds scary, it really shouldn't be. With the right treatment the disorder can be managed so well that if we were to go for another diagnosis we would not meet the criteria. It sounds daunting having to spend the rest of our life "managing" our illness. But it really isn't. The skills we learn in treatment become so ingrained in us that we will be able to manage the disorder unconsciously. The skills become part of our day-to-day life. We can be completely unaware that we are practicing the skills unless we consciously stop and take notice.

### If you can function at times, you do not have BPD.

BPD is very much on a spectrum—some people have it more mildly and others have it full-blown with all the traits. There are people with BPD who are able to hold down a job and give the impression to the outside world that everything is well with them; only their close family members may recognize that all is not as it seems. There are those with BPD who are considered to be "quiet borderlines" because they tend to internalize all their anger; their symptoms tend not to be externalized, and therefore they appear to be well to those around them. It must also be pointed out that BPD *can* go into remission. There are times when we can start to feel "normal" again and can function reasonably well. We can even start to believe that we have been "cured,'" only for it to come back with a bang and let us know it is still well and truly there.

### Those with BPD are nasty people.

Those with BPD may behave in a way that makes others believe that we must be nasty people. The fact is, we are not "nasty" people at our core—we are people in immense internal pain who are trying to survive. Unfortunately, as so many people are not educated when it comes to this disorder, others tend to take us at face value. They observe our behaviors and judge us on them, without truly understanding what we are going through.

### Those with BPD are violent and dangerous.

There are those who can be violent and a danger to others. However, it is far more common for someone with BPD to be a danger to themself. As mentioned in the previous chapter, there are nine traits, and to get a diagnosis someone must tick five out of the nine boxes. Not everyone with BPD has violent outbursts. To say that anyone with BPD is violent and dangerous is like saying anyone with a criminal record is violent and dangerous—it's simply not the case.

### Bad parenting causes BPD.

There is no 100 percent known cause of BPD. It is believed that a combination of things causes someone to develop it. Environment and biology can both play a part, *but* there are those with BPD who have no other family members with mental health issues and grew up in a loving environment. Unfortunately, due to the fact that a lot of people with BPD have suffered some form of abuse, parents very often feel judged and start to question whether it is all their fault. I personally do not believe there is anything to gain from blaming our parents or our parents blaming themselves. Yes, there are those of us who have truly suffered. And while it is important that we feel validated and are able to work with a therapist on our past issues, I think it is equally important to let go of the past in order to focus on our present and thereby create a better future for ourselves.

### People with BPD are manipulative and selfish.

Yes, our behaviors can be seen as manipulative and selfish, but the fact is that adopting these characteristics are our way of trying to survive. Manipulation is something that is premeditated and done consciously. We do not mean to manipulate—we do not do it consciously, and when we act it is done impulsively with no preplanning involved. We often behave like this when we feel desperate and are trying to do everything in our power to cope in that moment and get our needs met.

### The only therapy for BPD is dialectical behavior therapy (DBT).

DBT is a widely known and proven form of therapy for BPD, but it certainly isn't the only therapy. There are other effective therapies that are also available for the treatment of BPD. I discuss the various treatment options in more detail in chapter 17.

*BPD is not a valid diagnosis—personality disorders are not even real mental illnesses.*

BPD *is* a very real and very serious mental health illness that is recognized in the DSM (*Diagnostic and Statistical Manual of Mental Health Disorders*). For a long time, professionals could not agree on the various symptoms of BPD, which led to problems with diagnosing. But now there are nine traits that are recognized. Some studies have shown that those with BPD have brain differences compared to the general population.

*Those with BPD have a flawed personality.*

A personality is considered to be the way we think, feel, and behave. Those with a personality disorder think, feel, and behave in a way that causes us to relate to the rest of the world in a different way, which can lead to all sorts of problems in various areas of our life. Rather than having a "flawed" personality we have a "unique" one.

*Medication won't help if you have BPD.*

While there is no medication proven to cure BPD, it must be noted that most people who suffer from it also have co-occurring disorders (discussed more in chapter 24). Medication can certainly help alleviate some of the symptoms. In particular, antidepressant, antianxiety, and antipsychotic medication, as well as mood stabilizers, are all commonly taken by those with BPD. If someone is not given medication to help alleviate the symptoms common among sufferers, any other form of therapy becomes a lot more difficult to engage in. Thus, by easing certain symptoms, the sufferer will find it easier to engage in the relevant therapy and therefore reap benefits and learn skills to manage their BPD.

*Medication is the best treatment for BPD.*

Medication can ease some of the symptoms that commonly occur with BPD, but medication alone is not helpful. In order to manage BPD, we need to learn new skills to replace our old negative and unhelpful coping mechanisms. Medication does not give us these skills—we need therapy to learn the skills and we need to practice them in everyday life.

Medication can ease some of the symptoms that make it more difficult to engage in therapy, thus making it helpful, but medication is certainly not the best treatment and should never be the only form of treatment. It needs to be combined with both therapy and counseling.

### BPD is really rare.

Studies have shown that borderline personality disorder affects up to 2 percent of the population (Weill Cornell Medicine 2007), although some argue that this statistic should be closer to 6 percent. One study showed that up to 40 percent of those with BPD initially get diagnosed with bipolar disorder (Zimmerman et al. 2008). Even so, 2 percent of the world's population is 152 million people. BPD is certainly not rare. In fact, the number of people with BPD is larger than both bipolar and schizophrenia. It just so happens that fewer people are aware of BPD and therefore assume it must be rare.

### People with BPD do not know how to love.

Those with BPD are more than capable of love. The fact is, we experience emotions more intensely than the general population, including love. Problems arise when we are unable to regulate our intense emotions and then behave in a way that makes those around us question our feelings for them. When we love someone it often leaves us feeling incredibly vulnerable, as we are afraid that person will leave us. When this happens we tend to either become very clingy—which results in the person seeing as us more obsessive than loving—or push people away. Once we are able to regulate our emotions, our relationships can blossom.

### When someone with BPD attempts suicide, they do not really mean it.

Ten percent of those with borderline personality disorder commit suicide. Unless someone actually lives with this condition, they cannot understand how truly painful it is to live life on a day-to-day basis. The pain can be unbearable a lot of the time. It is no surprise then that out of all those diagnosed with BPD, 65-70 percent attempt suicide (Black, 2004). These suicide attempts are not merely a case of looking for attention, they happen because the sufferer feels there is no other way out of the pain they are living with. To believe that those with BPD do not mean it is both dangerous and untrue. In order to help deal with the issue, more needs to be done to understand why the suicide rate in BPD is so high.

### Anyone who has BPD suffered some form of abuse as a child.

As discussed in the "bad parenting" myth, the cause of BPD is still not known. Yes, many of those diagnosed with BPD have suffered some form of abuse, neglect, or trauma as a child and have grown up in an environment that has been detrimental to them. It must be noted, though, that there are also many people who have been diagnosed with BPD who never experienced abuse in childhood. Likewise, there are many people who have suffered abuse in childhood who grew up and never developed BPD.

### BPD disappears with age.

There are those with BPD who find that as the older they get, the more their symptoms seem to ease. This is certainly not the case for a lot of people though. Perhaps, as we age, some of us learn to start managing our symptoms without even being aware of it, thus feeling as if the BPD has disappeared. There are also people with BPD who find their symptoms worsen with age. This may come down to the fact that the longer our brain is subjected to cortisol the more our brain is being eroded away, therefore exacerbating our symptoms.

### People with BPD choose to be the way they are.

This is so far from the truth. Why would someone choose something that causes them such intense pain and constant chaos in their lives? It is not known whether we are born with BPD or develop it later on in life. What is known is that brain scans have shown that someone with BPD has a brain that is different than the brain of someone without the disorder. While BPD is not a choice, once we become aware of it we can make a conscious effort to learn how to manage it. The disorder is not a choice, but recovery is.

*People with BPD cannot lead a normal life.*

Certainly life is a lot more difficult when we have unmanaged BPD. We can go through times when we seem to function, often followed by times when we cannot. Once we start learning skills to help us manage our BPD we can go on to lead not only a normal life but also a very enjoyable and happy one.

*Children and teens cannot be diagnosed with BPD.*

Some professionals refuse to diagnose BPD before age eighteen, as they believe that some of the symptoms can be similar to what a normal teenager goes through. This is quite a dated view—nowadays more and more professionals are realizing that BPD can be diagnosed from a younger age, thereby enabling the child or teen to access the right help earlier, saving them and their families from years of pain and suffering. The DSM-5 does not state an age limit on this disorder.

*BPD and bipolar are the same thing.*

A lot of people seem to get misdiagnosed with BPD when they actually have bipolar and vice versa. It is true that there are many similarities between the two, but they are two completely different disorders. Treatment and medication for bipolar would not work on someone with BPD, and medication for BPD could in fact pose a danger to someone with bipolar. Bipolar disorder is discussed in greater detail in chapter 24, as it isn't uncommon for someone to have a dual diagnosis of both disorders.

*BPD and PTSD are the same thing.*

BPD and post-traumatic stress disorder (PTSD) are two completely different disorders. PTSD will be discussed in greater detail in chapter 24, as BPD and PTSD can co-occur, especially due to the fact many people with BPD have suffered some kind of abuse or trauma in their past, which can also cause PTSD to develop.

*All people with BPD are the same.*

Just like no two people without BPD are exactly the same, neither are two people with this disorder. We all have our own unique characteristics and personalities. Saying that all those with BPD are the same is the same as saying all those with cancer are the same. It is preposterous. To be diagnosed with BPD we must meet five of the nine criteria. Some people may have five of the traits, while others have six, seven, eight, or nine. The total number of combinations is 256. Even if two people meet the exact same criteria as each other, they may both display the traits in different ways from one another.

Throughout the next nine chapters I will be discussing each of the nine BPD traits. I wish to help those who do not suffer from BPD understand the thoughts and feelings behind our behaviors, so that they can better understand us. I am also hoping that those with BPD will be able to read the chapters and identify the traits that are an issue for them. Self-awareness is crucial in order for us to recover.

# PART II

# THE TRAITS—
# AND THE
# COPING SKILLS

Chapter 5

# FEAR OF ABANDONMENT

*"She wasn't scared to walk away.*
*She was scared he wouldn't follow."*
—Atticus

**What Is Fear of Abandonment?**

Fear of abandonment can affect anyone, not just those of us diagnosed with BPD. This particular trait, however, is a core component of borderline personality disorder. As the name suggests, it is a deep and overwhelming fear that those we love and care about will abandon us. There may be no evidence to suggest that our loved ones are going to leave us, but in our mind we believe that they are.

Some non-sufferers surmise that if we are living with something as distressing as the constant fear that we will be left, it would be obvious to us that we have this trait. Unfortunately, this is simply not the case.

I myself was completely unaware that I lived with this trait until I learned what it was and how it can manifest itself. I felt deep in my heart, mind, and gut that whoever I was close to was going to abandon me. But it never felt like merely a fear of what *might* happen. I never thought, "I *think* they're going to leave me." I thought, "They *are* going to leave me." There's a big difference in the two thoughts. In the first thought, I am giving some leeway to my fear—it is merely a possibility that they may leave me. In the type of thoughts that I was having, it was a *guarantee* that they *were* going to leave me. That's why, to me, my feelings felt as if they were perfectly justified and rational. Only with hindsight do I recognize that my thoughts, feelings, and behaviors were completely irrational.

This fear of abandonment can manifest itself in many surreptitious ways, often leaving us unable to even comprehend what is happening. For instance, whenever I entered into a relationship, trust was never something I first considered. I would enter a relationship with my heart on the table. I would literally dive right in and start planning our wedding on date number two and our children's names on date number three. In my mind, this person was "the one" and we were destined to be together forever. Like most relationships, we would go through the "honeymoon" period, which was always so exciting and fun—and one hundred times more intense than the average person's honeymoon period. Unlike a "regular" relationship, however, my honeymoon period was over almost as soon as it began. Why? Because my old thought pattern would reappear, and suspicious and negative thoughts would start popping into my brain, causing me to feel and behave in a way that would have the opposite effect of what I wanted.

The problem with living with this intense fear is that we start to behave in a way that inevitably pushes away those around us. Our deepest fear then becomes a reality, and in our mind we are convinced that we were right all along, rather than realizing that it was actually our behaviors that led to this outcome.

Before we can accept that what we are experiencing is an irrational fear of abandonment, we have to learn to consciously use our cerebral cortex, our rational brain, to scrutinize the facts.

Fear of abandonment can show itself in a variety of ways, rather than in the same way for everyone. The ways in which it can appear can sometimes seem to be polar opposites and yet the driving force behind both is the same.

## Our Thoughts

If only it was as simple as thinking, "I think this person is going to leave me." We do not necessarily consciously have this thought, even though subconsciously this is the prime factor behind all of our thoughts, feelings, and behaviors. Our fear of abandonment is sneaky and sly and can manifest itself in numerous different ways.

Before I jump into the types of thoughts that we have, I must warn you (especially if you don't have BPD) that you may find yourself thinking, "Do people *really* have these thoughts?" The answer is *yes*. Yes, we do, on a daily basis.

"They are probably still in love with their ex."

This thinking seems perfectly plausible to us. After all, they had once been together, so they obviously love one another (at least they used to, although our mind tells us that the love is still well and truly there). Once we have this particular thought, it will literally consume our mind. We picture them having sex, sneaking phone calls behind our back, contacting each other on social media for virtual sex, thinking of their ex while having sex with us, masturbating over their ex in private, and so on.

It always surprised me that when I was expected to sit and listen to a visualization meditation, I was unable to let my mind visualize anything. But when my mind was suspecting someone of something I seemed to become an imaginative genius with a brain that could literally zoom into the tiniest details and replay the images repeatedly in HD with surround sound so realistic that I felt like was actually there in person.

"They think I'm fat/ugly/thin/short/boring/not like their ex..."

As will be discussed in chapter 7, those of us with BPD tend to have an unclear or unstable self-image. It is no surprise then that this, combined with our fear of abandonment, can contribute to thoughts such as these.

Our mind immediately goes on the hunt for reasons why this person will leave us, and, due to our completely warped sense of self, it doesn't take us long to think of a million and one reasons why this person would leave us due to faults in ourselves.

"They think I am going to cheat on them, so they are going to cheat on me first."

This thought might seem contradictory considering our very low self-esteem. It must be remembered that our thoughts are not rational. This is merely us making up another reason in our head for why they would cheat on us.

"They like my best friend/cousin/next door neighbor…"

Our self-esteem is often nonexistent, our sense of self is distorted, and we compare ourselves to others. We constantly think that we are less than and question why someone would want to be with us when there are others out there who outshine us in every area.

"They would rather be at work than be with me."

Our partner may have bills to pay, a car to run, and so forth, but we disregard these factors. In our distorted mind we have the vision of us spending every hour of every day together. Work should not come between us, and, if it does, then it must surely mean they have chosen to put their work before our relationship.

"If they don't answer their phone, they are either: avoiding me on purpose, having sex with someone, or laughing at their phone as they watch it ringing and commenting to anyone who will listen, 'I'm not answering to this crazy bitch.'"

We do not consider the possibility that our loved one is actually working. That thought doesn't cross our mind. We immediately feel suspicious and our thoughts start to spiral out of control.

"They seem distant tonight. They must be thinking of leaving me."

Our partner may have been working flat out all week and is exhausted. When they get home from work, if they are not excited to see us, wanting to tell us everything about their day and asking us about our day, then clearly something must be seriously wrong in our relationship.

"They love their mum/dad more than they love me."

The problem with in-laws is that they usually have a close relationship with our partner. To a non-BPD person this would be a positive thing. For us, anyone with a close relationship with our partner is automatically seen as competition. We are not the sort who want to share our partner—even with their own family. Our thoughts may start out fairly harmless, with us feeling slightly irritated by a relative's closeness. Eventually we may be consumed with paranoid thoughts that the relative is trying to turn them against us. The relative goes from being the competition to the enemy, even when they haven't done anything wrong.

"They have changed—they're not the person I fell in love with."

People with BPD often think in black and white—there is no gray area. If we are in a relationship, we will either love or hate our partner, there is no in between. In our "black thinking" stage, we will compare partners to exes, friends, even their past self (bearing in mind that our partner may not have changed at all, it is just our perception of them that has).

Our thoughts can often appear to come out of nowhere with absolutely no trigger. Yet, there is almost always a trigger. What constitutes a trigger for us, however, may be seen as inconsequential to someone else. For example, let's say our partner is fifteen minutes home late from work. The average person thinks: Perhaps there is traffic, maybe they had to work slightly later, and the like. In our mind it means (a) they are never coming home again, (b) they are with someone else, or (c) they have been in a car accident. We consider these three options and realize that only if it is option c will we forgive them. We find ourselves hoping that it is option c, as that would mean we hadn't been abandoned on purpose.

Our perception of the world around us differs so dramatically from the average person. Seemingly minor incidences can absolutely destroy us. We constantly live in fear of being abandoned, and we are forever on the lookout for threats that might risk us being deserted. We start believing that there are threats all around us. We turn any situation into a possible threat in our mind. In a desperate bid to try to avoid abandonment, we start to preempt it.

If a loved one announces that they are going away for a break, our mind goes into overdrive. We panic that there will be a crisis in their absence and nobody will be there for us to turn to. We panic that they will realize life is easier without us and not return. We start to question whether they care about us at all, and our fear turns to anger. How can they do this to us? How dare they?

Our mistrust of those close to us causes us to disbelieve most things they tell us. If a loved one needs to cancel plans that we have made, we assume it is because they do not *want* to keep the plans, rather than that they can't. This leads to further scrambling for reasons why they don't want to see us, and our reasons can vary from the fact that they do not like us to them seeing other friends behind our back.

The thoughts that we live with daily can be described as obsessive, intrusive, suspicious, negative self-talk, paranoid, anxious, all consuming, and desperate.

## Our Feelings

With such negative thought patterns, it is unsurprising that we spend most of our days in a state of anxiety or depression. Our thoughts affect our feelings. It is highly unlikely that someone who is having anxious and paranoid thoughts is feeling happy and joyful.

It is not uncommon for us to spend weeks or months in anxious or depressive states. Our thoughts feed our feelings, and, with an inability to stop our thoughts, we must succumb to the negative feelings associated with them.

Every time a new intrusive thought fills our mind we feel as if we have taken a hard punch to the stomach; our emotional feelings also present themselves physically. It is no longer just our mind being affected but also our body.

For some, a state of sadness may cause us to feel physically sick and unable to eat; for others, we may eat more, hoping to fill the void within us.

Anxiety also causes us to suffer a multitude of physical feelings, from trembling hands and a shaky leg to fast breathing, sweating, and the constant need to look around at our surroundings. Some notice our odd mannerisms while others go unaware.

Anger is an extremely intense feeling that rears its ugly head often, although it can be portrayed in various ways among people. We are continually deciding on a fight-or-flight response. *Fight* means we get angry, whereas *flight* means we feel fearful. We swing between the two feelings, desperately fighting for our survival, completely unaware that our perception is wrong and our fight-or-flight response has been triggered unnecessarily.

To friends, our bouts of anger can seem to appear out of nowhere, for they do not understand what is going on in our mind and body. To the outside world, we can appear happy and well adjusted. When first in a relationship, we may be seen as intense, but intense good feelings rarely pose a problem. It isn't until later when our true selves' surface and those around us are shocked, for they cannot comprehend that we can appear happy one moment and a monster the next. Our fear drives our anger, and what appears as rage on the surface is in fact a deep hurt that is coursing through our body.

With those we love we feel protective, but the intensity of our feelings transforms that protectiveness into an obsessiveness and a jealousy that ultimately causes problems for us and those around us. Our feelings of protectiveness do not stem from our fear of something happening to them, rather it comes from a fear of them abandoning us.

Like a child who goes to school for the first time, who stands at the end of the day in the classroom contemplating whether anybody is going to be there to take them home, we feel helpless and dependent. Only we are not children, at least not on the outside. Our body may be twenty-plus years old, and yet our mind is like that of a three-year-old. Unlike a three-year-old, we are expected to fend for ourselves when we often do not know how, at least not emotionally. Just like the child who is waiting to be collected after their first day at school, when somebody is late turning up, we fear the worst. We feel our anxiety building inside; we start pacing the floor with an aching feeling in our gut and a lump in our throat. Only when our loved one turns up can we let all those built-up feelings erupt, either through crying uncontrollably or by turning on them in anger. Our loved one will look at us in confusion, wondering what bought on such a colossal outburst, for they have no way of feeling how we feel or thinking how we think.

## Our Behaviors

Our actions can vary from person to person and feeling to feeling. There are those who externalize their feelings and those who internalize them.

### Stalking

Our suspicious thoughts and feelings can lead us to become clingy with those we care about. We hang on to them for dear life with the fear that if we loosen our grip just slightly they will be gone forever. Our clinginess can turn quickly into obsessive behavior, with us stalking our loved one, either via social media or physically. Many a time, we drive around at night searching for our partner's car, trying to disprove the location they told us they would be. Hiding in bushes, searching their phone, hacking their email. These behaviors do not seem odd to us, rather they're a necessity. So long as we have both eyes on them, we believe we can stop them from leaving us when the time comes for them to choose to do so. To us, this simply seems like relationship maintenance. If a loved one questions our behaviors, our thoughts tell us that they are trying to hide something, and so we up our game, becoming sneakier and more controlling.

When we suspect someone of something, we will go to the end of the Earth to prove it, often dismissing any evidence that may prove that they have done nothing wrong and that our suspicions are unfounded. We lose all rationale and instead focus all of our attention on our end goal: preventing them from abandoning us. But before we can work out how to stop someone from abandoning us, we must first discover how they are going to abandon us, and this in itself causes a whole variety of behaviors.

### Accusations, Projection, Manipulation, and Violence

More often than not, we do not find what we are looking for. And then the accusations will start. We will force our loved one to tell us what it is that we are searching for. This often proves difficult, as what we believe we have "discovered" is in our mind and is not reality. For example, we may believe that our loved one is having an affair. There may be no evidence for this, but we think it and we feel it and therefore we only need to prove it. When our searching has not revealed anything to us, we take a new tactic. We may start up a conversation, putting words into our partner's mouth and twisting the words that they voice. We project on to them and start accusing them of wrongdoing. An argument will ensue, and the intensity of our rage may cause us to lash out physically. If our loved one turns to leave, we may threaten them with a suicide attempt or we may self-harm if they do leave. To the outside world, this appears to be manipulation at its finest. Manipulation, however, is calculated and thought through. Our threats are never rationally thought through; they're a desperate and impulsive attempt for us to try and regain control of a situation in which we have no control. We are despairing at this point and unable to think clearly. We are frantically trying to avoid the abandonment that we have feared all along. It is ironic, therefore, that we often trigger the abandonment ourselves. In the drastic measures that we take to protect ourselves, we actually push away those we love and cause them hurt and pain. We sabotage our relationship and are completely unaware that we are doing so. When we look back at the reality of what happened, we again look back with distorted vision. Rather than accepting our role in the breakup, we will instead believe that we were right all along and that our fear of abandonment is justified. We continue to carry that fear with us everywhere we go, causing destruction in any future relationship that we enter into.

### *Cutting Off Our Nose to Spite Our Face*

Our fear of abandonment can appear in any close relationship, whether with a friend, a romantic partner, a family member, or even our psychologist or therapist. We are often encouraged to build a close relationship based on trust with our medical caregivers. This bond takes time and effort on both sides to form.

But what happens when a bond is formed and later needs to be broken? I found out the hard way when my psychologist, who had worked with me for years and who I trusted implicitly, broke the news to me that she had to "hand me over" to another psychologist due to administrative changes beyond her control. The deep hurt and anger I felt came as a shock. I felt as if she were making a personal choice to let me go. My self-harming started to increase, as did the bulimia, but to anyone who knew me, I was coping surprisingly well—after all, why would I not? It was only a change of psychologist. What those around me failed to notice was the immense loss that I was feeling inside.

My next psychologist was nice enough, but the fear of abandonment had intensified ten-fold, and I no longer wanted to put my trust in the new psychologist. I couldn't bear the pain of being left again. Rather than get angry, I cut off emotionally. I would talk to my psychologist but I would never discuss the things that truly mattered to me. The hour would be wasted with pointless chitchat and yes/no answers. I carried the abandonment of my first psychologist into my next relationship with a medical professional. I put up barriers, and there was no way I was going to let them down this time. Not surprising, my mental health deteriorated. It would take years before I became aware of what I was doing and realized that I was risking my own recovery due to this resentment and fear.

### Hypochondria and Munchausen Syndrome

Hypochondria is yet another form in which our fear of abandonment can surface. It may start as simply wanting constant reassurance and attention. This constant giving of attention can become too much for most people; it is draining and they are unable to keep up with it. For those of us with BPD, we think that we need this constant attention, for in our mind if the attention stops so does their love for us. Drastic measures taken by us may include feigning illness. When we are ill we receive extra love and care, and we come to crave this type of attention. This leads to us inventing illnesses or purposefully making ourselves ill in order to be noticed. Although Munchausen syndrome is an illness on its own (known as factitious disorder in the DSM-5), it is not uncommon to be displayed by those with BPD. The attention we receive when we are ill, by both medical professionals and our loved ones, helps to soothe us; we like to feel cared for, and this makes us believe that we are loved.

Given our intense emotions and impulsive actions, there are times when we need to see our psychologist more often and times when we are admitted to a mental health unit as an inpatient. Both these outcomes cause our loved ones to rally around us and realize that we are actually suffering with a medical condition. Needing more intensive care acts as a reminder that the BPD is there and that we are sick people who need help. Problems surface when we begin to recover—we almost fear getting well because, to us, getting well will mean people will no longer fuss around us. It equals being abandoned, and we will go to any lengths to sabotage our own recovery for this reason.

### Moving from One Relationship to Another

People may wonder why, if we struggle with fear of abandonment, we seem to jump from one relationship to another. It is because we fear abandonment that we do this. We fear being alone and we fear the pain at the end of a relationship. Our solution is to move on quickly and without looking back. To those without BPD, this seems cold and heartless; in truth, it is understandable why it appears this way. We are not setting out to hurt anyone by doing this—we are cutting off our emotions so as not go through immense pain. We fear our emotions and we fear feeling out of control. Detaching from our emotions is an automatic self-protection response—it is our defense mechanism. For this same reason, there are those of us with BPD who avoid relationships altogether. We fear the fear of abandonment itself, causing us to withdraw from any relationships as a means of protecting ourselves. We refuse to let our barriers down and become intimate with anyone. Casual sex is the closest we will get to anybody, and if we feel somebody is getting too close to us, we shut them out immediately.

## Where Does This Trait Come From?

Fear of abandonment typically stems from childhood. Types of losses experienced by a child that can cause this trait to form might include the death of a loved one or divorce. If a young child experiences a loss they may be too young to comprehend, they can hold on to the feeling of losing someone and carry it into adulthood, never really understanding why it is there.

Abuse and neglect, although not experienced by everyone with BPD, are common contributing factors to this trait. Both abuse and neglect (which is a form of abuse) can lead to a child growing up with attachment issues. If a child is not shown the love and attention that they rightly deserve, their brains develop differently. Neural pathways that should have strengthened actually disappear and fade away from lack of stimulation. These children grow into adults who do not understand what a healthy attachment is. They may cling to a relationship for dear life or they may avoid relationships altogether.

Fear of abandonment, although commonly triggered in childhood, can also develop later in life. It isn't uncommon for someone who has been abandoned in a relationship in later life to also carry the fear, believing that it will happen again. There are many of us who take all of our insecurities and hurt from a past relationship into a new one.

## What Is Happening in Our Brain?

In early infancy our brain develops at a rapid rate, with neural pathways strengthening or disappearing. As mentioned in chapter 2, we are social creatures; separation is not supposed to feel good. When our caregiver put us down as babies, we would cry in the hope that they would pick us back up. If we cried and a parent went to us, we would then grow up knowing that, when we need someone, they would be there. If we were left to cry and cry, we would eventually stop crying, as we knew it wouldn't prompt anyone to come to us. Years ago it was the norm to let children "cry it out"; now we know how damaging this is for children. Children are helpless and need their parents. They cannot talk or communicate in any way other than crying to get their needs met.

If our parents came to us when we needed them, we grew up with healthy attachments. We grew up knowing that our parents could put us down and that they would come back if we needed them. If we did not get our needs met, we may have grown up with attachment issues. We might suffer from separation anxiety, which can lead to fear of abandonment.

Whenever we suffer any form of trauma, be it a loss of a loved one or abuse, the emotional and physical pain and hurt that we feel are stored in our amygdala as an emotional memory. If as a child we were left alone in a room to cry, the memory of being alone and it being emotionally painful is stored. Later in life, when a loved one leaves us to go to work or see friends, it triggers the emotional memory of us being "left" and causes us emotional pain. This is actually our brain's way of surviving. It is looking at past painful experiences to help us avoid them in the present and in the future. If a loved one leaves, our brain recognizes that as a painful memory and we start making frantic attempts to avoid the situation. We act impulsively—after all, our survival instincts have kicked in and we will go to any length to survive. The problem is that it isn't actually a life-and-death situation now that we are adults, but as a child it would have been. We needed to be cared for and loved, we were unable to fend for ourselves, and we depended on our caregiver to help us survive. Our brain does not consider this; instead it uses our past experiences to trigger the relevant response in the now.

As you can see, this is our "survival" part of the brain at work, our limbic system.

It may seem to us that our fear of abandonment is being triggered by a current event, when actually it is an emotional memory that has triggered it. This all takes place in our "emotional mind." Our prefrontal cortex, our "reasonable mind" or "rational mind," is not being used here, for if it were, we would be able to think rationally about the current event.

I have a theory about the origins of my own fear of abandonment.

When I was two years old my mum went to the hospital to give birth to my brother. Back then, when a woman gave birth she would spend a week or more in the hospital. All of a sudden, my mum was gone and my dad, who was usually at work for long hours, had taken over caring for me.

I do not have any memories of this traumatic time, but my mum tells me that when she left the hospital and got home, I was curled in a ball in the corner of the room and wouldn't talk. She said it left her deeply disturbed. I was too young to understand that my mum would be returning home. All I knew was that she had left, and when she *did* finally come home, she had a new baby! As a very young girl, I was left feeling very confused. Although my brother, Carl, and I are extremely close and I love him to the moon and back, I probably resented him just turning up as he did! My fear of abandonment may have been born then.

## How Does It Affect Those Around Us?

Our loved ones are unable to look inside our brain and see what is going on. They do not know what memories we have stored, what thoughts we are having, or what emotions we are feeling. All they observe are our behaviors, our actions. When looking at the actions alone, without any understanding of the influences behind them, we seem completely irrational and quite scary.

We can suffocate those around us with our presence or we can push them away. We are so intense and demanding that our loved ones can feel as if they are being smothered. To start with, we may just seem slightly needy or clingy. This may first become apparent when our loved one leaves to run errands and they find that we constantly phone them for no particular reason. Our sulky mood may progress into demands that they do not leave us, and, when they do, into threats to convince them to stay. Loved ones can be left feeling as if we are too much of a responsibility to look after.

We are not denying that we can be incredibly difficult to live with, but it is only with hindsight and forcibly using our rational brain that this becomes apparent to us. When our fear of abandonment is out of control, we are unable to see the damage our actions cause, unable to see it from the other person's point of view. All rationale goes out the window and we leave our loved ones feeling confused, angry, and as if they are walking on eggshells when they are in our company.

Our behaviors can cause anxiety within those we love and leave them thinking, "How much more can I take?" Loved ones are often left feeling completely helpless and torn between living their lives and not causing us hurt.

We must understand that it is our behavior, rather than who we are, that is a huge weight upon their shoulders. Although unconscious, our behaviors can seem manipulative to those who do not understand this disorder, causing our loved ones to feel tied down and trapped. This inevitably leads to them pulling themselves free from us; then we are left with "proof" that our abandonment fear was perfectly rational.

It is important that we become aware of our actions and the effect they have on those around us, just as it is important for those around us to understand the reasons behind our behaviors. When we are able to look logically at the harms we cause, rather than finger pointing and casting blame, we can start to understand how those around us feel. It is vital that we see things from our loved one's perspective. When we do this, we realize that they do not have a personal vendetta against us, they are merely responding to our behaviors in the only way that they know how.

## Skills for Dealing with Fear of Abandonment

When considering what skills to use to help us manage this trait, we should first ask: *Where do I think this trait has stemmed from? Has something in my past caused this fear to be triggered in me? If this is the case, can I now learn to accept and let go of the past?*

Once we can accept something that has happened in our past, we can then begin to separate the fears from our past from the reality of the present. It is imperative that we do this, for if we do not we will forever be living a life in which our past dictates our future—and we will be unable to move forward successfully.

## *Acceptance*

We cannot change our past, but we do have the power within us to accept it. Accepting our past does not mean that we agree with what happened. Nor does acceptance mean that we approve of our past. Acceptance is being able to look back and say, "This happened and I cannot change it, but now I am going to move forward." Whether we accept it or not, the pain will still be there. The difference is that by not accepting it, we are simply prolonging the pain and therefore causing ourselves to suffer. By having acceptance we can begin to heal. We cannot expect to heal while we are suffering.

Acceptance has played a huge role in my own recovery. In 2011, my marriage changed forever. My stepson was fifteen, my daughter had just turned two, and my son was three months old. I discovered that the person I loved and trusted more than anyone in the world had been having an "emotional" affair with my best friend. The months that followed were a blur. I turned to drink and drugs to get me through my days, and suicide attempts and self-harm followed. I had gone from believing that I had the perfect family and that I was living a life people could only dream of to wanting to die. I tried to make my marriage work—after all, this was the man with whom I had wanted to spend the rest of my life.

Both of them told me that nothing sexual had happened, they just talked daily on the phone. I believed them and I still do, but for me it was an even more heart-wrenching scenario. It wasn't a drunken mistake, a one-off thing that they regretted. It was a close emotional relationship that they had built up, a close bond for more than a year, all behind my back. I spent every day of the first six months crying. I have never in my life felt pain like it. The pain felt physical—I finally understood where the saying "heart-broken" came from. My chest hurt so much, as if my heart had been ripped in two.

More than a year and a half later I entered rehab because I was unable to stop my drug addiction. While in rehab I ended my marriage. I realized that I could not forget what had happened, and being with my husband was a daily reminder of the betrayal. I desperately wanted to stop using drugs, and I didn't see how I could if we stayed together.

My marriage breakup was again heart-breaking. I could see how much I hurt my ex-husband by leaving him, and that destroyed me. I never wanted to hurt him. He was the father of my two children and he was the man with whom I had imagined growing old, but I needed to focus on my recovery from drugs so that I could be the best mum that I could be.

Within two months I had met someone else and moved on quickly, which only caused my ex-husband more pain. It was then when I realized just how much anger I still held toward my ex. I hated him for what he did and I hated him for breaking up our family, even though I was the one who had ended it. I also realized that I carried all of my hurt, all of my anger and distrust, and all of my insecurities into my new relationship. Only a couple of months into my new relationship, I discovered I was pregnant. Pregnancy is hard for a lot of women, but having BPD made it so much harder. I was a complete mess, my new relationship was hanging by a thread, and I started self-harming.

When my beautiful baby boy was born, life only seemed to get harder. I argued with my ex about when he would see the children. I argued with my new partner because I was so insecure and I truly thought he was going to cheat on me. Things continued to worsen until my partner decided he couldn't take it and decided to move out. Unsurprisingly, I took this as complete rejection and nearly fell to pieces. He explained he didn't want us to break up but he needed space. I did not understand this need, and all the old pain that I had suffered came rushing back.

I was living alone with three young children, and I felt like my world was crumbling around me. I had two choices: Give up and let my world crash down or do something and fight back. I started to look back on my past relationships and realized there was a pattern. I had always been so very jealous of all my ex-partners, always believing they would leave me for someone else. When my then-husband had come along, I made such an effort to rid myself of that jealousy...and then he betrayed my trust. After that I reverted back to my old jealous self. I would start arguments with my partner over the slightest thing and was constantly pointing the finger and blaming him for things he had never done. My old temper had returned. Once, I even woke him in the middle of the night and gave him a black eye because I "thought" he had been unfaithful.

I finally started to become aware of my fear of abandonment and realized that this was something I had lived with as far back as I could remember. I started to look at where it could have all stemmed from, going all the way back to the day my baby brother was brought home from the hospital. When I was five my mum and dad divorced, and my dad went to live in Ireland. My mum had one other relationship in my childhood (with a man us kids named Mr. Popcorn!), which lasted for years. Then one day, when I was a teen, it was all over. The only other father figure I had known was gone as well. I could finally understand where my fear came from. Things started to make sense to me for the first time in my life. In all of my relationships I had carried this fear with me, letting it destroy my relationships in the process.

It had taken me years to let my guard down with my then-husband, and I felt as if he had thrown it in my face with the affair. My response was to pick up this fear that had now quadrupled in size and bring it into my next partnership, only for it to slowly demolish that relationship as well.

Now that I could see the fear for what it was, I felt I could do something about it. I realized that it was a fear carried from my past experiences. It was not the reality of my present relationship.

The first step I took was looking back at the men in my life who I felt had abandoned me. I had to accept what had happened. I realized that I had never truly accepted any of it: my dad leaving, Mr. Popcorn leaving, my then-husband leaving. So I started to focus on accepting things as they were. My dad leaving to live in Ireland was actually the easiest to accept, as both my mum and dad are now married to wonderful partners with whom I am very close. Had my mum and dad not separated, I wouldn't have these amazing people in my life. It was accepting what my ex-husband did that I struggled with. Then I realized, whether I accept it or not, it still happened, the only difference is I can either accept it and move on or not accept it and stay where I was, in emotional turmoil.

I looked back on my relationship with my then-husband and I realized that life with me hadn't always been easy for him. He never understood my BPD and often didn't know how to cope with me—as much as he tried. Our relationship had been like an emotional roller coaster from the beginning. I started to think of the positives that came out of our relationship: I had my wonderful stepson, my daughter and my son, none of whom deserved to be caught in the middle of me and their dad hating each other. I made the decision that I would accept what happened. Now, acceptance didn't happen overnight—it was a process that took many months. Previously I had always asked, "Why? Why did he do this to me?" I eventually stopped asking this question when I realized that I would never have the exact answer. Things happen that are out of our control. He told me it was a mistake, and I had to accept that it happened and that nothing could change that it happened. I have not yet learned how to go back in time and change circumstances!

In the beginning of the acceptance process I started saying to myself regularly: "I accept it. It happened and that's that." I also said: "I am letting this go, because if I don't, I will never have a happy relationship." Obviously there were times when I would feel the old hurt and anger coming back, and I would just say these phrases over again and again. I had to do this often, but I didn't give up.

I then started to become aware of my fear when I was with my partner. When a jealous feeling or an intrusive thought popped into my head, I would remind myself that it was just my fear rearing its ugly head. It was not my reality. This took a lot of practice, as I was having intrusive thoughts daily about him cheating on me, to the point where I almost felt as if he had. Every time a new thought would pop into my head, I would remind myself that it was "just a thought based on my past experiences and nothing to do with my current relationship."

Slowly, slowly we began to rebuild our relationship. This was harder than imagined, as it was not just fear of abandonment that was my problem—I suffered with all nine of the BPD traits!—but fear of abandonment was at the core of everything. It was therefore vital that I dealt with this trait.

Today I have an amicable relationship with my ex-husband. I've forgiven him, although I am not sure that he forgives me. I can look back with hindsight and see things from his perspective, and can now feel more understanding and compassion toward him.

My partner and I welcomed our second baby, a little girl, a year ago and moved back in together. Our relationship can still have its ups and downs like most relationships, but not the roller coaster ups and downs that we had become so accustomed to. I no longer suffer from intrusive thoughts of him cheating, and I no longer fear being abandoned. That is not to say I will never be abandoned again, because just as I can't go back in time and change the past, neither can I control what happens in my future. I can, however, accept life on life's terms. I cannot stop anything painful from happening to me, but I can prevent suffering by learning the skill of acceptance.

It is important that we recognize the fact that we have two options: We can hold on to past events and let them cause us pain and destroy any hope for the future, or we can make a conscious decision to let something go and free ourselves from the suffering we experience.

Accepting a horrific event from our past takes courage, but it is essential for our recovery. Rather than immediately trying to let go of our past, we can practice acceptance in day-to-day life. We are powerless against many things; therefore mastering this skill can lead us to have a more peaceful life.

Things we may start practicing acceptance with may include:
- Our cab not turning up
- A canceled appointment
- A bill
- Arranging a BBQ and then it rains

- Missing the train
- Someone canceling plans with us

These are all minor irritations that can happen to any of us and that we have no control over. We can either let them ruin our day or we can accept that they have happened and enjoy the rest of our day. Obviously practicing acceptance around minor irritations is a lot easier than accepting a major life event from our past, but by starting small we are making acceptance of bigger things more achievable.

Reminding ourselves that we have two choices is helpful, as we can then feel that we have some control over the situation. Yes, choosing acceptance seems to be a difficult choice to make, but isn't living with the pain of past events even more difficult?

We may then start repeating acceptance statements to ourselves. Statements that can help us with acceptance may include phrases such as:

- I cannot change what has happened to me
- I can accept and move on or not accept and stay where I am
- If I continue to fight my past, I will continue to suffer
- I have control over my present moment
- I am powerless over other people and events
- I am going to free myself from my suffering

We often have to fake it to make it, at least to start with. The more we repeat these statements to ourselves, the more we will start to believe them.

### *Separating the Fears from our Past from the Reality of the Present*

Our fear of abandonment stems from past events, yet we let it destroy our future by holding on to these fears. It is therefore vital that we are able to recognize when this is happening. Are we in a relationship with someone who we can't trust? Why can we not trust them? Have they betrayed us? The chances are that they have not. So why do we not trust them? If we look at past relationships, maybe there was a time when we were betrayed by someone else, or maybe we had a parent leave our family home when we were young. We must realize that our current partner is not our former partner, nor are they the same person who left us when we were a child; they are a different person and this is a different relationship.

Writing down our fears and where they stem from can be helpful. By writing them down we are:

1.  Acknowledging them
2.  Externalizing them
3.  Able to see them for what they are—fears from our past

For example, we can grab a sheet of paper and write down the fears that we have, followed by where they may stem from. Here's an example:

| FEAR | PAST EVENT |
| --- | --- |
| I'm not good enough | My parent was very critical |
| My partner will cheat | My first partner cheated |
| Nobody likes me | I got bullied at school |

Once we have created a list like this, we can then focus on the present moment. We can then question if our fear is justified today.

### Checking the Facts

If we want to determine whether our fears are justified in the present, we need to start checking the facts. We often let the emotional part of our brain run away with itself, and then we make decisions based purely on our emotions. This is a dangerous thing for us to do, because no decision based purely on emotion will be a good one, just as no decision based purely on facts will be a good one. It is imperative that we allow both parts of our brain to have their say before making decisions.

Again, we should put pen to paper and start by writing down what our fear is, followed by the facts that we believe make our fears justified. Here's my example.

**FEAR: My partner is cheating on me.**

FACTS: They were late home from work.

They are very friendly with my friends.

When I asked them outright if they are cheating they stormed out.

They took a private call that they claim is someone from work.

We must remember that due to our fear of abandonment, our brain is constantly on the lookout for threats, meaning that our perception of what we believe is a fact may be distorted. It is therefore imperative that we question our thinking rather than immediately jumping to conclusions.

For us to do this we need to take another look at each of the "facts" one at a time. We need to look at them objectively and without judgment. This can be difficult to do, as our emotions have already told us that each fact proves they are guilty. To do this, first we need to write down each fact again, but this time we need to think up different explanations for each one.

**Here are my examples:**

**FACT: They were late home from work.**
EXPLANATIONS:
> They were stuck in traffic.
> They stopped at the shop or petrol station on way home.
> They were asked to stay behind at the office.
> They stopped the car to take a phone call.
> They bumped into an old friend and had a chat.

**FACT: They are very friendly with my friends.**
EXPLANATION:
> They are a very friendly person and they get on with most people.
> They make an effort with my friends as they want to get on with them for my sake.

**FACT: When I asked them outright if they are cheating they stormed out.**
EXPLANATIONS:
> They did not want to argue with me.

They knew they wouldn't win the argument and so it
would be pointless to try.

They are fed up with being blamed for cheating.

They have had a hard day at work and are too stressed to argue.

**FACT: They took a private call that they claim is work-related.**
EXPLANATIONS:

They did actually take a call from the office and didn't want
to be disturbed.

It was a phone call from a close friend of theirs and the
friend asked to talk to them in private about something.

They are having a private call about what to buy us for our
birthday and didn't want us to hear.

As we can see, there are plenty of other explanations for someone's
behavior, and none of them are "threats" to our relationship. In fact, the
other explanations are often far more plausible, and yet we often dismiss them and focus on the one that seems to confirm our fear of being
abandoned.

The problem with this is that our constant blaming and criticizing
actually drives our loved ones away, causing our fear of abandonment to
become a reality, when it needn't be.

*Becoming Mindful*

So often nowadays we here about *mindfulness*, but what is it and how
can it help? In a nutshell, being mindful is being able to focus all of our
attention on something in the present moment without any judgment.
For example, if we are looking at a flower we may think to ourselves,
"that is pretty but I don't like the smell." Within that thought we have
made two judgments: The flower is pretty and the flower smells bad. To
look at the flower mindfully we would just notice it for what it is:

- It is a flower.
- It has a green stalk.
- It has a strong smell.
- Its petals feel soft.

- Its stalk feels slightly rough.
- There is a pink and yellow pattern on it.

These thoughts involve no judgment and only facts. The beauty of mindfulness is that it can help us refocus our mind and holds our attention. When we are caught up with intense emotions, our mind can fill with intrusive thoughts, causing us further emotional distress. How wonderful would it be if we could gain back some control of our mind and be able to momentarily halt our distressing emotions? This is exactly what mindfulness can enable us to do.

Many of us try mindfulness a couple of times and give up when we find that our intrusive thoughts fail to stop. The truth is that mindfulness takes both practice and patience.

I first learned about mindfulness when I was on a DBT course. Before every session we would do a ten-minute mindfulness exercise. We would sit quietly in a circle and each be given a photo or an object to hold and look at for five minutes, and then for the next five minutes we would discuss our experience. I hated participating in this exercise. I might hold my object for twenty seconds before either my mind would wonder or I would start having judgmental thoughts. I would then tell myself, "I can't do this." I felt like a failure, especially when others in the group could do it.

Those of us with BPD tend to live a chaotic life, and sitting peacefully and without judgment can seem an impossibility for us. This is simply not the case. To truly master the art of mindfulness we need to persevere with it rather than quitting at the first hurdle.

Another important point to mention is that it is okay if our mind wanders. In fact, it would be a miracle if it didn't, at least in the beginning. Rather than judging ourselves on this we can simply be mindful of it. As an example, here are my thoughts as I sit holding a stone:

*"This stone is hard and it has a very smooth surface. It feels cold to my touch. When I put it to my lip, my lip tingles. I forgot to buy milk earlier. I might have a coffee when I get home, so I'll stop at the shop first. My*

*mind just wandered. That's okay, I will just bring it back to the stone. The stone feels quite heavy. It is slightly more curved on one side and has a little point on the other. What time will my partner get home tonight? Shall I cook chicken tonight or something else? I feel like a salad ... I'll get some salad at the shop too. I might get some fish as well. My mind has just wandered again. This stone is a light shade of gray but has some darker speckles of gray on it too."*

As we can see, my thought process wandered a couple of times. But rather than being judgmental or giving up, I would just notice the fact that it wandered and bring my attention back to the stone. The more we practice mindfulness the more we will find that our mind will stay focused on whatever it is that we are being mindful of.

It isn't only objects that we can be mindful of either; we can also learn to become mindful when it comes to our emotions. So rather than let an emotion consume us, we can simply notice it and not judge it. Getting into a habit of recognizing what feeling we are experiencing is helpful, as doing so takes the power out of it. By saying to ourselves, "I have a feeling in my tummy. I am feeling anxious," we are describing a physical and emotional sensation but not judging it in any way. If we were to think, "I have a *horrible* feeling in my tummy. I *hate* feeling anxious," then we would be making judgments and we would be feeding the emotion. When we notice the emotion that we are experiencing, we should also remind ourselves that it will pass. Did you know that an emotion only lasts ninety seconds? If this is the case, then why do our emotions seem to last for so long? Our emotions last longer because we allow them to do so! When an emotion hits it will intensify, fade, and then pass—all within ninety seconds. But instead of letting the emotion run its natural course, we, however, rethink what made us feel that emotion to begin with and often act out on it, only causing it to intensify again and again.

Wouldn't it be amazing if we could simply allow the emotion to run its ninety-second course and then be over? Well, we can—and mindfulness is the key. When we experience an emotion we should first make a conscious choice to name it, whether it's sadness, fear, anger, or any other uncomfortable feeling. We should then become aware of the physical effects it is having on our body. Are we trembling, has our heart rate or breathing increased, or do we feel ourselves getting hot? By being mindfully aware of our physical and emotional feelings, without judging them, we can allow them to surge through us and pass without them causing further suffering. We can also begin to focus on our breathing, slowing it down and noticing every deep inhalation and every slow and controlled exhalation. By doing this we are able to calm ourselves, and our mind is then occupied on the here and now rather than feeding our emotions further and prolonging them.

The more we practice being mindful, the easier it becomes and the more beneficial we find it to be in times of need. We can begin to become mindful of absolutely anything we are doing: washing the dishes, taking a shower, going for a walk, eating dinner, and so forth. When our mind is focused on the present moment, we are prevented from reminiscing on our past or focusing on what will happen in the future—both things that those of us with BPD spend a lot of time doing.

### Communicating

One of the biggest problems that our fear of abandonment causes us is the way in which it affects our relationships. We make accusations, we become clingy or distant, and we argue—a lot. How many of us actually take the time to sit down with those closest to us and explain this trait to them? Not many of us. There are a few reasons for this: it may be because we ourselves are not even consciously aware of it, we feel ridiculous even saying it out loud, or we are putting ourselves in a vulnerable position by admitting it. The next time we accuse our partner of something we certainly do not want them blaming our fear of abandonment on our feelings rather than their behaviors.

If we continue as we are, however, the chances are extremely high that we will damage our relationships beyond repair. If we allow ourselves to open up about this trait with those closest to us, they can begin to understand why we behave the way that we do.

We must also become aware of how we communicate our feelings with our loved ones:

"You have ..."

"You make me feel ..."

"Why did *you* ...?"

"You" statements can cause our loved ones to automatically jump on the defensive, and very often an argument will ensue. This is because by saying "you," it sounds as if we are personally attacking the person with whom we are speaking.

Imagine a partner has returned home late from work. They walk through the door and we immediately say, "Where the hell were *you*? *You* didn't even call to say *you* would be late! *You've* made me so angry!"

Now imagine we word it differently. Our partner walks through the door and instead we say: "*I* wish you had called me, as *I* have been so worried. And now *I* feel so angry!"

Both statements explain how we feel, but the second one does so in a way that is far less likely to cause our partner to become defensive.

By making simple changes in the way in which we convey what it is that we want to say, we are less likely to come across as confrontational, allowing us to avoid conflict.

### *Coping in a Crisis*

A crisis point is reached when our emotions become so unbearable that we feel as if we have lost control and are desperate for the pain to go away. Those of us with BPD often find that we reach a crisis point often, and it is far more likely that, when in this state, we act impulsively and recklessly. Our fear of abandonment is a common cause of us reaching a crisis point; therefore it is important for us to include skills that we can put in place at times of crisis.

Finding something that works for us in our time of need takes practice and patience, and a coping skill that works for one person may not work for another. When thinking about what new coping mechanism might work for us, we must also be open-minded to trying new things. Something that we may think has absolutely no chance of working may in fact turn out to be our go-to choice when trying to cope in a crisis at a later date. The more different things we try, the more things we are likely to find that work for us.

Distraction is a technique that has some major benefits for us. Not only can it relieve us from the pain that we are experiencing, it also buys us time to calm down and reassess the situation. Sometimes a time-out is all we need to avoid the crisis completely. What we may at first perceive to be the end of the world may actually be seen in an entirely new way when we come back to it.

The ways in which we can distract ourselves are numerous. First off, exercise is a wonderful distraction if we are feeling anxious or angry. We are able to let out all of our pent-up energy in a healthy way, and the release of endorphins in our brain can leave us feeling slightly euphoric. A simple fast-paced walk will suffice, a fast sprint or jogging on the spot—something that allows us to release energy. When using exercise as a distraction technique, we should try and focus solely on what we are doing rather than exercising and still focusing on our problem—remember, we are trying to distract.

Exercise isn't the only way in which we can distract. We can also consider a hobby, whether cooking, writing, painting, playing golf, or reading. Of course, when we first start using hobbies as a way of distracting in a crisis it is highly likely that our mind will wander back to the actual crisis. This is why practicing these coping skills when we are *not* in a crisis is helpful. The more we practice them, the stronger the neural pathways we build in our brain will be and the easier it becomes to use these skills when we need them most. It is important when taking part in such activities that we do so as mindfully as possible. Yes, mindfulness should be used here as well! The more we focus on what we are doing, the less we can focus on the problem.

There are times, due to the nature of BPD, when we actually push people away to the point that they leave us. Our fear of abandonment becomes a reality and we are left distraught. The sadness can overwhelm us, and all we want to do is curl up into ball and disappear. If we had

71

a friend who was suffering like this, what we would do to help them? Would we tell them to go and self-harm or use drugs? No. We would treat them with kindness and compassion, and this is exactly how we should treat ourselves: with kindness and compassion. So how do we do this? Again, as with all the skills, different things work for different people. Some people may want to cuddle up in bed with their pet whereas others may prefer to go for a walk in the countryside.

We can help calm and soothe ourselves by using our senses: sight, sound, touch, taste, and smell. We should consider which things stimulate our senses and which senses we prefer to stimulate. If we are someone who prefers visuals for stimulation, we may consider going for a walk somewhere beautiful, visiting an art gallery, or watching a film. If it is sound that we find more helpful, listening to music or a guided meditation are things to consider. If touch is our thing, then stroking an animal, having a nice bath, or taking a relaxing swim may work. If we find taste soothing, then enjoying a nice meal or a drink can help soothe us. If we like to use our sense of smell, then baking a cake or smelling a scented candle, flowers, or freshly cut grass are all options to try.

How many of us actually know which senses we find the most soothing, though? It isn't until we try using all of our senses in various ways that we gain insight into what works and what doesn't. Even if we think something will not work for us, it won't hurt for us to try it. We must remember that the more tricks we have up our sleeve for coping in a crisis, the better.

### Building Self-Esteem

Our fear of abandonment is not helped by our insecurities and low self-esteem. If we believe that we are useless, how can we possibly believe that others see us any differently? Therefore, it makes sense that if we want to help conquer this fear, we should include building our self-esteem.

Just as fear of abandonment often stems from our past, so does our low self-esteem. Perhaps we got bullied at school, had a critical parent, were abused, or had an ex-partner who would belittle us. Thinking about where our low self-esteem stems from is helpful, as we can then understand the reason it is the way it is. The reason isn't that we are not good enough or that we are horrible people, rather that someone else in our past has made us feel that way about ourselves.

Positive affirmations are important, as we can use them to replace the ongoing and intrusive negative self-talk that we subject ourselves to.

| Negative Self-Talk | Positive Affirmations |
|---|---|
| I am a bad person. | I am a good person. |
| I am ugly. | I am beautiful. |
| I don't deserve to be happy. | I deserve to be happy |
| I hate myself. | I love myself. |

We need to replace every negative comment about ourselves with a new positive one. When thinking of a positive affirmation, consider using the exact opposite of what you usually tell yourself. At first, yes, we may not believe what we're saying, and yes, we will feel ridiculous saying it, but we owe it to ourselves to do this. If nothing changes, nothing changes. In time, we start to notice that we don't feel so silly reciting these affirmations to ourselves, and further down the line we eventually start to believe them ... and this is our self-esteem growing.

### Building Solid Relationships

When living with a fear of abandonment, we may find that we distance ourselves from other people, fearing that they will hurt us. Sometimes we do the opposite and surround ourselves with so-called friends, all the while never truly showing them our true selves. There are also those of us who tend to pick people who are not necessarily good for us but perhaps subconsciously remind us of someone from our early years. Consider a young woman who searches out an older man who is emotionally distant, like her father was when she grew up, or a man who gets with a woman who verbally abuses and attacks him, just as his mother did when he was young.

Many of us who were raised in a dysfunctional family eventually replicate the household in which we grew up. This happens because of the attachments we formed in childhood, whether they were positive and healthy or negative and unhealthy. As we grow up, we do so believing that the attachments that we have are normal, so we carry them into our adult relationships with us.

If we are trying to gain some control over our fear of abandonment, it is very important that we surround ourselves with good, positive people. Not "so-called" friends who we only see when we are out socializing and drinking. Not toxic "friends" who put us down at every chance they get, and not "friends" who only see us when they choose to. When starting recovery, it is vital that we take a look at our friendship circle. Maybe we have a friend who always seems to be there for us when everything is going wrong in our life, but on closer inspection we realize that when things are going well for us they are not there for us at all.

The saying "quality over quantity" applies very much to our friendship groups. Having two or three solid relationships is so much more valuable than having ten fickle ones. When building solid relationships, we must also take a look at ourselves. If we continue to wear a mask and never reveal our true selves to someone, the relationship is based on a lie. It is important that we learn to be authentic—not with every single person we meet but at least with one or two people to start with.

We must also ask ourselves, *What is it that I expect from a friendship?* We probably want a friend who we could trust, one who would be there for us when we need them, a friend who doesn't keep canceling plans we have made, someone who can make us smile, a friend who does not judge us and is supportive and understanding.

Then we must ask ourselves, *Can I, too, be all those things to another person?* We cannot expect a friend to be all these things and yet not reciprocate. If we make plans with a friend, we need to do our utmost to stick to them. We need to listen to them rather than always being the one who wants to be heard. Yes, we have BPD, and the problems that come with that are abundant. But that doesn't mean our friend doesn't also have problems of their own. In fact, we often find when we are able to reach out and help a friend it also benefits us; we are distracted from our own problems and we feel useful, which helps build our self-esteem.

We must also think about our romantic relationships. Ask yourself, *Do I treat someone the way I would like to be treated? How would I feel if I were constantly being blamed for things?* Just by putting ourselves in the other person's shoes, we can begin to understand the effect we have on them.

We must know that a solid relationship is not built overnight. It takes time and effort on both sides. A one-sided relationship is sure to fail, leaving us with an even bigger fear of abandonment. Whether it is us putting all the effort into our relationships and getting nothing in return or the other way around makes no difference—if it is one sided, it won't work.

### *Getting Professional Help*

There are those of us who have suffered such emotional or physical abuse or neglect that no matter what skills we learn, we still struggle with regular flashbacks of traumatic events, avoid anything that may remind us of a past event, or suffer from hyperarousal due to previous trauma. This does not mean that learning new skills will never benefit us, only that we may need a bit of professional help along the way. It may very well mean that we are suffering with post-traumatic stress disorder (PTSD), as well as having borderline personality disorder.

One type of trauma therapy is trauma-focused CBT, which is particularly helpful for those who suffer from PTSD. A more recent therapy for trauma is eye movement desensitization and reprocessing (EMDR). This involves recalling the traumatic event while making rhythmic eye movements. Doing so affects the way our brain processes memories and experiences. Although this treatment is fairly new, it has shown to be extremely helpful when treating patients who have suffered trauma.

### Skills Checklist

In this chapter we have learned an array of skills for identifying, noticing, managing, and decreasing the power of your fear of abandonment. We can call on these skills when we feel this fear rising.

- Acceptance
- Separating the fears from our past from the reality of the present
- Checking the facts
- Mindfulness
- Communication
- Coping in a crisis
- Building self-esteem
- Building solid relationships
- Getting professional help

Chapter 6

# UNSTABLE RELATIONSHIPS

*"Relationships don't last because of the good times.*
*They last because the hard times were handled with care."*
—Anmol Andore

## What Are Unstable Relationships?

To understand what is meant by "unstable relationships" it is help-ful to contemplate what a "stable" relationship is. Most relationships have periods of ups and downs, good and bad times. People in a sta-ble relationship can still argue and have times when they disagree with one another, but they will often work through these issues together in a healthy manner. In healthy relationships, the ups and downs appear sporadically between long periods of stability. Those who are in an un-stable relationship also have ups and downs, good and bad times, but rather than the rift being an occasional event that appears and sends a slight ripple through the stability of the relationship, it is the opposite: the whole relationship is like the waves in the ocean, constantly moving up and down and rarely showing any signs of stability.

When we look at the various traits of borderline personality disor-der, it seems an impossibility that our relationships could be stable. For how can a relationship be balanced and secure when one of the partners lives with a fear of abandonment, intense anger, impulsive behaviors, and mood swings? We know not everyone with BPD necessarily has these particular traits, but even having just one of them is surely enough to cause a relationship to be volatile. Right?

It is therefore unsurprising that unstable relationships is one of the criteria for BPD.

## Our Thoughts

Many of us with BPD think in black and white—something is all good or all bad, right or wrong, positive or negative, ideal or imperfect. There is no in between, no gray area, no middle ground. This style of thinking is also known as *splitting* and it can have a profound effect on our relationships.

If a young child is told they cannot have candy, they may say, "I hate you." They are extremely angry and hurt, and they see their parent as the villain rather than as someone who loves them and is saying no for their own good. Children often can't think logically when upset and therefore can't see the gray area of the situation. Those of us with BPD can react in the same way as a young child would with our families, partners, and friends. These loved ones are either in our good book or our bad book; we don't have neither-good-nor-bad books, because people are *always* in one or the other in our eyes. Those in our good books we place high up on a pedestal, only to knock them off when they do anything that we consider to be "bad." An example of a "bad" behavior is when our loved one changes plans that they made with us. We don't consider the fact that they may have a genuine reason to change plans, instead we immediately deem them to have done us a wrong and instantly remove them from our "good book" to our "bad book"—until the time comes when they redeem themself. We think in extremes and without logic, and yet we believe we are being totally logical and rational; not until we become consciously aware of this trait and recognize when it shows up can we then start to question our own thought pattern.

Due to the many different traits of BPD and the numerous reasons behind our unstable relationships, our thoughts can seem never ending. Here is just a sampling of thoughts we have almost continuously.

### Fear of Abandonment Thoughts
- *They are going to leave me.*
- *They are cheating on me.*
- *They think I am ugly.*
- *I have to change so they do not leave me.*

The thoughts brought on due to our attachment and abandonment issues are abundant. See chapter 5 "Fear of Abandonment" for more information on this topic.

### Splitting Thoughts
- *I love them.*
- *I hate them.*
- *They are amazing.*
- *They are the scum of the earth.*
- *How can they do this to me?*
- *I never want to see them again.*

As mentioned above, we think in extremes. It is almost as if our mind closes off to any other information that is available to us. If a loved one has taken a week off work to spend time with us, but on day six they tell us they actually need to go back to work a day early, we completely forget all the time spent together and instead zoom in on the fact that they are now leaving us.

Likewise, if we are in an abusive relationship with a partner who treats us badly 99 percent of the time but one day comes home with flowers for us, we close our mind to the fact that this person is awful most of the time and focus just on the 1 percent of the time that is good. The abusive partner immediately goes into our good book, and our family member who spent time with us all week except for one day, goes straight into our bad book. Irrational, yes, but to us our thinking seems rational, as we are unable to examine all the actualities, instead focusing on a one-off event as opposed to the surrounding circumstances.

### Obsession and Jealousy Thoughts
- *I need to know everything about them— their past,*

*present, and plans for the future.*
- *They* will *fall in love with me.*
- *We* must *be together.*
- *I will catch them fooling around.*
- *I know they are up to no good.*
- *I must know what they are doing at all times.*
- *I can tell what they are thinking.*
- *I must stop them.*

Our mind can often fill with intrusive thoughts, and although a thought does not equal a fact, we struggle with this concept, tending to believe that our irrational thinking is justified. Our obsessive and jealous thoughts can also be linked with our fear of abandonment and can cause us to make frantic efforts to avoid rejection.

Another reason behind our obsessive nature may be the fact that we are so unhappy with our own lives. Obsessing over another person causes us to focus our attention on someone else rather than looking inward at ourselves. Obsessing over someone can also make us feel as if we have control over a situation when the truth is that we do not.

### Trust Issues Thoughts
- *Please like me.*
- *They are going to leave me.*
- *They do not like me.*
- *If they do not give me attention constantly it means they don't care about me.*
- *I don't deserve to be loved.*
- *They like other people more than they like me.*
- *My partner likes blondes and I'm a brunette so he must find me unattractive.*
- *I need to be richer/skinnier/more muscly/funnier/more clever/and so on.*

Trust is yet another thought pattern brought on by our fear of abandonment and our unclear self-image. This thought pattern is heightened by our inability to see and recognize the gray area. Due to those around us so regularly going from black to white and back again, we struggle to achieve trust in a relationship, believing that if someone can go from black to white so often they have not earned our trust. We struggle to realize that our idealization and devaluation of others is something we create in our mind and is a distorted perception of reality. Once we are able to tackle our black-and-white thinking and are capable of observing the gray area, we can then challenge our perception and slowly learn to trust others.

Our low self-esteem and unclear self-image also heighten our distrust of others. If we do not like ourselves how can anybody else like us? Projection is one of our defense mechanisms; rather than focusing on what we do not like about ourselves we put the blame on our loved ones and assume they think the same way about us as we do about ourselves.

## Our Feelings

Relationships seem to be the fuel powering our turbulent feelings. The effect others have on our emotions is gargantuan. What we fail to realize is that other people cannot make us feel anything; it is our own choice how we let others affect us. Our perception of others' intentions isn't necessarily accurate. It is our distorted view of the world and those in it that inadvertently bring on feelings that do not correspond with the reality of the situation.

We think in extremes, and our feelings match our thoughts: intense in nature and seeming to appear out of nowhere. While it is our thoughts that trigger our feelings, it is our intense feelings that spur us on to act in a way that we deem appropriate for the internal feeling; but the truth is that our actions are often extremely inappropriate.

Our feelings can range from one extreme to the other within relationships, and we are likely to go through every feeling imaginable over the course of time. Our feelings at the start of a relationship tend to be more positive. It seems we enter into new relationships, whether romantic or otherwise, with positive feelings for our future. We can feel as if we are on a high due to the intensity of the feelings. Love, happiness, joy, and sex are all words we can use to describe the initial feelings we have at the beginning of a relationship.

As a relationship takes its course, however, those positive "white" feelings are replaced with "black" ones. We begin to feel insecure and less than, leading us to lose any trust we may have previously thought that we had built in the relationship. Our fear of abandonment resurfaces, and we are left feeling anxious and scared for our future. Jealousy, like resentments, literally eats away at us, destroying our self-esteem and damaging our already unstable relationships.

## Our Behaviors

While it is our thoughts and feelings that cause us the most pain, it is our actions that cause the greatest pain to those around us. Our actions, although justified in our mind, are nearly always caused by an irrational thought and feeling. To the person that is unfortunate enough to feel our wrath, we appear out of control, irrational, and downright scary. Our actions are both impulsive and fierce, as we are desperately trying to control a situation we have no control over.

Here are some of the driving forces behind our action, followed by the actions themselves.

### Fear of Abandonment Behaviors

- Frantic efforts to avoid abandonment (see chapter 5 for examples)
- Cutting off emotionally, becoming emotionally detached
- People-pleasing
- Violent outbursts
- Changing who we are in order to prevent rejection
- Testing our partner

People-pleasing isn't necessarily an action that will cause harm to others, at least not at first glance. We go above and beyond with our people-pleasing in an attempt to avoid rejection and to make people see how wonderful we are, which seems contradictory, as we personally see ourselves as anything but wonderful. The problems arise when we do not see our actions reciprocated or we start to feel taken for granted. A resentment will start to form, and we begin to feel unloved; eventually our anger will come to the surface.

Years ago, I started making a partner the most lavish lunches for them to take to work. The first few times I did he couldn't thank me enough and praised me to anyone who would listen, telling them about his amazing lunches made by *moi*. After a few weeks, the thanks and the praise started to dwindle until it was nonexistent. I continued to make the extravagant lunches, but inside I started to feel angry. How dare he not thank me for his lunch when I put so much effort into it? I started to see him as an ungrateful good-for-nothing git. I then started to question if we should even be together.

There are those of us who cut off emotionally from other people, a defense mechanism to protect ourselves from emotional pain. Doing so can cause hurt and confusion for our loved ones, especially if we had appeared warm and loving at the beginning of our relationship. We have the ability to make people feel on top of the world, due to our intense feelings of love and passion. Our partner can then be left feeling unloved and unwanted when we go from being intensely in love with them to cutting off from them, with no explanation. While we may realize we are simply protecting ourselves, our loved one doesn't, and they may take the rebuff as rejection. We do not always consciously realize that we are doing this, and it can happen gradually over time, with us becoming more and more distant.

My own relationship history illustrates some of these dynamics. When I first got in a relationship with someone, I would mold myself to be whatever I thought they wanted. If I felt they wanted a homely, stay-at-home, and clean-the-house sort of person, then that is who I would become. If I thought they wanted a sex-mad party girl, I would take on that persona as easily as changing my outfit. I was a chameleon to the extreme. My problems would start a few months into the relationship when I felt the "chase" was well and truly over. They were my partner now, and slowly I would let my mask slip. Gone was the girl they thought they had, replaced by the real me, a complete stranger to them. I went from having sex daily to not wanting it at all, cuddles in bed to "this is my side—stay off it," and from saying yes to everything to saying no to everything.

### Splitting Behaviors

- Making our loved one feel as if they are the most important person in the world and then switching, causing them feel as if they are the most hated person in the world
- One day talking and engaging with a loved one and ignoring them completely the next day
- Being genuinely nice one moment, then making subtle, not-so-nice remarks or back-handed comments the next

Our black-and-white thinking can sometimes be in-your-face obvious, but other times it is far subtler. While we know that we have gone from liking someone one moment to not liking them the next, the other person may be completely unaware of this. They may have an idea that something isn't quite right, due to our subtle, disparaging remarks about them, but they may put this down to a "mood swing" rather than splitting. There are also times we can go from liking someone one moment to not liking them the next and have no valid reason for the shift in feeling.

To illustrate this splitting, I could wake up one morning and start noticing lots of negatives about my boyfriend. He wouldn't have done anything wrong, of course, but I wouldn't be able to help but focus on all the things I don't like about him: the way he blows his nose, the way he leaves his socks lying around, his laugh, the way he calls me "babe." The previous day none of these things had been an issue, but throughout this particular day they are—and they could grate on me as much as someone scratching their nails down a blackboard. I could look at my boyfriend with contempt, unable to even give him a smile. Then, at night, when lying in bed with him asleep next to me, I could look at his face and feel such anger toward him. Without even a thought, I could fling my arm over and whack him in the face. He would jump up not knowing what the hell had happened, and I would pretend to be asleep.

Yes, this is pretty shocking behavior, especially when we consider the fact that this guy hadn't actually done anything wrong. As easily as he had moved into my bad book, the following day he could move back into my good book—and the socks and his laugh would no longer irritate me.

### Obsession and Jealousy Behaviors

- Stalking someone, either physically or on social media
- Accusing our loved one of something
- Looking for physical evidence against our loved one as proof they have wronged us, such as checking emails, phones, and so on
- Playing mind games
- Verbal and/or physical abuse

Obsession and jealousy can take us to a very dark place. They are incredibly painful to live with, and so we act out, often impulsively, causing harm either directly or indirectly.

In the beginning of a relationship, I usually wanted to be the cool, chilled-out girlfriend who never nags. A few months in, however, I would transform into the girlfriend who would phone multiple times a day, turning up at his work and following him in the car. I literally became any guy's worst nightmare.

My jealousy was intense from back when I was fourteen and I had my first boyfriend. One day I discovered that he had a collection of magazines of females in their underwear. I can remember feeling as if I had been punched in the stomach. My reaction? I tried to throw myself off a motorway bridge, but he wrestled me to the ground.

Another time, when I was twenty, I was seeing a guy who went out for a lads' night. When I phoned him, he told me quite honestly that he was in a strip club. My response? I cut my wrists, trashed the house and overdosed.

When I was twenty-two, I had started seeing my soon-to-be husband. One night he told me he couldn't see me. I immediately felt paranoid, as if I knew he was up to something. I drove around looking for his car for hours. When I was unsuccessful in finding it, I went on a drink and drug binge for days.

A week before our wedding, my fiancé went out for his stag do and, unsurprisingly, his friends took him to a strip club. I cut the crotch out of his trousers and destroyed his clothes as punishment for "betraying" me.

I could write a whole book on my jealous and obsessive behaviors, but I think we get the picture. My thoughts and feelings were so intense and I would react in an intense, impulsive, and destructive way.

My jealousy didn't always emerge in such a spectacularly explosive way, though. In fact, my jealousy, which was eating away at my insides, could cause me to be cunning and clever, in my actions—mind games.

**Mind Games**

In nearly all of my relationships—not just the romantic ones—mind games were my hidden treasure. Playing them was something I could do without being blatantly obvious. I wasn't explosive; I was controlled and shrewd, and I could play with anyone I fancied without it being immediately noticeable.

Tests of love were a firm favorite of mine, and I would play this game often, adapting it as need be. For example, I would subtly phone a family member and ask them to grab me a fizzy drink on the way home, without specifying what drink I wanted. If my loved one came home with the drink I wanted, they passed the test. If they came home with a drink I didn't usually drink, they failed. In my mind, I thought they clearly didn't know me at all, which was proof they didn't love or care for me. I wouldn't necessarily have an outburst if they failed; rather, I would just file away their failed test in my mind along with any other failed tests, ready to use against them at a later date.

If a loved one asked me if I wanted dinner as they were cooking, I would often say no. This was a test. Obviously, I wanted dinner—was I just not going to eat, for goodness' sake? If they then prepared themself dinner and not me (even though I had said no), they failed the test. Surely they should be able to read my mind and make me dinner anyway, cover it in cling film ready for me to eat later?

I would sometimes start up a conversation about a famous actress or singer (who usually looked the opposite of me) and mention how beautiful she is. This was a trap. If my partner agreed with me, I decided that he couldn't possibly find me attractive if he thinks someone else looks attractive. This game could be played while walking down the street. I would simply point out a pretty girl and say something like "she has a great figure." If he agreed with me, he would have hell to pay and I would accuse him of looking at other women.

With a family member I might bring up a time when I had been naughty as a child and start discussing the memory. If the family member agreed that I had been hard work, I would flip out, accusing them of still holding it against me and screaming that they didn't love me back then and they don't love me now.

Yes, these tests of loves can be seen as manipulative and selfish. But they are acted out impulsively, not planned ahead; they're done out of desperation, when we are trying to do everything in our power to cope in that moment and get our needs met.

Tests of love are not the only mind games that we play, however. We are known to blackmail our loved ones, especially when we feel we are losing control of a situation. If we have an argument with a loved one and they go to walk it off, we take this as abandonment and may resort to blackmail. We might yell, "If you walk out this door you will never see me again!" "If you leave you will regret it!" and so on. Blackmail is most commonly used when we feel backed into a corner and are feeling particularly desperate. It is not calculated or premeditated; it's a tactic used impulsively out of desperation.

Many of our loved ones will say that we also project onto them, which we often do. Without realizing that we are doing so, we take all of our own insecurities and faults and blame someone else for them. For example, if we feel insecure about our body we may begin shouting at our partner and telling them that they think we are fat and ugly. We also twist words. We might ask a loved one if they like this new outfit we have bought, and when they say they are not too keen we scream at them, telling them that they said we look a mess. It is no wonder that our loved ones can be left feeling as if they are walking on eggshells around us. Loved ones become afraid to talk around us in case they say the wrong thing, causing us to erupt at them.

## Codependency

We are so desperate to feel loved that when it does happen we often cling to the relationship for dear life, becoming extremely dependent on that person, whether a family member, friend, partner, or therapist. We start to believe that this is the person who can save us—a huge responsibility for someone to take on. We do not realize that it is only we who can save ourselves. We believe that we are not whole without this person in our life, and we look to them for reassurance persistently.

For many years I saw men as my medicine; I believed that to be happy I had to be in a relationship. When I was single I felt lost, so I would quickly jump from one relationship to another. I feared being on my own, as I was unhappy in my own skin and needed to have a man in my life to make me feel validated. Once in a relationship I became a leech, sucking the life out of my partner and refusing to leave their side. If a partner went to work they could either expect to have multiple calls from me hourly or dread that I would unexpectedly turn up at their work. Once they got home, I would follow them around the house like a puppy dog! They couldn't go to the bathroom without me following them.

Codependency can happen both ways. We may get ourselves into a relationship with someone who thinks that they can save us. They believe that they can be the one to change us and make us truly happy. If only it were as simple as that. We may also find ourselves getting into relationships with someone who has their own problems: alcoholism, addiction, narcissism, gambling, sex addiction, or just your general "bad" boy or girl. When we get into a relationship with someone with their own troubles, we can focus our attention on them rather than on ourselves. We have low self-esteem, and by trying to "fix" another person we feel better about ourselves.

So why do we get into relationships such as the ones mentioned above? A lot of it stems from our childhood. As we know, many people with BPD have suffered some form of trauma or abuse. We may have grown up in a dysfunctional family where addictive behaviors or shouting was the norm. We grow up with the idea that that is what love is, and we then seek it out in adulthood. Maybe we grew up having to look after our parent or siblings. Perhaps we had a parent who overly mothered us so that we never learned any form of independence. When a parent shouted at us we may have become submissive, or we may have desperately tried to please them, thinking that we would earn their love. Within our adult relationships we will often continue to carry the same traits that we had as a child.

## Friendships

Friendships can be as difficult as our romantic or family relationships. We become clingy and under the illusion that we ought to be our friend's only friend. If they enjoy other friendships, we consider it disloyalty. We think in black and white with our friends, and can blow hot and cold. We may make plans with them and then cancel at the last minute, but they must not do the same to us. We play mind games with our friends to test their loyalty, and we can become jealous of our friends and even obsessive over them. We will find that, over time, we lose many of our close friendships, as people believe us to be attention seeking, demanding, and even abusive. We must understand that our friends are only able to view our behaviors; they can't read our thoughts or understand our feelings. They do not grasp the nature of this illness and often withdraw from us in order to protect themselves. For us, losing a friendship is yet another abandonment in our eyes, and we can take it very personally and hold a grudge, unable to recognize the reasons behind them unfriending us.

Those of us with BPD may also suffer from unstable moods, depression, and anxiety. These traits impact our day-to-day lives and our friendships. How often do we make plans with friends only to make excuses and cancel? Friends can get tired of our unreliability, as we very rarely divulge our true reasons for not seeing them. We seem unable to disclose to people that we are feeling down or suffering with our mental health, preferring to fabricate details about not meeting with them. We believe that if people were to know the truth about us they would not understand—and we risk being judged. In reality, though, it is the lies that we tell that result in us losing our friends.

## Where Does This Trait Come From?

Our childhood and our upbringing possibly play a part in certain aspects of our unstable relationships, such as our codependency or fear of abandonment. If, however, a child grows up in a stable and loving home and yet still goes on to develop BPD in adulthood, unstable relationships will more likely than not still be one of the traits that they have. The reason for this is simple: it is unlikely that anyone who has at least five BPD traits, and therefore has a diagnosis of BPD, can have stable relationships due to the fact that all of the traits, whether singularly or combined, have a devastating impact on the person's life. Each of the nine traits is destructive and overwhelming, either to those around us or to ourselves. It therefore seems highly unlikely that someone with BPD will have no instability in their relationships.

BPD is characterized by the intensity of our emotions and our inability to manage them. Other people have a huge impact on how we feel and, depending on how we feel, determine how we will react. It is a vicious cycle; our unstable relationships cause us to feel and react a certain way, and how we feel and react cause us to have unstable relationships.

## What Is Happening in Our Brain?

The relationships we seek out in adulthood tend to be replicas of the relationships we had as a child, whether we are aware of it or not. Our stored emotional memories, conscious or unconscious, have a profound effect on our relationships. Emotional memories can trigger us to behave in a way similar to the way we did when the memory was first formed.

As previously mentioned, our brain is made for survival. Those of us with BPD have a hypothalamus that is constantly aroused and high levels of cortisol in our bodies, meaning we are constantly on high alert and looking for threats. It is more than simply a case of anxiety.

Here's a story that shows what a strain this high-alert mode can create, both for us and for those we love. When I was twenty-five and living with my then-husband, I had a friend come over for dinner. We had a lovely evening, laughing and joking and enjoying the good food (made by myself!). After dinner we decided to put on a funny movie and chill, before my friend's partner came to collect her. It was during the movie when I suddenly noticed that my friend and my husband were laughing a lot together and at parts of the film that I didn't find funny. I immediately thought to myself that they must be sharing a private joke. This thought progressed into me thinking that they were laughing at my expense and the joke was on me. Half an hour later, my friend exclaimed that she had wet herself because she had been laughing so hard. Rather than believing what she said, I came to the assumption that she was wet because she had secretly had sex with my husband. I told my husband I needed a word with him, and once in the kitchen the accusations were thrown at him. He obviously denied it and even asked, "When was I supposed to have had sex with her? You have been with me the whole time!" I then proceeded into the front room and started accusing my friend. She was horrified, called her partner, and left.

So what was going on in my brain here? My hypothalamus was already on high alert, searching for threats. It didn't take long for me to find one when I noticed my then-husband and my friend laughing. This may have something to do with the hippocampus retrieving an old emotional memory of myself and my partner laughing like that. The laughter equated to love in my mind. The fact that it was my friend laughing rather than myself meant it was a threat, and this flawed threat was then sent to my overactive amygdala. My amygdala then activated my hypothalamus, which in turn set off my fight-or-flight response. I needed to act, I needed to do something. As we know, the prefrontal cortex (thinking, logic, rational) in the brain of someone with BPD is underactive when under stress. So rather than thinking through the scenario and questioning it, I just reacted, with no thought of the consequences, verbally attacking my then-husband and my friend.

There are so many different aspects to unstable relationships that different parts of our brain are responsible for certain thought patterns and behaviors. In chapter 5, the brain and fear of abandonment is discussed.

Within our relationships we may struggle with other issues, such as addiction, eating disorders, self-harm, mood swings, and extreme anger, to name just a few. How our brain works in each of these instances will be discussed in the relevant chapters.

## How Does It Affect Those Around Us?

Anyone who has a relationship with us—whether friends, family, or romantic partners—knows only too well the difficulties that come with loving someone with BPD. Just as those of us with BPD can feel that we are on an emotional roller coaster, so too can our loved ones feel as if they are strapped into the seat next to us for the turbulent ride ahead.

With our ever-changing moods and black-and-white thinking, loved ones never really know where they stand with us. Just as they start to feel as if things are taking a turn for the better, we act out in a way that drags them back to the reality of the situation—the BPD is still there and our brief moments of stability are just that—brief.

Our family members, friends, and partners may love us to the moon and back, but there are times when they will question everything. There is only so much people feel they can take, and we are forever pushing them to their limits. Those that love us but do not understand this disorder are likely to leave, deciding that we must be bad people if we are able to treat them in this way. Even for loved ones who do understand BPD, it can be hard. We can be vocally and physically abusive, we can make those around us feel as if they are the problem, we can leave them feeling helpless when we turn on ourselves, and we can be totally embarrassing.

I once had an argument with my then-husband and called my mum, screaming at her to come and collect me from my house. My mum turned up and proceeded to wait an hour, yet I still didn't go out to her. When she decided she had waited long enough, she drove away, going to the gym as she did every Saturday morning.

When I eventually came out and saw she had left without me, I worked myself into such a rage that I walked all the way to her gym. When I didn't see her I stomped down into the changing rooms. I started screaming, "Where the fuck are you?! How *dare* you leave me! Show yourself, you bitch!" There was no answer and finally I left, assuming she wasn't there.

It was only recently that I discovered that my poor mum had been there the whole time, hiding away in a changing cubicle, scared to make a sound in case I discovered she was there. Luckily now, both my mum and I can look back and laugh about the moment and see how ridiculous it was, but at the time my poor mum was absolutely mortified. She told me she waited another thirty minutes before coming out of the cubicle, as she didn't dare face anyone in the changing room in case they knew I was related to her.

We can show up family members in front of complete strangers. It is not that we consciously choose to do this, it is that we do not think of the consequences before we do it. We act so impulsively and erratically that loved ones fear being in our presence in case today is the day that we choose to humiliate them. Due to our behaviors, our loved ones can start to isolate themselves, not wanting others to see us at our worst. This isn't necessarily because they are embarrassed of us, but usually because they do not want people to judge us. Yes, they can be mad at us and think and say unpleasant things about us at times, but they also love us and do not want others to think badly of us. Our loved ones, family members, and partners in particular can be left feeling very alone.

Loved ones also spend an enormous time worrying about our safety.

BPD is a disorder in which 10 percent of those who have it actually commit suicide and 70 percent attempt it. It is sad that family members often feel they are left to deal with us on their own, with no support for themselves. It can be a huge weight on their shoulders, never knowing what we are likely to do to ourselves and being powerless to stop us.

## Skills for Dealing with Unstable Relationships

Due to the fact that this trait involves other people, it is no surprise that communication skills are one of the most important skills we need to learn.

### *Communication*

Our unstable relationships are almost always made worse by the way in which we communicate. Our intense relationships can lead to our intense emotions, which then cause us to react in an equally intense way. Not many of us can say that we try to sit with someone and calmly explain how we are feeling. We are far more likely to erupt and say the first thing that comes to us, no matter how hurtful. We believe that our internal pain is caused by another person, and so we cast blame and point the finger accusingly. Our loved ones step gingerly around us, fearing another eruption. This actually irritates us, as we do not understand why they are playing the victim and tiptoeing around, when as far as we are concerned it is them who have hurt us.

How we talk to others can either negatively impact our relationships, as it so often does, positively impact them, which is what we want to aim for.

So why do we communicate in the way that we do?

- **We let resentments build up.** Someone may hurt us and we do not say anything, preferring to bottle it up, but when we do this the hurt only grows bigger.
- **We people-please constantly.** And then we get annoyed when it isn't reciprocated, leading to another resentment.
- **We are not assertive.** We often just can't say no to people, yet again leading to a resentment building up. Our lack of assertiveness also leads to us being aggressive or passive-aggressive.

- **We misperceive things.** Our perception of events also triggers us to communicate in a way that causes conflict.
- **We act out impulsively.** This is due to the intensity of our feelings.
- **We lack communication skills.** We did not learn good communication skills when we were growing up.

So in order to change the way in which we communicate, we must also try to tackle the above obstacles. For starters, we should try and discuss our feelings often, rather than supressing them and hoping that they will go away. If someone has said something to us that we find hurtful, we should discuss it with them immediately. We may find that although we try to stay calm, we still use "you" sentences.

"When you said ..., *you* hurt me."

You sentences will cause the person we are trying to talk with to go on the defensive. Instead we should use an "I" sentence such as:

"When you said ..., *I* felt hurt."

This lets the other person know what they said and how it made us feel, without them feeling as if we are pointing the finger at them and casting blame. We are far more likely to get a calm reply and an explanation.

If we are people-pleasing, we should recognize when we are doing it and make the choice to either carry on not expecting it to be reciprocated or stop it.

Learning to be assertive is important, as it enables us to express our thoughts and feelings effectively and without being passive-aggressive. It also helps us build our self-esteem and allows us to get our needs met. To be assertive, we need to speak confidently and respectfully. Being assertive is not about always getting what we want but about us being heard by the other person. It helps us to communicate healthily within our relationships, without the other person feeling vilified every time we speak to them. If we really need to have a conversation with someone about something that is bothering us, and we have no idea how to start the conversation, we may consider writing a script beforehand. Reading through the script will help us feel more confident about having the conversation and can help ensure that we do not go off course.

If we find that we have absolutely no idea how to communicate orally without there being an almighty row, we should consider writing a letter, which can be done in peace without anyone commenting as we speak. Just as when speaking, when writing we should refrain from using "you" statements. After all, we want the other person to actually read our letter and respond courteously, rather than rip it up and think that we have personally attacked them.

### Questioning our Perception

The way in which we perceive the world seems to differ from others and causes us numerous problems. Our perception of the world around us stems from childhood and the attachments that we did or didn't make.

The relationships we formed in early childhood have a huge influence on how we perceive relationships once we have grown up. If, for example, we had a parent who neglected our emotional needs, we are likely to enter into relationships believing that we won't get our emotional needs met. We may feel rejected at the slightest thing and therefore overreact. Except we don't see it as overreacting, as this is how we genuinely feel, and if we are told we are overreacting, we feel as if we are being invalidated.

Our perception of events can affect all of our relationships: our romantic relationships, our work relationships, our friendships, and even the style in which we parent.

Of course, there may be times when our perception is spot on. But the chances are, if we have BPD, more often than not our perception of something in the present stems from a belief that was formed in the past, whether that be that we believe that nobody can be trusted, we are not good enough, or everyone is out to hurt us.

To find out if we struggle with a distorted perception, we should ask ourselves this: *How many times have I been told that I have completely overreacted to something that someone has said?*

| Someone said... | I reacted by: | My perception: | My core belief: |
|---|---|---|---|
| "I think your hair looked nicer longer." | Going home and crying. | They think I look awful. | I am not good enough. |
| Someone said... "I can't make lunch today, as something has come up." | I reacted by: Not talking to them and building a resentment. | My perception: They just don't want to see me. | My core belief: Nobody likes me. |
| Someone said... "Your friend is really nice." | I reacted by: Accusing them of fancying my friend. | My perception: They prefer my friend to me and are going to cheat on me. | My core belief: The opposite sex can't be trusted. |

It is helpful for us to write down some of the core beliefs that we have about the world around us. Our list may look something like this:

- The opposite sex cannot be trusted.
- All marriages end in divorce.
- It is wrong to show our emotions.
- If I am not perfect at everything I do then I am a failure.
- I am not lovable.
- I must never show my true self to others or they will leave me.
- The world is a dangerous place.
- I am different to everyone else.
- It's always my fault.

If we grow up with beliefs like these, they are bound to negatively impact our relationships. The way we perceive the world will be driven by these core beliefs. If we do not believe we are lovable, we will always perceive what people say to mean that we are not lovable. If we do not trust the opposite sex, we will always be on the lookout for deceitful behavior and will often perceive things in such a way that confirms our core belief to be true.

Of course, nobody likes to think that their beliefs are wrong, after all, that is why they are called beliefs—because we believe them to be true. For those of us with BPD, however, it is imperative that we do question our beliefs and our perception of events. If we do not do this, our relationships can never improve. Instead, we will carry on feeling wounded at the most innocent comments, offended when someone looks at us in a way that we construe to be demeaning, and our relationships will continue to hang by a thread.

### Questioning Our Black-and-White Thinking

Just as we need to question our perception, we must also observe our black-and-white thinking. The fact is, nearly everything in reality falls into a gray area. By categorizing everything into either all or nothing, good or bad, right or wrong, we are not actually seeing the reality of the situation. To look at the bigger picture we need to be able to examine all of it—not just one small side of it.

Our black-and-white thinking is the emotional part of our mind at work, the survival part of our brain. When fighting for survival it is important that we do think in black and white, as we need to react quickly. Imagine walking down a dark street at night and hurried footsteps are approaching quickly from behind us. We certainly don't want to start thinking "Hmm, well maybe it is just someone in a hurry. What if this person approaching means no harm?" This thinking would risk our survival, so it is important that we react quickly and without the part of our brain responsible for reasoning jumping in to help us look at the gray area first!

Most of the time, however, our survival is not at risk. If a friend cancels plans with us, our survival is not at risk. If a family member decides to go on holiday, our survival is not at risk, and if our partner forgets our birthday, our survival is not at risk. Yet, we still think in a way that suggests that it is.

If we want to see the gray area, we must first look at the language we use when thinking in black or white.

| Black | White |
|-------|-------|
| NEVER | ALWAYS |
| NO | YES |
| SHOULD NOT | SHOULD |
| MUST NOT | MUST |
| NOTHING | EVERYTHING |
| TERRIBLE | PERFECT |
| BAD | GOOD |

We can see from the words above that they are of the dramatic kind. The words "never" and "always" are far more dramatic than "sometimes," which is a gray area word. In general, the gray area seems boring to us as first, as we are so accustomed to thinking in extremes. Our extreme view of the world around us is rigid, and so we must rid ourselves of this thinking pattern in order for us to see things as they actually are. To do this, we must force the rational part of our mind to work and to start looking at things more logically. To change how we think takes time, practice, and lots of questions. We need questions to help us challenge our thinking. Questions such as "What if?" enable us to become more open minded.

Whenever we find ourselves saying "I hate them" or "I never want to see them again," we must stop and consciously recognize that we are thinking in black and white. Becoming aware of our black-and-white thinking is the first step we need to take. Once aware of it, we can then begin to challenge it.

### Accepting That We Are Powerless over Others

We are powerless over other people, and we are powerless over many things, but until we can accept this, we will continue trying to control the outcome of situations. The amazing thing is, once we can admit powerlessness, we actually empower ourselves.

We spend so much time worrying about things over which we have absolutely no control. *What if they cheat on me? What if my friend doesn't like me? What if no-one talks to me? What if a loved one dies? What if, what if, what if?* We must understand that no matter how much we worry about something, if it is going to happen, it is going to happen—and nothing that we do can prevent that. Worrying over such things only causes us pain and prevents us from focusing on the present moment.

By accepting that we are powerless, we are freeing ourselves from the compulsion to control everyone and everything. We no longer need to carry the weight of the world on our shoulders. We can learn to let go—rather than spending our days focusing on the behaviors of other people, we are able to focus on ourselves.

When first considering what we are powerless over, it helps for us to write it out as a list.

**I am powerless over:**

Other people's behaviors

The weather

Organizations, i.e., government

Death

War

Poverty

The law

Other people's opinions

The truth is, maybe we do not agree with the way that someone else behaves, maybe we cannot bear the thought of a loved one dying, and maybe we are unhappy with our government. Recognizing and admitting that we are powerless over these things does not mean we have to like them. Just as accepting something doesn't mean we agree with it, so too does admitting we are powerless over something doesn't mean we agree with it.

### Letting Go of Minor Irritations

For many of us, the idea of "letting something go" is ludicrous. To let something go sounds as if we are simply putting up with it. This is not the case. When letting go of something, we are acknowledging that we have a choice in how we let it affect us. For example, our partner always forgets to put the milk back in the fridge after using it. We ask them politely to please stop doing this, but every day it continues to happen. This infuriates us and we take this to mean that (a) they do not listen to us, and (b) they do not care about us, as they continue to do something that we have specifically asked them to not do. Perhaps we get angry and argue with our partner, but still this behavior continues. Where do we go from here? Are we going to end the relationship over milk?! Well, we have a choice. We are powerless over what our partner does, but we are not powerless over ourselves. We can choose to end the relationship (which is rather extreme considering the circumstances) or we can choose to not let their behavior affect us. We can "let it go."

What if we are in a relationship with someone who is physically violent? Should we let that go? Absolutely not! Domestic violence is not a minor irritation. When in this position, we also have a choice, and it is up to each of us to make the choice that is best for our well-being.

Obviously, leaving milk out is nothing like being in a violent relationship, but our choices are the same:

1. We can stay in the relationship and continue to be annoyed.
2. We can stay in the relationship but take responsibility for how we let things affect us and make the conscious decision to let it go.
3. We can leave.

When we look at our choices, we realize just how simple a choice "letting it go" is when it comes to *minor irritations*, and yet we are masters at overcomplicating everything. If we choose the first choice, then we are choosing to continue to live in pain. If we choose the third option for every little annoyance, we will never learn how to build healthy and meaningful relationships.

When it comes to bigger problems, such as abuse, letting it go is never the right option. In fact, to simply "let something go" that has a serious detrimental effect on our well-being, is akin to being a doormat.

### Admitting When We Are Wrong and Apologizing for Harms Caused

For those of us still in the grips of BPD and with no recovery under our belt, to admit we are wrong is laughable. After all—we are never wrong! How dare someone even suggest it? What if, however, we have perceived something in such a way that we have caused someone harm because of it? Are we right then? Surely that is not our fault, as it was our perception that caused us to react in the manner in which we did. But the fact still remains that we have caused harm to another person. If we continue to go through life causing harm to others, never taking responsibility for it and never saying sorry, we are likely to alienate a lot of people.

We should ask ourselves, *How often do I harm others, hate myself for doing it, and then continue to live with the guilt and shame afterward?* It is an extremely painful place to be but one that can be made better by ourselves.

There are times when we may apologize to someone only to have them not accept our apology. Although we would love it if every time we apologize to someone they would throw their arms around us in an embrace and tell us that we are forgiven, that is not realistic. If we find that someone does not want to forgive us, we must understand that we have hurt them. Some people take longer than others to heal. For us, it isn't necessarily the acceptance of our apology that is important but the fact that we are finally taking responsibility for our actions.

Admitting that we are wrong does not mean that we have to go through every day apologizing to everyone we have hurt, either. Just being able to recognize when we may be in the wrong is enough to begin with. If we are unable to ever admit that we are wrong, how are we supposed to moderate our behaviors? If we truly believe that we are never in the wrong, we have absolutely no reason to make changes, and our life and relationships will stay stagnant.

Being able to admit when we are wrong takes courage. We have to take a good hard look at ourselves and the effect that we have on those around us. For many of us, it isn't pretty—in fact, it is extremely painful. But it is through confronting our shortcomings head on that we are able to free ourselves from them. Every time that we admit, either to ourselves or to another person, that we are wrong, we are becoming evermore self-aware of our behaviors and therefore more proficient at recognizing when the more harmful ones show up. Through doing this, we discover that, as time goes by, the amount of harm we cause lessens, and the guilt and hatred that we have toward ourselves also diminishes. We have less to feel guilty for, and our relationships can begin to be rebuilt.

So how do we know when we have done something that we shouldn't have done? At the end of each day we can ask ourselves the following questions:

*Have I…*
- *Been angry at anyone?*
- *Blamed someone?*
- *Been dishonest?*
- *Purposefully tried to control a person or situation?*
- *Ignored someone?*
- *Been closed-minded?*
- *Gossiped about another person?*
- *Been jealous?*
- *Made someone feel guilty?*
- *Expected perfection from someone?*
- *Been selfish or self-centered?*
- *Been prejudiced?*
- *Projected onto someone else?*

If we can answer yes to any of the above, chances are we have caused harm to someone. The more we ask ourselves the above questions and answer them truthfully, the quicker we will be able to recognize these behaviors as and when they appear. Only then can we do something about them.

We may ask ourselves, *But what if someone causes us harm?* This is a very reasonable question. After all, there is no guarantee that we will never get hurt by another person; we know that we are powerless over other people. Learning to recognize when we are in the wrong has nothing to do with other people's behaviors. This skill is all about us taking responsibility for ourselves and our own faults.

### Taking Care of Ourselves

Many of the problems in our relationships stem from our impulsive and reckless behaviors. Drinking alcohol is a major culprit in our relationship problems, as is using drugs or spending too much money. In chapter 8, impulsive and reckless behaviors are explained in more detail. Due to the impact it has on our relationships, however, it is important to also mention it within this skills section.

If we want to have more-stable relationships, it is imperative that we start taking care of ourselves more. If we struggle with impulsive behaviors, it is vital that we learn the skills that can help us to deal with them. Is drinking or gambling affecting our relationships? If the answer is yes, we need to take action to stop these behaviors. Rehab, accessing alcohol and drug services, and 12-step meetings are all there to help those who struggle with addictive behaviors.

### Quality Time

We often find that our relationships are so unstable that we actually fail to invest time into them, instead either taking them for granted or neglecting them completely.

How often do we cancel plans? How often do we spend time with our loved one having fun? Relationships are two sided, and if we want them to flourish, we must ensure that we are playing our part in them fairly and not just expecting the other person to make all of the effort.

We actually find that when we do something nice for our loved one, it not only makes them feel good but we also feel good as well. We may cook them a nice meal or put together a picnic to have in the park. Below are some ideas of ways in which we can have quality time with someone.

- Plan a movie night (at home or at the cinema)
- Share a meal
- Go for coffee or ice cream
- Spend a day out at a zoo, theme park, museum, or art gallery
- Have a spa day
- Go swimming
- Go miniature golfing
- Do a hobby together, like gardening or painting
- Try a new activity, like yoga, horseback riding, or golf
- Go on a picnic or have a barbecue
- Train for a marathon
- Listen to music
- Play a board game or a game of cards
- Look through old photo albums
- Lie on the grass watching the stars
- Have a short break away

We often find that we get so caught up in day-to-day life that quality time with loved ones goes out the window. Spending time together helps us to reconnect—away from the rat race of everyday life. Even if it is only an hour a week, we will benefit from it.

**Skills Checklist**
- Communication
- Questioning our perception
- Questioning our black-and-white thinking
- Accepting that we are powerless over others
- Letting it go—particularly of minor irritations
- Admitting when we are wrong and apologizing for harms caused
- Taking care of ourselves
- Quality time

Chapter 7

# UNCLEAR OR UNSTABLE SELF-IMAGE

*"A flower does not think of competing*
*with the flower next to it. It just blooms."*
—Zen Shin

**What Is an Unclear or Unstable Self-Image?**

If we were to look up "self-image" in a dictionary, we would see that it is the idea a person has about their own abilities, looks, and personalities. Basically, it is how someone sees themself. There are some people whose self-image is based purely on how they see themselves, others who base it upon how others view them, and still others whose self-image is based on how they think others perceive them.

Someone with a negative self-image sees themself entirely in a negative light. Somebody with a positive self-image will view themself in a positive way, able to see their shortcomings in an accurate but rational way. An unstable self-image is when a person continuously swings from a positive self-image to a negative self-image and back again. An unclear self-image is when a person is unsure of who they are. Someone with an unclear self-image may question everything about themself. *Who am I? What do I like? What am I good at?* Most people are able to answer these types of questions relatively easily. Someone with an unclear self-image may struggle to answer one, if any, of these questions, as they just do not have the answers.

## Our Thoughts

When we have an unstable self-image, our self-talk can alternate between being positive and being negative. While in the positive self-image stage, we feel happy with our life and who we are. We may start thinking that we are capable of achieving whatever we set our mind to. It is often while in this phase that we start making plans for our future—after all, we believe the world is our oyster.

Soon enough, however, our self-image flips and we are crippled with self-doubt and/or self-loathing. We relentlessly pick faults in ourselves; typical things we may say to ourselves are: *I'm too fat* or *I'm too thin. I'm stupid. I can't do anything right and nobody likes me.* We are unable to remember the positive thoughts we previously had about ourselves, and if we do recall them we dismiss them, asking ourselves, *What was I thinking?* We think of ourselves as being flawed, inferior, and terrible.

The mirror's reflection that stares back at us is different than what others see when they look at us. We may be underweight and yet look in the mirror and see a much larger image of ourselves looking back. We may be young and healthy and yet think we are aging and weak.

Our negative self-image causes us to compare ourselves to others; we long to be different, more desirable. Our continuous negative self-talk only batters our self-esteem further, resulting in us thinking that we are beyond repair and that there is no hope for our future.

## Our Feelings

When our thoughts are of the more positive nature, we may have feelings of hope and happiness, even euphoria, although these feelings tend to be brief and rarely last a very long time.

For the majority of the time, we are crippled with insecurity. We feel insignificant and undesirable most often. Our feelings of worthlessness can lead us to spiral into a deep depression. Being in the company of other people heightens our feelings of inadequacy, and we can begin to feel jealous of those around us. We feel anxious in the company of others and embarrassed at ourselves, always questioning whether we said or did the right or wrong thing. Our frustration can lead to us feeling angry, sometimes at others but more often at ourselves. Life is particularly hard when we feel like a piece of shit.

We struggle to find any joy in life, and we start feeling hopeless. We have an emptiness in the pit of our stomach. Even if we are in a room full of people, we feel lost and lonely.

Imposter syndrome is common among us. Even if we are doing well in our jobs or relationships, we are under the illusion that we are unworthy and are unable to comprehend how we got there. We feel like a fraud and begin to feel scared that we will be "discovered" and found to be undeserving. We so desperately want to feel accepted, and yet we do not accept ourselves, for how can we when we don't even know who we are?

Living with a negative or unstable self-image causes us to feel out of control of our own life and scared for our future. We start to feel desperate for a way out, and life becomes more and more painful as each day goes on.

## Our Behaviors

Our inferiority and inadequacy can manifest in various ways. There are those of us who isolate and prefer to avoid others completely to save ourselves the embarrassment and anxiety. Some of us become dependent on our loved ones, feeling that we are incapable of doing anything on our own and instead rely on those around us to do things for us.

Those of us who suffer from an unclear self-image may find ourselves adapting who we are to suit who we are with. Like an ever-changing chameleon, we mold ourselves into who we believe others want us to be.

Throughout my life I have been able to change myself to fit in with the friends I hung around with. If I was with a friend from London, my voice would change to mimic theirs—my walk, my demeanor, everything would change. If I was with a friend who had a posh accent, I would modify my own accent to be more like theirs.

It wasn't just my characteristics that would change either. I would alter my entire personality to fit in. If my friend liked a certain musical artist, I too would say I liked them (even if I had never heard of them!). If there was a television series that I enjoyed but then found out my friend hated it, I would hate it too!

With any romantic partners I would completely reinvent myself to be who I thought they wanted me to be. If they liked blondes, I would become blonde. If they liked girls with no makeup, I would stop wearing makeup. They like a girl that looks like a walrus? Hell I'd make myself look like a goddamn walrus!

When I went into a treatment center in 2013 for my drug addiction, I was given an assignment to work on my self-image and self-esteem. I discovered that my self-esteem was on the floor and my self-image was unclear. I had spent my whole life molding myself to what I thought others wanted me to be. I had absolutely no idea who I was. Was I confident or was that a mask I wore? What were my likes? What were my dislikes? I just didn't know. I was a stranger to myself.

Wearing so much makeup that we look completely different, constantly taking selfies and posting altered or filtered images on Instagram, and obsessively using Snapchat are all signs of our deep insecurities. Unfortunately we are living in an age of the image-obsessed, and this only heightens our feelings of inadequacy.

We constantly need reassurance from our loved ones. We doubt ourselves so much that we need to hear that we are loved. This trait, combined with our fear of abandonment, leaves us feeling vulnerable, so we may find ourselves people-pleasing for recognition and acceptance.

Intimacy: into me you see. Intimacy is more than being sexual with someone. It is opening ourselves up and showing someone the real us. But we do not like the real us, and so we pretend we are someone we are not, preventing people from seeing our true selves and thus blocking us from being intimate with anyone. Intimacy is not intimacy if we are telling a lie. Yet we do not set out to be false; it is never done intentionally, it just seems to happen. Most of the time we are unaware that we are even doing this, believing instead that we are being authentic. We can take on a persona and wear a mask for so long that even we believe that is who we truly are, becoming unable to distinguish between our true and false selves. There are times when intimacy seems an impossibility—after all, how can we show people the real us when even we don't know who the real us is?

Our negative self-image can cause us to feel angry at ourselves and our situation, leading to us self-harming or acting impulsively to alleviate the pain that we feel.

## What Is Happening in Our Brain?

As mentioned previously, our brain starts developing from the moment that we are born, with neural pathways either strengthening or weakening. Our environment has a lot to do with how our brain develops. While young and dependent on others, we look around at those closest to us to help us learn and grow. Depending on what kind of upbringing we have had, various core beliefs are formed. If, for example, we had a mother who was never happy with anything we did, we may have grown up with the belief that we are useless.

Our core beliefs are so deeply ingrained in us that most of the time we are not even consciously aware of them. The beliefs that we carry around with us are stored in our brain as truths. We do not question them, we simply live by them, often to the detriment of ourselves.

## Where does this trait come from?

Our self-image starts forming when we are children and entirely dependent on those around us to get our needs met. As a child, even with a loving family around us, we are aware that we are helpless and unable to fend for ourselves. Back when we were tiny, our self-image was possibly more factual based, but our environment played a huge part in how it formed, and this is when things started to become distorted.

If we had one parent who told us how wonderful we were and another parent who ignored us most of the time, we may have grown up with an unstable self-image, sometimes believing in ourselves and other times not.

Perhaps we had a parent who suffered with anxiety and passed all of their fears on to us. We then grew up with the belief that the world is a dangerous place and that we aren't equipped or capable of dealing with it.

There are many of us who grew up constantly being put down, sometimes through unkind words and other times through our caregivers' actions. When we start to believe what we are told, our whole self-image is based upon other people's negative opinions of us.

We may then attend school where we encounter bullies who only further bash away at our self-esteem and seem to confirm the negative self-image that we have of ourselves.

By the time we are old enough to be independent we still feel like incapable children, never having grown up. How many of us feel like a child trapped in an adult's body? We step out into the big bad world not knowing who we truly are and carrying with us a brain full of negative beliefs.

There are people who we may meet along the way who do not see us in the negative light in which we see ourselves. However, rather than make us feel better, this only adds to our confusion of who we really are.

Our self-image is also based on how we *think* others see us. We know that those of us with BPD have brains that are on the constant lookout for threats; a major threat is that people do not like us, causing us to think that we are not likeable. We then try to hide our true selves, preferring to imitate others who we believe are likeable.

Throughout our life we may have many different circumstances that assist in shaping the way that we see ourselves, often in a way that isn't truly representative of who we are.

### The effect our self-image has on those around us.

Our lack of self-esteem and our unclear and/or unstable self-image causes us to cling to those around us for reassurance. We believe ourselves to be unpleasant and useless, but by having "friends" around us we can pretend that we are likeable. In order to do this, we often mimic those close to us, much to the frustration of others.

When I was thirteen, I was a student at a girls' school. Girls can be very competitive, and I never felt that I really fit in. But there was a girl in my year who, in my opinion, was both popular and pretty, and I decided that I wanted to be just like her.

First, I befriended her through flattery, telling her how pretty she was. Once we started hanging around together, the copying started. When she put red dye in her hair, I did the same. When she bought a new dress, I went out and bought the exact same dress. It didn't take long before I heard from others that she was annoyed with me because I copied everything she did. Our friendship did not last very long.

My imitating others continued into my late teens. I met a girl in my local pub, and we became firm friends—still are to this day. I was in complete awe of her; she was so beautiful and confident and everything that I felt I was not. I soon started listening to the music she listened to, wearing the same makeup and clothes as her, and even changing my voice to mimic hers. I was extremely fortunate that this friend took my copying of her as a compliment and, rather than dismissing me, she understood me; bizarre that fifteen years later she too got diagnosed with BPD! When we talk now we laugh that we were actually both as insecure as each other back then, though neither of us had discussed it with one another.

Our loved ones can find interacting with us tiring, constantly thinking they must reassure us or risk us having a meltdown, constantly questioning whether they have said the right or wrong thing. The people we cling to and start copying can begin to feel stifled by us. We must realize that spending a lot of time with any one person can produce problems; although we are social creatures, it is healthy for us to socialize with a variety of people rather than just one person all of the time. It is also healthy to be able to spend some time alone, something that we take to the extreme, spending either all our time alone and isolating or being unable to be left alone for any amount of time, no matter how short.

To those around us, we can feel like a huge burden and responsibility. Although friends want to spend time with us, they may not want us to live in their pockets; yet they fear telling us this, knowing exactly how we will react. So instead, they carry on allowing us to smother them until they can take it no more and they erupt, telling us that we can no longer be friends.

Our family members struggle with our changing personas, believing that we are insincere. The outside world has no idea what we are dealing with internally; outsiders only witness our behaviors, observing that we change as often as the weather and therefore must not be genuine. The fact that we can change so dramatically and in such a short space of time, constantly copying others, can cause loved ones to believe us to be shallow, which is, of course, inaccurate.

Our lack of intimacy can also pose a problem; partners conclude that we are cold and distant. There are times when we do detach emotionally, and loved ones are left questioning our feelings for them. This can lead to them feeling insecure and unsure about the relationship.

## Skills for Dealing with an Unclear or Unstable Self-Image

Whether we have an unclear self-image or an unstable one, chances are our self-esteem is extremely low. How can we build our self-esteem when we do not even know who we are most of the time? By first discovering who we are and gaining a strong identity, we are then able to build our self-esteem.

### *Discovering Ourselves*

We spend so long wearing a mask in order to disguise our true selves from others or to fit in that we often lose our own identity. When first setting out to discover who we are, we need to ask ourselves questions. Lots of questions.

Imagine that we are asking a stranger these questions, which isn't entirely a charade, as we kind of are strangers to ourselves. We should take our time with each question and answer as truthfully as possible. When answering, we must remember that nobody but us is going to read our answers. This is important, because if we believe others will read it, we might elaborate our answers, wanting them to sound interesting rather than being honest.

When asking ourselves questions, we can go into as much detail as possible. We want to find out every small facet of what makes us, us. Here are a just a few questions to get us started, but we need to keep adding to it in order for us to truly discover who we are.

What is my favorite color?

What is my favorite food?

What is my least favorite food?

What are my pet peeves?

What are my hobbies?

What is my favorite smell?

What genre of books do I like?

What is my favorite film?

What is my favorite animal?

If I could do anything, what would it be?

Once we have completed our list as truthfully as we can, we may then read through it and ask ourselves, *Are any of my answers things that I incorporate into my daily life?* For example, if our hobby is swimming, do we go swimming or have we not swam in years? If our favorite genre of film is comedy, then why do we only seem to watch thrillers?

Chances are, we do things that we think others like rather than what we like. Maybe we are embarrassed to admit that we only really like comedies, as none of our friends watch them. Perhaps we listen to a certain type of music because that is what our partner is into. Learning who we are and what we like is wonderful, but only if we truly become who we are. If we write down all of the answers to the questions and yet we carry on living our life in a way that isn't true to who we are, then what is the point of the exercise?

### *Goal Setting*

Once we have an idea about what truly makes us tick, we are ready to start setting small, realistic, and accomplishable goals. We start small, as we do not want to set ourselves up for failure. Goals may include:

- Saving $5 a week for a month to treat ourselves to something we like

- Eating healthfully for one week
- Taking up a new hobby
- Practicing a skill once daily to help with our BPD
- Making our bed each morning
- Contacting an old friend
- Writing a letter to someone
- Doing something nice for ourselves once a week
- Walking more

The feeling we get when we have achieved our goal is wonderful—and not only do we feel good, we are also building our self-esteem in the process. We can use the questions listed in chapter 26 to help us plan our goals.

### Building Self-Esteem

Having an unclear or unstable self-image can be caused by our low self-esteem, and our low self-esteem can be caused by our unstable or unclear self-image. So what should we tackle first? It is a good idea to treat them as a package; they come together, and working on one can help the other.

### Stop the Negative Self-Talk

The first thing we need to do when trying to build our self-esteem is to end the negative self-talk. When we notice ourselves doing this, we need to stop it immediately. Negative self-talk doesn't necessarily mean that we sit there thinking that we are ugly all day. It may come in the form of us comparing ourselves to others. We may be scrolling through Facebook or Instagram and all the while have this sinking feeling in our stomach. Why do we feel this way? Most of the time, this feeling, this jealousy within, arises because we just don't feel good enough. Once we recognize that comparing is something we do, we need to make the conscious decision to stop it. If that means taking a break from social media, so be it. Other forms of negative self-talk can include beating ourselves up whenever we make a mistake or constantly focusing on the things that we can't do, as opposed to the things that we are good at.

As Albert Einstein said, "Everybody is a genius. But if you judge a fish by its ability to climb a tree, it will live its whole life believing that it is stupid."

### Focus on the Positives

Second, we need to start focusing on our positives. Our negative self-talk needs to be replaced. We do this in the form of positive affirmations. Now, it is highly likely that we will feel both embarrassed and a bit stupid doing this to start with, not to mention a bit of a fraud. We cannot expect to go from constantly thinking badly of ourselves, to all of a sudden thinking that we are the next best thing since sliced bread! Rather than thinking, *I can't say nice things about myself*, we just need to inhale deeply and do it. We mustn't overthink it, as this only causes us to think up reasons why we shouldn't say it. The positive affirmations that we choose are up to us. If we don't want to say, "I am absolutely amazing," then we don't have to. Try these more subtle positive affirmations:

"I deserve to be happy."

"I am a kind person."

"I am not my illness."

"I am a good friend."

"I have a lot to offer."

These are all ways to be positive about ourselves without feeling as if we are bragging too much. It is okay to start small and build up our affirmations later. And while we may not believe them when we first start, eventually we will.

### Surround Ourselves with Positive People

Third, we need to surround ourselves with good people who love us and are there for us. All too often we hang around with toxic people who sap our energy and leave us feeling emotionally drained. It is our life, and we can choose who we want in it and who we do not. Do we have a friend who loves to be around us when we are having a major meltdown but seems to disappear when things are going well? Do we have a family member who constantly criticizes us? Do we know someone who always makes us feel less than? Do we have a friend who causes us to feel as if we are walking on eggshells when we are with them (yes, we too cause people to walk on eggshells around us, but that is discussed in the family section!)? These types of people will hold us back from building our self-esteem; it is wise for us to distance ourselves from them for this reason.

### Giving Ourselves a Gold Star

We need to learn to give ourselves a pat on the back when we have achieved something. We can take a cue from parents who reward their children every time they do something positive, whether it be they smiled, they said "Please" or "Thank you," they remembered to take their shoes off before traipsing mud throughout the house, or they went to bed without a fuss. This is something that we need to start doing for ourselves.

Only those of us with BPD understand just how difficult accomplishing the smallest daily task is. Sometimes we struggle to even get out of bed. On the days when we do get up and bother to clean our teeth, we don't have someone there to tell us "Well done!" Why would they? To other people, getting up and brushing their teeth is done automatically, without a second thought. But we are not other people; to us, these seemingly minor tasks can seem like gigantic hurdles. We need to recognize that every time we *do* achieve something, no matter how small, is a cause for celebratory recognition. We need to buy a pack of shiny star stickers and a black piece of cardstock. We need to hang the card where we will see it regularly throughout the day. Next time we achieve something, we give ourselves a star. We make the bed—gold star. We answer the phone—gold star. We go to the store to buy milk— gold star! When we look at the black card and see it filling up with stars, it will be a constant reminder that we have achieved something.

## Skills Checklist

- Discovering ourselves
- Goal setting
- Building our self-esteem
- Stopping the negative self-talk
- Focusing on the positives
- Surrounding ourselves with positive people
- Giving ourselves a gold star

Chapter 8

# IMPULSIVE, SELF-DESTRUCTIVE BEHAVIOR

*"We often throw rocks not realizing that*
*they're going to land somewhere."*
—Craig D. Lounsbrough

### What Is Impulsive, Self-Destructive Behavior?

To act impulsively means to act without any forethought and without any consideration of the consequences that our actions may produce. A self-destructive behavior is one that will cause damage and harm to oneself. Simply put, impulsive, self-destructive behaviors are actions that we do not give any thought to prior to acting upon them and that are likely to cause harm to either ourselves or others.

The variety of impulsive, self-destructive behaviors is numerous and varying in severity. At one end of the severity scale we have suicide attempts and self-harm (which are BPD traits), followed by drug use, drunk driving, gambling, eating disorders, and so on. At the other end of the scale we have social media usage, shopping, and the like. The latter may not appear to be actions that are at all that reckless, yet they too can have a devastating effect on the person engaging in these behaviors. Just ask the person who keeps taking out credit cards to feed their clothing addiction, racking up thousands of dollars of debt and risking losing their home.

There are also those of us who constantly feel the need to post on social media, continually upping our game in order to receive more "likes"—and yet this doesn't make us happy. We live in a digital world that isn't our reality, yet treat it as if it is, comparing ourselves to others and in the process damaging our already broken self-esteem. When our emotions are running high, we turn to social media to post a status that we later regret sharing.

Social media is also the perfect place for us to do some stalking, especially when it comes to either our ex or our partner's ex. We want to see them worse off than we are. But we forget that people are more likely to post the most beautiful pictures of themselves, laughing and having fun. We wind up causing ourselves further pain.

There are impulsive behaviors that are obvious to those around us and others that we keep hidden, sometimes only disclosed when they finally cause us devastation, for not all of our impulsive behaviors cause us outright destruction straightaway. How many of us can get along reasonably well while also drinking daily or using drugs? We have all heard about the high-functioning addict or alcoholic, able to live their lives while concealing something as huge as addiction. It must be added, however, that rarely can those of us with BPD hide our impulsive behaviors for very long. That isn't the nature of borderline personality disorder. It is often our extreme emotions that cause us to act impulsively, and, as we all know, our emotions just explode out of us in the most dramatic fashion a lot of the time. Of course, there are those who experience BPD quietly, internalizing everything as opposed to externalizing everything. Those of us who do internalize our feelings can often go under the radar, undetected due to the lack of outward eruptions.

So why are impulsive, self-destructive behaviors so common among those of us with BPD? The answer seems simple and yet it can vary among each of us enormously.

First, to live with borderline personality disorder is both soul destroying and painful. Normal, everyday events are debilitating and leave us struggling to just get through the day. Our extreme emotions force us to act even though our actions often leave us worse off than before.

We are unable to control the intensity of our feelings and are unable to regulate them. Over the years, we develop our own coping mechanisms that we believe will make us feel better, and in the beginning they usually do the trick. Next time we have a crisis, we are far more likely to repeat whatever we did previously that seemed to help us. Maybe we turn to drink, sometimes we self-medicate with drugs (both the illegal and the prescription kind), other times we may seek out casual sex or we may self-harm. Some of us have a bag of tricks up our sleeves that we can use at any moment to relieve us from the pain that we are feeling, whereas others may just have one go-to solution that is used in moments of emotional turmoil.

Second, many of us with BPD suffer from chronic feelings of emptiness (trait seven in the DSM-IV-TR). This trait will be discussed more in the relevant chapter, but it is important to mention it here as well. Living with this emptiness, this void inside of us, can cause us to seek out ways to fill it. This is when our impulsive self-destructing behaviors come in. These behaviors cause us to "feel" something and momentarily fill the void. We can also consider all of the other BPD traits, as I have mentioned before, one trait can set in motion other traits. Fear of abandonment, unstable relationships, explosive anger, and our unstable or unclear self-image can all cause us to act impulsively and recklessly.

Third, impulsive behaviors can become habitual and incredibly addictive. Once we start acting out in this way, seeking "rewards" as a way of making ourselves feel better, it becomes easier for us to slip into this pattern of behaviors and far more difficult for us to stop them.

## Our Thoughts

It needs to be noted that in this chapter our thoughts are few. This is because we act impulsively—we do not think before we act. Any thoughts we do have tend to be fleeting and often unconscious.

"I need to stop/change how I am feeling."

This thought is barely even a thought, as it is certainly not one that we consciously think. It is, however, the key reason that causes us to act. This thought can be brought on due to either our intense emotions or our chronic feelings of emptiness. It is also the thought that we have that drives our addictive behaviors, as we are constantly trying to "fix" ourselves.

"Fuck everyone."

"Fuck you."

"I'll show you."

When we are in a state of rage we will often cut off our nose to spite our face, going into self-destruct and self-sabotage mode. We get the fuck-you attitude and will often behave in a way that we know will anger those around us. After acting on our impulse we may then think to ourselves, *Look what you made me do*, turning the blame onto those who angered us in the first place.

"They can't leave me."

This thought stems from our fear of abandonment and can drive us to make frantic attempts to avoid being abandoned. Although this is a trait all on its own, it is also another reason that we may act impulsively.

"I want someone to love me."

"I hate how I look."

These thoughts are triggered by our low self-esteem. Again, they are not conscious thoughts. They drive us to seek out love and attention, but not in the healthiest ways.

"I can't go on any more, I've had enough."

This thought is what precedes our most damaging self-destructive behavior: suicide attempts. This will be discussed in more detail in the following chapter.

## Our Feelings

As with many of the BPD traits, it is our thoughts that actually cause our feelings to be more intense. With impulsive, self-destructive behavior, it tends to be the other way around. Our excruciatingly painful feelings drive us into action, sometimes with the briefest thought, but most of the time without any.

Almost any intense feeling imaginable can be felt preceding our actions. That includes feelings of joy. Here's an example from my own life.

One day in 2005, I woke up and felt okay—not good, not bad, just okay. This was amazing for me, because for as long as I could remember I had woken up wishing that I never had. I got out of bed and went downstairs. It was one of the first days of spring, so the sky was finally blue, rather than the gray I had become accustomed to. An upbeat song was on the radio and I felt a rush of good feeling flow through me. Usually in the morning I would walk around like a zombie, but that day I actually felt like dancing. I felt as if I was on a high and I didn't want it to end.

I jumped in the shower, got dressed, did my hair and makeup, and hopped in the car. I drove to the local mall and went on a shopping spree, buying a ridiculous amount of clothes that I really didn't need. My buzz was getting better and better, and I decided to call my dealer and get him to meet me at my local pub.

At the pub, I immediately bought a bottle of wine for myself, called a friend to meet me, collected the cocaine from my dealer, who was waiting in the car park, and went on a bender. That evening I was completely smashed on drink and drugs, but I can remember all of a sudden going from feeling as if I was on the top of the world to crashing back down to Earth with a bang. All of my happiness was gone, instead replaced with a feeling of guilt, shame, regret, and anger at myself. The reality hit me: I had just used up my overdraft on clothes that I didn't need and on drink and drugs, which were quickly disappearing, and with no money I couldn't restock my supplies. I felt like shit.

When I got home, I had a blazing row with my partner and stormed out of the house. I don't remember the rest of the night. I don't know if I drove off in my car, walked, got a cab...who knows. I woke up the next day at my mum's feeling shittier than I had felt in a long time. The worse thing was, I didn't learn from my mistakes—that day I went out and bought more drugs and went on another binge. This time my impulsive actions were bought on by my negative feelings.

Of course, most of our impulsive and reckless behaviors are bought on due to the painful negative feelings that we experience, but that's not to say that is the only reason, as we can see from my story. Our feelings of happiness are so rare that when we do experience them we want to do everything we can to make them continue. Our feeling of happiness can also begin to make us feel as if we are on a high and we are buzzing, causing us to behave in a way that isn't our normal behavior. We may be so full of energy that we talk faster, move more quickly, and generally behave as if we are under the influence of an illegal substance, when we are not.

A sudden dip in mood is a common feeling that comes before our impulsivity. We can go from feeling relatively okay to extremely low and miserable abruptly, and we'll do anything that we can to try and lift our mood. We feel desperate for the pain to go away, and our intense emotions cause us to feel out of control, which essentially we are.

Anger is another emotion that can lead to us acting impulsively, especially when our anger is directed at or caused by another person. We often perceive things in a different way than those without BPD. We often feel as if people are out to get us, and therefore we can become very defensive. We may feel insulted and become angry. For many of us, anger is actually our secondary feeling, although we are not aware of this. If someone has said something that we perceive to be offensive, we may retaliate in anger. The primary feeling, however, is hurt; we feel wounded and turn that upset into anger so quickly that we are unable to process what has happened. We believe rage is what we are feeling, which it is, but the rage stems from us feeling hurt.

How many of us spend most of our time yearning for other people's approval? This yearning may stem from our fear of abandonment or our unclear self-image and low self-esteem. When we are with others we feel insecure and keen to please or impress them, which may include acting impulsively, with the intention of getting people to like us or fitting in.

Addictions, such as drug use, alcoholism, sex, gambling, and eating disorders, can all lead to us feeling as if we *need* them to make us feel better. Eating disorders often start as a way of us either needing control of something in our life or due to our bad self-image and feeling as if we are not good enough.

Boredom and loneliness are also two feelings that can lead to us impulsively doing something, simply as a way of distracting ourselves.

## Our Behaviors

We must remember that our impulsive and reckless behaviors are our coping skills. We behave in this way in order to survive a crisis. What signifies a crisis for someone with BPD, however, may appear to be a minor hindrance to someone without this disorder.

While we often act impulsively on our own with nobody else involved, if the reason for our impulsivity is caused by another person, we will often lash out with either verbal or actual physical abuse, with no thought of the other person and no consideration of the consequences. We say the most unkind and insensitive things with the intention of hurting both the person our comments are aimed at as well as ourselves. We fail to realize in the moment that we cannot go back in time and take back the words that we say. The damage is done.

I used to feel that other people were my biggest triggers in regard to my BPD traits, especially close family members and partners. For instance, one time I was arguing with my then-husband in his car. I could feel myself getting angrier and angrier, and I started verbally abusing him, saying the most hurtful things. He was getting more and more annoyed with me, and we kept going over the same argument again and again and not getting anywhere. Before I even knew what was happening, I had opened the car door while the car was moving and threw myself out. I then ran and hid in some bushes.

Another time, when I was nineteen, I had an almighty row with a boyfriend in a pub. He stormed out, so I jumped in my car and started trying to run him over. Not once did I consider what would happen if I had succeeded in running him over. Luckily for both of us, my attempt at hitting him with my car was unsuccessful. Believe it or not, that wasn't even the end of the relationship.

The methods of impulsivity that we take are not always big and dramatic events, however. We may be sitting at home feeling bored when we have the sudden urge to do something. So we might decide that we need to buy something completely random—and right now. Maybe scented candles, cleaning products, makeup, a book, stationery, a lock for our bike, plants for the garden, a lampshade, new bedding, clippers, seat covers for our car … the list is endless. When we decide we "need" this item, we are not able to postpone going to get it—"anticipation" and "patience" are not words in our vocabulary! We immediately either head out to a shop or go online to make our purchase. Of course, this is not immediately self-destructive, but over time it can be, especially if we are constantly repeating this behavior and do not have the money to fund it.

Some of the impulsive, self-destructing actions that we take become addictions. At first, we use drugs to give us a high when we feel low. The problem arises when we become so used to using drugs that the high we get becomes the norm for us, so when we stop using them and come down to where we should be, we feel as if we are on a massive low, triggering us to pick up the drugs again. Alcohol is another common thing that we turn to when we feel down. The problem here is that alcohol is a depressant and inevitably only makes all our negative feelings feel ten times stronger.

Gambling, sex with strangers, social media—these addictions initially give us the high that we crave, but they're never long lasting; we always end up feeling worse than before. Social media, although amazing in many ways, can be so damaging for us. For instance, we have an argument with a loved one and immediately put all the details on social media, looking for sympathy from others but not always getting the reaction that we were hoping for. There are those of us who change our status from "in a relationship" to "single" and back again so often that even we lose track of what it says unless we check it.

Drunk driving is not uncommon among us. If we suspect someone of something or we "need" to see someone straightaway during a crisis, we do not stop to think of the consequences of getting behind the wheel while over the limit. All of our focus is on getting to wherever we need to be, without any consideration of the dangers that we are putting ourselves and others in. We are running purely on emotion; any logic goes out the window.

Many of us go through difficult periods with our eating habits, whether it is because we suffer from other addictions, have a poor body image, or suffer from depression. Binge eating is yet another way of us acting impulsively. We binge eat not only for comfort but to feel as if we are in control of what we are doing—we may not be able to control other people, but we can certainly control how much food we eat or don't eat. Binge eating is an impulsive action that is particularly triggered by our strong emotions. So much food nowadays is high in sugar, which can be addictive; we eat sugar as a way to make us feel better. Unfortunately, after the sugar has spiked in our body, we then have to face the sudden drop in our mood and energy.

Our impulsivity can cause us to behave in a manner that seems like the right thing to do at the time but is actually very embarrassing and cringe worthy when we look back.

As another example, one time I was having a blazing row with a boyfriend as we were walking down a busy street. I was getting angrier and angrier, and the next thing I knew I had pulled my top up, my bra came down, and I had squished my boobs against the window of a packed restaurant as I screamed at my boyfriend, "Look what you've made me do! Happy now?!"

**What Is Happening in Our Brain?**

As we grow up and start going through painful experiences, our brain builds neural pathways every time we develop a new coping mechanism. For example, when we are sad and we eat a load of junk food and find that it (temporarily) masks our pain, we have built a neural pathway. Next time we feel sad, we immediately go for junk food. Every time we do this, that neural pathway gets stronger and stronger, to the point that the next time we are sad we do not even think that we "need" to eat junk food, we just do it. Obviously, talking things through with a close friend or taking some time to relax would be more helpful, but unless we do these things regularly when we are sad, our brain is going to take the easiest route to make us feel better, which is eating junk food or whatever other unhealthy coping mechanism is used regularly.

Our neurochemicals are also at work here. We have chemicals that make us feel good, such as dopamine, oxytocin, serotonin, and endorphins, but we also have chemicals that make us feel not good, such as cortisol. All these chemicals have a job to do in helping us survive.

- **Dopamine motivates us to get what we need.** For example, our prehistoric ancestors likely had hunted for food to the point of exhaustion. But when they suddenly heard an animal in the distance, dopamine was released to get them excited and push them toward their goal of getting food.

- **Oxytocin helps us build trust with others.** As mentioned in chapter 2, Personality and the Brain, working well with others socially was absolutely vital to our survival as a species.

- **Serotonin motivates us to get respect from others,** which was important years ago for the leader of the tribe. They could not lead if nobody respected them.

- **Endorphins momentarily block physical pain.** This was hugely important when our prehistoric ancestors were alive. If someone was hurt while trying to escape an animal, they needed to have that pain blocked so they could continue to flee and escape unharmed.

- **Cortisol helps us avoid threats.** Like an internal alarm system, this stress hormone helps us scan our environment for threats, which was absolutely vital for the survival of our ancestors. Cortisol would both motivate and fuel their fight or flight response, enabling them to react quickly and without delay, giving them a better chance to survive. The problem for those of us with BPD is that we are being alerted to threats constantly, even when the threats are imagined.

The first four "happy" chemicals feel good when released. Cortisol, however, does not feel good. Because we have so much cortisol pumping through us already, we desperately seek out ways to release our happy chemicals. The problem is that our happy chemicals don't last, and it's not long before we have our bad feelings back, so yet again we seek out a way to feel good, continuing the vicious cycle.

Exercise can give us a rush of endorphins, as can self-harm. Drugs such as cocaine give us a rush of dopamine, causing us to experience that feeling of excitement without us having to do anything hard to get it. Heroin and other opiates release our endorphins and give us that feel-good euphoria. Touching another person can release oxytocin. Do we see why we turn to the "quick fixes" that we do? We tend to look for things that give us a reward (feel-good chemical hit) straightaway rather than doing something that is better for us long term.

**Where Does This Trait Come From?**

Impulsive self-destructive behaviors stem from our intense emotions and our other BPD traits. Living with BPD is so incredibly painful that we are constantly looking for ways to help ourselves cope and survive. From a very young age, we developed beliefs and learned behaviors from those closest to us—our caregivers. Some of us saw how our parents coped in difficult times, watching them drown away their sorrows. Some of us were told that we shouldn't show our emotions or discuss how we feel. Because we were not taught how to deal with the intensity of our emotions when we were growing up, as adults we are left to fend for ourselves. Along the way we picked up quick fixes that helped us feel slightly better but only for a moment. It is unfortunate that most of our quick fixes are actually self-destructive—and if they're not immediately damaging, they're most likely going to cause damage long term.

I've had times when I wanted to die. I hated my life so much and couldn't deal with the pain of living. I felt that I had two choices: I could commit suicide or I could drink shit-loads of alcohol and use cocaine. I chose the latter.

**How Does It Affect Those Around Us?**

Our impulsivity can cause an enormous amount of concern for our loved ones, leaving them fearful of what we might do next, either to them or to ourselves. Living with the unpredictability of someone with BPD is draining and exhausting.

My mum tells me that during my hardest years she would go to bed every night not knowing whether she would receive a call informing her that I had done something bad or, worse, that I was dead.

Loved ones can be left frustrated, believing that we behave the way that we do for attention. To people without BPD, the thought that we behave like this for survival seems absolutely ridiculous. Who in their right mind would turn to drugs or sex to help them cope when their life is already so problematic? Those around us believe that our addictions and self-destructive behaviors are the problem. This is not true. Yes, our behaviors are problematic, but for us, the BPD is the problem—it is our intense emotions, our fear of abandonment, and all the other traits that we may have that are causing us trouble. Our impulsive behavior seems to briefly solve all these difficulties for us, at least temporarily, and thus we continue with them.

## Skills for Impulsive, Self-Destructive Behavior

Drinking copious amounts of alcohol, using drugs, gambling, and all the other self-destructive and impulsive behaviors that we partake in are our *solutions* to our problems; they are not the main problem themselves. It is, however, unfortunate that these "solutions" actually cause us further harm.

Bearing in mind that our negative impulsive behaviors are our "solutions," it is imperative that we must replace them with positive actions. For if we do not have a replacement solution, we are left with nothing—and it will not be long before we are continuing with our old unhelpful ways to help us cope in a crisis. That is why we must not think of *stopping* impulsive behaviors but *replacing* them.

We must also remember that we have built up neural pathways in our brain; when a crisis hits, we automatically do what has become habitual. In order to build new neural pathways, we must practice our new replacement coping skills as often as possible. The more we practice, the stronger that new neural pathway will become; eventually, in the event of a crisis, we will be much more likely to use the new skill as opposed to the old unhelpful one.

### Learning to Cope with Our Painful Emotions

If we are unable to cope with our painful emotions in a healthy way, we will try to cope them with them in an unhealthy way. Therefore, learning to cope positively in times of distress is something that we must learn to do.

It is good to keep in mind that an emotion lasts a mere ninety seconds—that is only one and half minutes! Of course, our emotions seem to last so much longer than this, but this is because we "feed" them and, therefore, allow them to continue. By reminding ourselves of this fact repeatedly, we can become a lot less fearful of our emotions and also realize that we can have some control over them.

For years we have lived in fear of our emotions, as they seem to control us completely and leave us feeling powerless to stop them. While it is true that we are unable to prevent ourselves from feeling something, we do have some control over how *long* we feel them for. Imagine a huge wave in the ocean. We have two options: fight against it and possibly go under or ride the wave. It is the same with our emotions: we can fight them and feel as if we are drowning in them, or we can ride them out, letting them pass naturally and with ease. To do this, we need to put into practice the skill of *mindfulness*. Mindfulness allows us to accept the emotion, without judgment.

When we feel an emotion coming on, we should sit down and focus entirely on *how* we feel and not *why* we feel like this, as this will cause us to judge the emotion and set off our negative thinking. We may notice the physical feelings in our body, our breathing, any funny sensations that we might be experiencing. To do this nonjudgmentally, we must simply notice the feeling rather than adding judgments to it. For example, we would notice "My hands are shaky and feel warm," rather than judge with "I hate how my hands are shaking—they feel horrid and warm." Just notice, do not judge.

Of course, as with all the skills that we learn, this takes practice and getting used to. We are people who suffer with intrusive and forceful thoughts, and our feelings are driven by them. Learning to switch off the internal chatter is possible, and it is through repeating mindfulness exercises again and again that we can achieve this.

Once we are able to "ride" an emotion and let it pass through us, we are less likely to act on our emotions, as they will have already passed without impacting us too negatively.

### *Distraction*

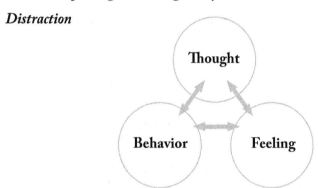

This diagram shows how our thoughts trigger our emotions, which then influence our behaviors. Our behaviors then lead to new thoughts, and the cycle continues.

Let's apply an example to the diagram:

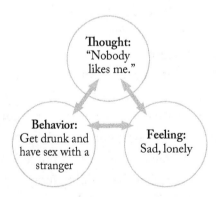

By getting drunk and having sex with a stranger, we set off a new cycle:

The diagram below shows how we can have a thought that triggers an emotion, which triggers another thought, which feeds the emotion and makes it bigger, leading to more detrimental thoughts. And the cycle continues. It is when our emotion becomes unbearable that we impulsively act out in a detrimental way. By distracting ourselves from the emotion, we also distract ourselves from the thoughts that we are having, which in turn allows our emotion to dissipate.

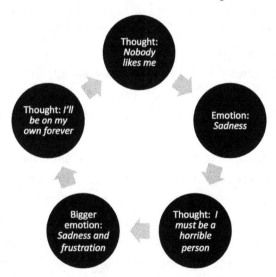

One way to break this cycle is to question our beliefs and change our thoughts, a skill taught in *cognitive behavioral therapy* (CBT). For many of us with BPD, however, our feelings seem to just appear so rapidly and so intensely that we miss the opportunity to change our thoughts. We therefore need to be able to put something in place between our feelings and our behavior. This is where *distraction* comes in. If, when we are overwhelmed by emotion, we are able to momentarily distract ourselves from them, we are able to prevent ourselves from acting out in a destructive way. By distracting ourselves, we are also able to interrupt the negative thoughts that are feeding our emotions.

As soon as an intense emotions strikes, we must instantly jump into action and distract ourselves. How we choose to distract ourselves is up to us. There are copious amounts of ways in which we can distract, and no one way suits all.

Some of us find that releasing a large amount of energy in a short span of time works best, whereas others may find that something more soothing over a longer period works best. When learning new ways to distract, we should try as many different things as possible and practice them often, especially when we are *not* having a crisis. This enables us to build new neural pathways in our brain, which is vital if we want to eventually use them with ease and without resorting to older, unhealthier coping mechanisms.

The next time we feel a surge of emotion we can remove ourself from our surroundings, maybe getting outside. We may decide to sprint around the block a couple of times or we may prefer to take a relaxing walk and get back to nature.

Surrounding ourself with others is beneficial by allowing us to distract while also keeping us safe in the process. We are less likely to act impulsively when surrounded by others.

Something to consider when deciding on possible distraction techinques is hobbies. Doing something that we enjoy makes distracting less alien for us. If you are a person who hates to read, then reading a book to distract will unlikely work for you. Sports, relaxation, music, dancing, seeing friends, walking the dog or playing a game are all possible distractions.

### Recognizing Our Triggers

Many of us can agree that when it comes to our impulsive and reckless behaviors, whether abusing alcohol, using drugs, gambling, or having sex, they tend to be addictive. We then discover that we turn to these habits even when we are not in a crisis. The problem is that these behaviors cause us to feel "high." When we come down off the high, we feel as if we have hit a low, when the reality is that we have returned to a normal level. A normal level feels extremely low compared to the high that we feel when engaging in these behaviors, so we repeat them, hoping to feel the same high as before.

If we are suffering with an addiction or a really bad habit that we just can't seem to break, we need to think of what our triggers may be. Once we become consciously aware of what our triggers are we can then do our best to ensure that we avoid them.

Remember the acronym HALT: Hungry, Angry, Lonely, and Tired. These four things can all trigger us into acting impulsively. It therefore makes sense that we try to avoid feeling any of these things by making sure we look after ourselves.

Other triggers may include:

- Stress
- Certain people
- Places
- Dates, such as anniversaries
- Smells
- Talking about our addictive behaviors
- Too much responsibility
- Emotions
- Certain times of the day

Identifying our triggers is important if we want to recover. Everyone's triggers vary greatly and are personal to each of us. Once we are aware of what they are, we can plan ahead so that we can avoid them wherever possible.

If we are suffering with an addiction, there are a few options we may consider, which are discussed in chapter 21.

*Exercise*

Exercise is hugely beneficial for us, as many of us neglect our physical well-being. We may drink, smoke, and generally make unhealthy lifestyle choices. Our physical body and our mental health are directly linked, with one affecting the other.

Exercise releases feel-good chemicals in our brain, allowing us to get that "high" that we so desperately crave to make us feel better. Exercise also allows us to release energy in a no harmful way. This is favorable to the choices that we tend to make impulsively.

Exercise has both short- and long-term benefits. The long-term benefits include a new and healthier physical body, which positively impacts our mental health. When learning to regulate our emotions, exercise is an important tool to include.

The exercise we choose and how often we do it is up to us. Some of us, especially those who have never exercised before, may prefer to start light and just walk. Others may benefit from a sport such as boxing, as this allows us to release pent-up energy and anger. Swimming is another great choice, as we can decide whether we want to go hard at it or have a relaxing, slow swim. If we suffer with low self-esteem or anxiety, a workout video that can be watched in the comfort of our own home is a good idea to consider.

By choosing to incorporate exercise into our daily life, we begin to make healthier choices all around. We may even find that we have made a complete lifestyle change, cutting out the things that are no good for us and being much more aware of how we treat our body.

When deciding to make lifestyle changes, we should do things gradually. If we decide all at once to eat healthily, cut out alcohol, stop smoking, and work out daily, chances are we will be setting ourselves up for failure. Instead, we should focus on one thing at a time. If we choose exercise first, deciding to do twenty minutes of exercise three times a week is both reasonable and accomplishable. If we manage to stick with this for the first month, it will get easier and easier to do. At a later date we may then decide to start cutting back on the amount of sugar we consume.

## *Weekly Planning, Routines, and Balance*

We know that feeling hungry, angry, lonely, or tired (HALT) are triggers for us to act impulsively and recklessly. By planning the week ahead, ensuring we have a good routine to stick to each day, and making sure we have balance in our life, we are able to avoid these triggers. chapter 25 discusses the importance of planning, routines, and balance in much greater detail. If we have a plan for each day of the week and we stick to it, we are far less likely to go off course.

## Skills Checklist

- Learning to cope with our painful emotions
- Distraction
- Recognizing our triggers
- Exercise
- Weekly planning, routines, and balance

Chapter 9

# SELF-HARM AND SUICIDAL BEHAVIOR

*"Never make permanent decisions
on temporary feelings."*

—Wiz Khalifa

**What Is Self-Harm?**

Self-harm, or *non-suicidal self-injury* (NSSI), is different than suicidal behavior and therefore we will look at them separately. Those of us who self-harm do not intend to kill ourselves. Just as our impulsive self-destructive behaviors are a solution to our problems, so is NSSI. It is one of our coping mechanisms when struggling with our intense emotions.

The ways in which we self-harm can vary greatly in both severity and approach. At one end of the scale are those of us who literally try to gouge chunks of skin out of our body with a knife and cut so deeply that medical attention is needed. At the other end are those of us who scratch our skin obsessively or pull individual hairs out of our head. No matter what end of the scale we are at, self-harm is self-harm; unless we learn new healthy coping skills, NSSI is unlikely to stop.

*Our Thoughts*

Prior to self-harming, typically our mind is racing and we don't know what to do about it. The thought process preceding self-harm is difficult to pin down, because when we do turn our anger inward, we

141

do so impulsively. Self-harm is not usually something we think about prior to doing it, it just seems to happen reflexively. The more frequently we self-harm, the shorter the thinking process beforehand, until the act almost becomes habitual.

The first time that we self-harm, we may consider it first. But this consideration is happening when our logical brain has shut down and we're running on our emotional brain, therefore not thinking rationally. All we are thinking is that we have to do something immediately to stop the pain that we are feeling. Once we have self-harmed and found some relief from doing so, we are more likely to use it as a coping mechanism the next time we are in a crisis.

### Our Feelings

Many of us who self-harm do so because of those intense emotions flooding through us. But it is also true that some of us self-harm because we feel so numb and dead inside. These feelings will be discussed in chapter 10, Chronic Feelings of Emptiness. One of the ways we cope with a lack of feelings is by acting out in ways that make us "feel" something, and self-harm can be one of those ways.

Many of us feel extreme emotional pain when we choose to self-harm. This emotional pain may come in the form of sadness, despair, anger and hatred, to name but a few. There are many times when our hate and anger is directed at ourselves; we hate who we are and we see ourselves as bad people who deserve to be punished.

When our anger is aimed at someone else, we can self-harm through frustration or as a way of punishing those who we are angry at. Of course, we are really only hurting ourselves. Rather than our loved ones feeling as if they have been punished, they think we are being manipulative or attention seeking. While manipulation is not the reason we self-harm, looking for attention can be. So often we are crying out in desperation for help but are unable to communicate our distress to others, and so we turn to self-harm as a method. The words "attention seeking" have such negative connotations, when really all we are doing is crying out for help.

With our borderline personality disorder traits, we can feel as if our life is spiraling out of control. It's as if we are on a bike speeding downhill with no brakes. We feel so afraid and desperate to get off the bike that we just jump, causing injury to ourselves. Self-harm is our means of jumping off the bike; it is our way of trying to control the situation before it gets out of hand.

I tended to self-harm after an argument, which often led partners to believe I had done it to spite them. This wasn't the case. I just felt so absolutely devastated, believing that I had caused the argument to escalate (which I so often had). I'd be so angry at myself, thinking that I had irreversibly damaged the relationship and that they were surely going to leave me. I would get so upset that I would self-harm, causing myself physical pain, which would momentarily replace the emotional pain. After self-harming, I would be able to go straight to sleep. I never once considered that my sleeping partner in the bed next to me would wake up to a blood-soaked bed, not knowing what the hell had happened. Looking back, I can see how traumatic that must have been, but at the time I was too emotional to focus on anything other than the pain I was experiencing.

### Our Behaviors

The manner in which we harm ourselves varies with each individual. Here are the most common forms of self-harm:
- Cutting skin
- Burning skin
- Head-butting
- Scratching skin
- Picking skin
- Pinching self
- Pushing objects (pins, etc.) into skin
- Hair pulling
- Making self vomit

All of the above can vary in severity; there are those of us who cut deeply and those of us who cut superficially with razors. There are those of us who pull out small amounts of hair out and those of us who pull out great chunks.

Our self-harming is not always obvious to those around us. Many of us self-harm privately and cover the marks so that nobody else knows what we have done. Self-harm is particularly prevalent among those of us with "quiet BPD," as we internalize our anger rather than externalizing it. In other words, those of us with quiet BPD do not have impulsive self-destructive behaviors as a coping mechanism, so self-harm becomes one of our primary solutions to our problems.

By cutting or harming ourselves physically, we are distracting ourselves from the intense emotional suffering we are feeling. When we harm ourselves, we can then focus on the physical, which in turn stops us from focusing on our emotional pain.

Eating disorders, drug use, alcoholism, and so on are all forms of self-harm; but they also an impulsive, self-destructive behavior; these are discussed in chapter 8.

## What Is Suicidal Behavior?

Suicidal behavior is when someone acts with the intent of dying. Unlike self-harm, it is not a coping skill. Someone who attempts to behave in a way that will end their life does not want to cope and get through the difficult times, rather they are putting an end to their suffering. Suicidal attempts are a last resort when the person suffering feels they can no longer go on living any more.

Living with borderline personality disorder is an everyday struggle. Those of us suffering with it go through severe emotional pain, our relationships are usually in tatters, and our life is chaotic. To us, seconds can seem like hours and hours like days, with no end in sight and no way out. Unfortunately, a lot of the times when we attempt suicide, we are acting on impulse without thinking things through rationally. If we took the time to rationalize things in our mind, we would see that suicide is not the right answer. The truth is, just because in that second of crisis we want to die, it doesn't mean that we truly want to die. We just get to a point when we have had enough of struggling through each day, are sick of our unhealthy coping mechanisms that no longer work for us, and are tired of not being able to see how anything can change for the better.

## Our Thoughts

Our thinking prior to a suicide attempt will be extremely negative. Sometimes we think to ourselves that we wish we could tell someone how we feel, but we usually conclude that either nobody will understand or nobody will care.

I have attempted suicide multiple times throughout my life. I never actually planned any of them, although I did spend many years wishing I were dead. My suicide attempts would happen in a time of crisis without much consideration of the action I was about to take.

There were a couple of times when my attempts seemed to be pre-planned, as I had written a note to say that I was sorry and explain why I was doing it, but, again, the notes were written impulsively. I never actually planned ahead and thought, *I am going to commit suicide on this day and in this way.*

When we attempt suicide, we usually believe that we have nobody and feel incredibly alone. We may think that if we attempt suicide people will realize that we are desperate and reach out to help us. The suicide attempt itself may be a last cry for help; it is a very dangerous way to ask for help though, considering 1 in every 10 of us with BPD is successful in their suicide attempt.

Suicidal behaviors occur when we can no longer think of a way out of our situation. We have given up trying to solve our problems and think that suicide is the only answer.

## Our Feelings

When we attempt suicide, we feel so desperately helpless. We feel such intense emotional pain that we don't believe anything else can make the pain stop.

While we can experience a whole range of different emotions, ranging from sadness and anger to anxiety and hopelessness, when in a crisis, immediately prior to a suicide attempt we often feel as if we have detached. Calmness may come over us, as we have resigned ourselves to the fact that this is our only option, which of course it isn't, but at the time it seems that it is.

Other times we may be so caught up in our anger that we impulsively attempt suicide in a fit of rage, either at ourselves or at someone else.

When we reach the point that we decide we no longer want to go on, we can feel as if we are drowning in our emotions, desperately out of control and just wanting everything to stop. We feel alone and believe that we have nobody to whom we can turn, even if this is not actually the case. We feel that even if someone were there to help us, they would be unable to do so; therefore we choose not to reach out and not to tell someone how we are feeling.

### Our Behaviors

For the sake of this chapter, I am not going to discuss the ways in which we may attempt suicide, as I do not believe it will be beneficial.

It is difficult to pinpoint our behaviors prior to suicide attempts, as they can vary greatly. If a suicide attempt is taken impulsively, it will be when we are having a crisis; we may self-harm, use drugs, or drink alcohol beforehand. These are our first attempts at trying to cope in the situation that we are in. If we do not feel they have helped, we may then impulsively attempt suicide.

There are times when we may slip into a deep depression beforehand, isolating ourselves from the outside world, stopping engaging in therapy, and losing interest in things we used to find interesting. We have given up. The deeper we fall into the depression, the harder it seems to be able to get ourselves out of it. We may hit rock bottom, and when this happens we have a choice: fight back or give up. Unfortunately, there are those of us who do not feel we have the energy to fight anymore, and so we give up.

## What Is Happening in Our Brain?

When we self-harm, it causes endorphins, our body's natural pain relief, to be released in our brain, giving us a momentary high; we therefore believe that we have made ourselves feel better. We have also then created a neural pathway in our brain that tells us that the next time we are feeling low or are having a crisis, we can self-harm and the emotional pain will go away. The chances of us self-harming next time we have a crisis will increase each time we succumb to that mode of coping, as the neural pathway that we created is being strengthened.

Having endorphins released is also addictive, as we are getting a high from it. Endorphins are like morphine, a natural pain relief that makes us feel nice and calm.

## Where Does This Trait Come From?

Living with borderline personality disorder is extremely hard. Every single minute of every single day feels like an uphill struggle.

BPD often co-occurs with other mental health conditions, such as depression. This too can make life even more challenging for those of us with BPD.

As we grow up and experience difficulties in life, we learn to adopt our own coping mechanisms. Because we are not taught in school or at home how to deal with our intense emotions, we have to find our own way of coping.

If, as a child, we suffered some form of abuse, we can grow up believing that we did something wrong and that we deserved the abuse that we received. If we then take this belief into adulthood, we may believe that we still deserve to be punished, and self-harm can become a form of self-punishment.

## How Does It Affect Those Around Us?

Having a loved one who self-harms or attempts suicide is extremely upsetting. Family and loved ones can be left feeling so incredibly helpless. To watch someone we love harm themself or not want to be here anymore can be tremendously distressing. My own mum puts it this way: "Every night I would go to sleep with the worry that I would wake up and I wouldn't have my precious daughter here anymore."

It is a scary place for family members to be, unable to help their loved one and never knowing what will happen the next time they have a crisis. Parents of a child with BPD will want to wrap their child in cotton wool and yet they can't, leaving the parent feeling powerless, unable to save their child, and feeling completely out of control.

Family members can feel very confused; they do not know what goes on in our head, and this trait is very difficult for loved ones to understand. How can somebody cut themselves to help them cope? Why would a loved one attempt suicide when there are people who love them so much? It just doesn't make sense.

Unfortunately, this trait isn't as simple as just answering the above questions; borderline personality disorder is a very complex disorder. Those who suffer with it can get to a point when they will do whatever they can to stop the pain they are going through, even though the coping mechanisms they turn to tend to be self-destructive.

## Skills for Self-Harm

Just as impulsive, self-destructive behaviors are our coping mechanisms, so is self-harm. It is therefore vital that rather than just stopping self-harming, we find a healthy replacement instead. We cannot expect to remove all of our methods of coping and miraculously manage to cope in a crisis without having learned skills to replace them. That would be absurd and impossible.

We need to learn new skills that actually work and are healthy rather than self-destructive. Once we do this, we will be able to get through a crisis and tolerate the pain rather than succumbing to it.

If we want to self-harm or attempt suicide, it is evident that we have reached a crisis point. Learning how to manage in a crisis is therefore a high priority.

### Distraction

If we are able to distract ourselves momentarily from acting on the urge to self-harm, we can potentially avoid the harmful behavior altogether. When considering different distraction techniques, it is important to question what feeling it is that is driving the urge. Depending on the feeling, certain distraction techniques are better than others. It is a good idea to identify the various feelings that we experience and write them down as a list. Next to each feeling we can write down a few distraction techniques. Next time we are in a crisis, we can look at the list rather than wondering, "*What should I do?*"

**FEELING: Fear or sadness**
**DISTRACT BY: Soothing ourselves**

If we are feeling down, we should consider how we would treat a friend in this situation. We would likely give them a hug, allow them to cry, or make them a hot drink. These are the exact same things we need to be doing for ourselves.

Soothing techniques include:

- Cuddle a soft toy, blanket, or duvet
- Stroke a pet
- Listen to a relaxing guided meditation
- Have a warm bath or shower
- Listen to relaxing music
- Give ourselves a massage with cream or oils
- Light candles and focus on our breathing
- Allow ourselves to cry
- Phone a friend
- Go for a relaxing stroll
- Sleep

**FEELING: Anger or frustration**
**DISTRACT BY: Physically letting out energy**

When we are angry we have a lot of pent-up energy. By doing something physical we can healthily release that energy and hopefully some of the anger with it. Those of us who self-harm do so for the endorphin release. Exercise or doing something physical can mimic the feeling, as it also releases endorphins.

Physical ways to release anger and frustration:
- Scream into a pillow
- Punch a pillow or punching bag repeatedly
- Run
- Tense all of our muscles really tight and hold for ten seconds, release, and repeat
- Jump about and dance
- Stamp our feet

**FEELING: Emptiness, numb**
**DISTRACT BY: Using our senses**

When we feel numb and self-harm, we do so in order to "feel" something. It makes sense, therefore, that we need to simulate ourselves, but in a more helpful manner. It is with our five senses that we are able to "feel" the world around us, so a good distraction technique for feeling numb or empty inside is to distract by stimulating our senses intensely.

Ways to use our senses:
- Put a cold ice cube on our skin or in our mouth
- Flick an elastic band on our wrist
- Have a cold shower
- Squeeze a stress ball
- Eat something spicy
- Listen to rock music

**FEELING: Need to have control**
**DISTRACT BY: Doing something we can control**

So often our lives feel out of control, but even when we feel this way there are always things we can do that we do have control over. If, when we are feeling out of control, we do something productive we can take back the control and feel better for it.

Ways to do something productive:
- Clean the house
- Have a clear out and throw things away

- Sort old clothes and give some to charity
- Wash the car
- Write a to-do list
- Do some gardening
- Delete emails
- Rearrange furniture

**FEELING: Self-hatred and wanting to punish ourselves**
**DISTRACT BY:  Expressing our anger healthily**

Self-hatred is a form of anger at ourselves. Although certain physical activities may help release that anger, we need to be aware that we may purposefully try to hurt ourselves while engaging in such activities. A healthy way to express our self-hatred is through art. We do not need to be artistic to do it either.

Ways to express self-hatred through art:
- Write an angry letter to ourselves and then tear it up
- Write a poem
- Draw or paint a picture
- Write words on our arm in red ink
- Write in a diary
- Make a collage

**FEELING: Guilt or shame**
**DISTRACT BY:  Using positive reminders and reasoning self-talk**

When we are eaten up by guilt or shame, we continually bombard ourselves with negative self-talk, constantly reminding ourselves that we are "bad" people. Our negative thoughts only exacerbate our feelings, and the longer we sit with these thoughts without taking action, the worse we feel.

It is crucial that we try and distract our minds. One way of doing this is to focus on our good qualities. When we start thinking how terrible we are, we must follow it with a statement such as, "But I am a kind person." We must challenge our unhelpful thinking. We may also reason with ourselves, reminding ourselves that self-harm will not help in the long run.

Statements to say to ourselves:

- "I am only human and we all make mistakes"
- "I suffer with an illness that causes me to behave in certain ways—it doesn't mean I'm a bad person."
- "If I self-harm, I will only feel worse afterward."
- "I do not want to end up in a hospital."
- "This feeling will pass—I do *not* need to act on it now."
- "I am a good person."
- "I am a loyal and loving friend."

### The Five-Minute Rule

Next time we want to self-harm we should say to ourselves, "I'm not going to self-harm for five minutes." This buys us valuable time in which the urge to self-harm may disappear. If five minutes is too long a time for us, we can give ourselves two minutes, a minute, or thirty seconds. Once the time is up, we need to say it again to allow us even more time. The thought *I won't self-harm* seems an impossibility when we have the urge to do so. The thought of holding off, just for a short space of time, does not seem so impossible. We can keep repeating this until the urge has gone.

### Telling Someone

All too often, when we self-harm we do so in private. It becomes our own dirty secret that we are too embarrassed to discuss with anyone. We then spend weeks wearing long sleeves, even if the weather outside is roasting. The problem with keeping this secret is that the longer we leave it, the harder it will be to talk to someone about it. By opening up to another person, someone we trust, we often feel as if a weight has been lifted. It is a step toward our recovery. Talking is yet another way to express how we are feeling, rather than expressing it through self-harm.

Who we talk to is up to us, but we should bear in mind that although telling someone we love is extremely important, there is only so much support they can give us. Once we have opened up to a loved one, we should consider discussing our self-harming with a professional. If we feel too nervous about going alone to see a therapist or doctor, we can ask our loved one to accompany us. By seeking professional help, we may then be referred to services that aid in our recovery from self-harm.

If we have a support network, whether it's a family member or a few close friends, we should call or text one of them when we have an urge to self-harm. We do not need to disclose what we are planning on doing, but we can tell them that we are having a hard time and need to talk to someone. There are two benefits to this: (1) we are able to express how we are feeling, and (2) we allow ourselves time for the urge to pass.

### Crisis Box

All of us with BPD should have our own crisis box. How big our box is, what it looks like, and what is in it will be unique to each of us. A crisis box is simply a box that we can open up when we are having a crisis. It contains all the things we could possibly need to help us once we reach breaking point.

When learning to manage our BPD symptoms, many of the skills we pick up along the way include objects. For example, if we find that distracting with music helps, we need the music. If we find writing helpful, we need pen and paper. When in a crisis, the last thing we need to say to ourselves is *"I wonder where my stress ball is?* If we do not have easy access to the things that will help us in a time of crisis, we are likely to turn to an unhelpful coping mechanism. Having everything that we could need altogether in an easily accessible box enables us to be more likely to use a new coping skill.

Items in our crisis box may include:
- Diary
- Coloring book
- Colored pens or pencils
- Pen
- List of emergency phone numbers
- Spare phone with battery and calling credit

- Stress ball
- An elastic band
- CD of favorite music
- Scented candle
- Chocolate
- Inspirational quotes (print favorites off the Internet)
- Bubble bath
- Stickers
- Photos
- Calming pictures
- Book of crosswords and word games
- Cuddly toy
- Spare change
- List of skills to use now!
- Spiritual or religious book
- Herbal tea
- Face mask
- DVDs
- Packet of cigarettes or vape
- Magazines
- List of affirmations
- Play-Doh
- Mints
- Bubbles
- Pebbles or crystals
- Glue

The list is endless! Whatever we choose to put in our crisis box is personal to us. Another distraction technique when in a crisis is to actually decorate our crisis box. This can be done with markers, paint, stickers, photos, or whatever takes our fancy.

### Recognizing Triggers

If we are able to recognize the thing or person that triggers the urge to self-harm, we are then able to either avoid the trigger or learn skills to overcome it.

The easiest way for us to start recognizing our triggers is to keep a diary that we fill in every time we experience an urge to self-harm or after we have self-harmed. The table below shows an example of what a diary might look like.

| Where was I? | Who was I with? | What was said or happened? | How did I feel? | What did I do? |
| --- | --- | --- | --- | --- |
| At home | On my own | A friend texted to cancel going out tonight | Let down, angry | Self-harmed |
| In car | On my own | Song on radio | Angry at my ex because he left me | Went home, self-harmed |
| At home | On my own | Watched a sad film | Sad, reminiscent, lonely | Phoned friend then put on a happy film |
| At work | Colleagues | They were in a group talking and laughing | Left out, alone, angry | Went to toilet and self-harmed |

From reading through the above, we can work out a number of triggers for the person who wrote it.

The triggers are:

- Being alone
- Feeling left out or abandoned
- Listening to or watching something sad
- Reminiscing on the past

Of course, it is impossible to avoid every single trigger. This person cannot just give up work if they feel left out, nor can they prevent people from canceling plans. This person with BPD can, however, try to avoid stimuli that might make them feel sad. The person can also practice the skill of mindfulness to keep them in the present moment rather than thinking back on painful events. It would also be a good idea for them to work on their fear of abandonment and self-image, as this person clearly feels rejected by others. We can see that when this person had an urge to self-harm and phoned a friend and then watched something happy, they were able to resist the urge.

Over time, we are able to look at our own self-harm diary and notice patterns emerging. We can then analyze the patterns and begin to understand why we have the urge to self-harm and work on ways to prevent it in the future.

### Making Our Home Safe

We should remove anything that could be used to harm ourselves: sharp knives, lighters, scissors, razors, and so on. If items aren't on hand when the urge to self-harm comes, we have bought ourselves some time in which we can decide to use a coping skill instead.

## Skills for Suicidal Behavior

Suicidal tendencies arise when we feel that our means of coping are no longer working for us. It is often a last resort when we are overcome with feelings of desperation and hopelessness.

### Building a Support Network

Having a support network is vital, so when we feel as if we have hit rock bottom, there is always someone we can turn to. Each of our support networks will be unique to us; typically they include family, friends, school support staff, crisis professionals, mental health nurse, GP, social services staff, a suicide hotline operator, or the Samaritans. No matter how alone we feel, there is always someone we can talk to.

When we are in a place of despair, we can so often believe that we are completely alone and that nobody else out there feels as we do. We are not alone, yet there are so many of us who feel this way at some point. Having others talk to about our feelings is particularly valuable, as it allows us to communicate what is going on in our heads and the way we feel rather than letting it build up inside of us.

If we feel unable to communicate verbally with someone, we can write a letter or send a text. When we are going through a particularly bad time, we should inform a few close people and ask them to check in with us regularly. If someone reaches out to us, we should accept their help rather than believing that we can do this alone. Accepting help is not a weakness, it shows strength. Many of us feel anything but strong when in the thick of it, but it isn't until we come out the other side that we can look back and appreciate just how strong we were all along.

### *Giving Ourselves Time—The Five-Minute Rule*

When we are about to self-harm, or wish to act impulsively in any way, we should give ourselves some time. Not an hour, as that seems a lifetime away when in a crisis. We should try one to five minutes. If we still want to act on the urge when the time is up, we repeat the process and give ourselves a little more time.

### *Understanding Feelings*

Understanding that feelings do not last forever is also effective. A feeling lasts only ninety seconds; however, we feed the feeling, which causes it to last longer. Just knowing that feelings do not last is important. Yes, we may feel as if the world has ended right at this moment in time, but tomorrow is a different day and will bring with it different feelings. Remember, we should never make a permanent decision on a temporary feeling.

### *Keeping Busy*

When we are kept busy we do not have time to mull over the way we feel. Keeping busy is a wonderful distraction when we feel as if our mood is dipping. The problem is that, when our mood dips, the last thing we want to do is do something or see someone. We have a choice, however. We can choose to do absolutely nothing and have nothing change, or we can fight back. We know how much pain our emotions cause us, and most of us would agree that we would do anything to make the pain go away. Well, we can. Keeping busy might seem like a temporary distraction, but it can become a healthy, long-term habit if we work at it. Keeping busy doesn't have to mean we are out and about socializing all day. It just means we structure our days to include plenty of distraction. Each night we can write up a plan for the next day. An example might look like this:

| | |
|---|---|
| 8:00 am | Wake up, eat breakfast, get showered and dressed |
| 9:00 am | Check email |
| 9:30 am | Do household chores |
| 10:30 am | Go food shopping |
| 11:30 am | Meet friend for coffee |
| 1:00 pm | Go home, have lunch, and watch film |
| 3:30 pm | Walk in the park |
| 4:30 pm | Read a book |
| 5:30 pm | Make dinner |
| 6:30 pm | Practice skills for BPD! |
| 7:00 pm | Phone family member |
| 7:30 pm | Have a relaxing bath |
| 8:15 pm | Watch TV |
| 9:15 pm | Write in a diary, draw, do a word search |
| 9:30 pm | Get into bed and read |
| 10:00 pm | Go to bed |

If we create a daily plan and stick to it, we leave ourselves no time to reminisce on the past or worry about the future. Our mind is kept busy and prevents us from falling into a deeper depression. There are also other benefits of having structure and routine in our day, which is discussed in chapter 25.

### Preempting It and Having a Safety Plan

If we have previously gotten to a point where we feel there is no way out, chances are increased that we will experience it again. Preempting our suicidal actions before we reach this point is therefore essential.

The first thing we can do is clear our home of any dangerous objects: knives, guns, pills, and so on. We need to make our home as safe as possible, so if the time comes when we are a danger to ourselves, we have minimized the ease at which we can act out. We will have given ourselves valuable time—time to think things through logically and realize that suicide is never the answer.

We should also devise a safety plan for emergencies. We can write up or type out our plan, which should include: what to do in a crisis, important phone numbers, and a list of skills we can do. We can even make a crisis box, which is discussed in the self-harm skills section. When feeling suicidal we can reach for our crisis box and trust that the things inside will calm us.

## Skills Checklist

### To Prevent Self-Harm

- Distraction
- Soothing ourselves
- Physically letting out energy
- Using our senses
- Doing something we can control
- Expressing our anger healthily
- Using positive reminders and reasoning self-talk
- The five-minute rule
- Telling someone
- Crisis box
- Recognizing triggers
- Making our home safe

### To Prevent Suicidal Behavior

- Building a support network and accepting help
- The five-minute rule
- Understanding that feelings do not last
- Keeping busy
- Preempting it
- Creating a safety plan and using a crisis box

Chapter 10

# EXTREME
# MOOD SWINGS

*"Not to brag, but I haven't had a mood swing
in like seven minutes."*
—Unknown

## What Are Extreme Mood Swings?

Anybody in the world can suffer with mood swings, going from feeling good to feeling bad and back again. The difference between the general population's mood swings and those of us with BPD is that BPD mood swings happen quickly and often. We may find that our mood swings from being positive to negative multiple times in a day, often abruptly and without any warning. We can go from high to low in an instant, rather than feeling a gradual decline in mood.

We also have the "extreme" part of the mood swings, meaning that our moods, which are intense and unstable, tend to be at one end of the spectrum or the other—extremely low or extremely high with very little in between. Our black-and-white thinking does not help our moods, contributing to them being black or white.

## Our Thoughts

Our thoughts can certainly trigger us to have mood changes, especially in regard to how we perceive things. Our perception of the world around us is often distorted, triggering us to feel a certain way. We can love deeply and forcefully, but due to our fear of abandonment, we are constantly thinking and worrying that those we love will leave us.

I remember a time when I was at a restaurant with my then-husband. We were laughing and joking and generally having a really nice evening. In the car on the way home I started thinking to myself, *What if he only took me to dinner because he has done something that he feels guilty about?* My mood dropped in an instant, and I sat in silence for the rest of the journey.

We may be out with friends and feeling generally well and happy, when out of the blue our thoughts change to negative ones, causing our mood to change also. We are people who not only live with fear of abandonment issues but also negative self-talk due to our self-image, paranoia, and feeling empty inside. All of these other traits contribute to our rapid mood shifts, as can our perception of events.

Events that can cause our mood to change can range from the most menial thing to a huge crisis: having clothes that don't fit, spotting an attractive person, a friend getting a job promotion, an ex-partner meeting someone new, someone canceling a date with us. These are all events that can make us feel as if we are not good enough. We become jealous and resentful. Although we want to be happy for those around us, other people's success is just a bitter reminder that we want what they have: to be happy, free, successful, and confident. The fact may be that we are some of these things, yet we are not able to see it in ourselves. Instead, we mentally compare ourselves to others and always find that we are lacking.

There are times in our lives when our mood can shift suddenly without any trigger. We can go from one extreme emotion to an opposite one in the space of a minute, not knowing the cause and seemingly unable to prevent it. Perhaps we have had thoughts that we are unconscious of and therefore are powerless against. For example, we may be happily sitting in a car when a song comes on the radio; our mood unexpectedly shifts and we want to cry. There was no particular thought prior to this, it just seemed to happen unconsciously.

## Our Feelings

In a typical day we may experience happiness, sadness, anxiety, anger, hopelessness, hopefulness, desperation, and euphoria. Our roller coaster of emotions is completely out of our control and we feel powerless to stop them.

When our feelings are euphoric, we feel as if we are buzzing with joy and love, we feel on top of the world and it is bliss. When going through this phase, we tend to have a distant fear: we know our pleasant feelings are not going to last. We know at some point our mood is going to crash, and yet we try to block this thought and instead try and ride the good feelings.

Inevitably our mood will crash. Many a time our mood has not actually fallen as far as we think; it has simply returned to a normal baseline level. However, due to the extreme and intense high that we have been on, it feels as if our mood has plummeted. Once here, our negative feelings start to multiply until our mood has fallen further still.

It isn't only the velocity at which our moods change that is the problem but also the force at which we are hit. Our feelings are concentrated and strong, and have the power to devastate us in seconds. Sadness is not just sadness—it's a feeling as if our insides are being twisted and crushed, as if our mind is drowning in melancholy thoughts, utter desperation, with no end in sight. Anger is not just anger—it's like a volcano bubbling inside of us, needing to erupt before it consumes us. Anxiety isn't just butterflies in our stomach—it's more like gigantic frogs having an ecstasy rave in our stomachs, a fear that something so terrible is about to happen that we feel the need to run far away and hide. Happiness isn't simply feeling joyful—it's feeling such intense love and bliss, sensing that we will burst with excitement and wanting to throw our arms in the air and squeal with elation.

Although our positive feelings seem idyllic, they do not last—we know a crash will always follow. The better we feel, the harder we crash.

## Our Behaviors

The sheer intensity of our feelings is what forces us into action; we just want the pain to stop, and we go to any lengths to make this happen, not caring if we are self-destructing in the process. We need immediate relief and do not consider the long-term consequences of our actions.

When we face a sudden and dramatic drop in mood, we hit a crisis point and feel out of control. We try and cope in the best way we can, grabbing at any old coping habit we formed over the years: self-harm, drugs, sex, gambling, purging. These are all unhealthy and yet the momentary relief we gain from them cause us to believe they are effective.

As our moods shift so precipitously, the way we act seems to also come without any warning. We may act erratically. As an example, one night, I was queuing to get into a nightclub with two of my friends. The club was full and so the bouncer was only letting someone in every time someone left. Two people left the club and so the bouncer let my two friends in. I explained to him that I was with them, but he said I needed to wait until someone else left the club. I can remember going from being happy to being embarrassed and then being furious. I could not understand how it was such a problem to let just one more person in. I can remember feeling as if it was a personal attack on me. All in a matter of ten seconds I thought, *He thinks my friends are prettier, and that's why he has let them in. He doesn't like me. Well, fuck him, I am going in.* I then tried to barge past this huge bouncer. He obviously stopped me and I just flipped out, verbally and physically attacking him. The police were called, and by the time they got there I was a heap on the floor bawling my eyes out.

To the general population our behaviors are seen as dramatic and attention seeking, due to the intensity of our actions. What others do not understand is that our actions are in equal proportion to how we are feeling. It is not a case of wanting to cause a scene to receive attention. Our actions are not thought through and planned, they happen impulsively in accordance with our emotions. Unfortunately, our emotions are intense and therefore our actions mirror that intensity.

There are times in our lives when we go through periods of calm. This may be due to depression, chronic feelings of emptiness, or even the BPD seemingly going into remission. But eventually we find that we miss the chaos that we have become so accustomed to. Life seems quiet, dull, and flat. It can feel so out of the ordinary that it almost seems as if it isn't reality. We can become disorientated and start to feel on edge. We may act out purposefully in order to create the familiar and comfortable chaos that we are so used to. Not that chaos is ever truly comfortable, but to us it almost becomes habitual, and we long for it when it is not there, for we feel lost without it.

## What Is Happening in Our Brain?

Scientists who study BPD brain connections still do not fully know what is going on when it comes to extreme moods. Studies have shown that those with BPD have a fight-or-flight response that is easily triggered (Redmayne 2015). This makes sense, as our mood can shift so rapidly with a very small trigger. We also have both functional and structural differences in areas of the brain that are responsible for emotion regulation.

Studies have also shown that those with BPD tend to have low serotonin levels (Jogems-Kosterman et al. 2008). Serotonin is a neurotransmitter, and low serotonin levels can lead to depression and anger, which are both symptoms we can suffer with.

## Where Does This Trait Come From?

In some parts of the world BPD is known as emotion dysregulation disorder. This is because we are unable to regulate our emotions. When very young, all children are unable to regulate their emotions. But we learn from our caregivers how to regulate our emotions so that eventually we grow into adults who can. If a child suffers from abuse or neglect, however, this learning is compromised and the child can grow into an adult who suffers with emotion regulation.

Fear of abandonment as well as other BPD traits can also impact our inability to regulate our emotions. Due to the different BPD traits, we often live a lifestyle that negatively impacts our moods and can cause them to fluctuate wildly.

As mentioned earlier, differences in our brain also play a part in our mood swings.

## How Does It Affect Those Around Us?

Our extreme mood swings can leave our loved ones confused and asking, "What the hell?!" We must consider what we would think if we were with someone who is laughing and smiling one moment and in floods of tears the next. We too would wonder, "What just happened?" Nobody but ourselves knows the thought processes going on in our head. Nobody else knows how we are feeling. Outsiders simply observe us externally; to them we can appear fickle. For how can somebody's mood change so suddenly? Surely it is not possible. Yet, of course, we know that it is very possible, as we go through it daily.

Friends and family may believe that our mood swings are put on, a way of us gaining attention. Those of us with BPD find this incomprehensible, as the last thing we aim to do is draw attention to ourselves, but draw attention to ourselves we do, often causing us the utmost embarrassment once we have calmed down. Loved ones face the embarrassment during the episode, whereas we are so caught up in emotion that we are unaware of the impact of our actions on those around us.

## Skills for Dealing with Extreme Mood Swings

### Making Healthy Choices

We know that our mind and our body are linked. Just as our mental health can affect us physically, our physical health has an impact on our emotional well-being. If we want to regulate our emotions, it makes sense that we take a look at our lifestyle choices. Do we get enough sleep, do we eat regular meals, do we incorporate any kind of exercise into our daily life? Becoming aware of what positively impacts our mental health and what things negatively impact it is the first step toward us making changes where needed.

Most of us probably agree that we tend to tick more of the boxes in the column to the right. If we want to learn how to regulate our emotions, however, it is vital that we take steps to eliminate things from our life that negatively impact our moods and incorporate more things that positively impact them.

| Good for our mental health | Bad for our mental health |
|---|---|
| Taking prescribed meds on time | Taking prescribed meds sporadically |
| Fruits and vegetables | Sugar |
| Regular meals | Skipping meals |
| Exercise | No exercise |
| Getting outside (sunshine!) | Staying indoors |
| Healthy food | Junk food |
| Water | Alcohol, energy drinks, or soda |
| Herbal tea | Too much caffeine |
| A decent night's sleep | Too much or too little sleep |
| A balanced life | Too much of one thing |
| Friends | Isolating |
| Meditation/relaxation | Stress |
| Laughter/having fun | No fun in our lives |
| Yoga | Drugs |

## *Becoming Self-Aware*

Although our moods can seem to shift suddenly and without warning, if we look a bit closer we can usually notice either a trigger or a very gradual shift, so small that we are unaware of it happening. It may feel as if we have gone from 1 to 10 in mood intensity, when actually over the past week it had crept up from 1 to 6. When we then go from 7 to 10, we are under the impression that we have gone from 1 to 10, when this isn't the case.

If we can get into the habit of rating our mood each day or after any significant event, we are slowly able to recognize the very small shifts.

| Mood Intensity | How It Feels |
|---|---|
| 1 | Calm—everything is good |
| 2 | Quite calm |
| 3 | Okay |
| 4 | Not good, not bad |
| 5 | Not so great |

| Mood Intensity | How It Feels |
| --- | --- |
| 6 | Not good at all |
| 7 | Bad |
| 8 | Really bad |
| 9 | I'm going to explode |
| 10 | Breaking point—explosion! |

Most of us spend much of our time floating around levels 5 and 6 without even being aware of it. Getting from 1 to 6 can take days or weeks, whereas going from 6 to 10 can take minutes.

When we are able to recognize where we are on the chart, we can then take steps to reduce our level. Up until level 6, we can quite easily reduce the intensity. It is once we are at level 7 that it becomes more difficult. This is why it is important to become aware of where we are—so that we can catch it before it gets out of hand. The sooner we take action the less likely we are of reaching explosive levels.

Just as the intensity of our moods increases gradually, so do our moods when we are trying to reduce them—we cannot expect to go from 6 to 1 immediately after taking action to reduce it. Instead we should aim to reduce our mood intensity down to 5, then 4, and so on.

It is said that those of us with BPD are actually born with a higher mood intensity, and, as we go through life challenges, the intensity increases, never coming back down to baseline level. Those without BPD also suffer life difficulties in which their mood intensity increases; but once the problem subsides, their intensity level drops back to where it was prior to the problem. This is not the case for those of us with BPD. It seems as if once our mood increases, although it may drop slightly afterward, the intensity is still raised. This accounts for why we constantly seem to be going through a crisis. If the intensity level of our moods never decrease lower than a 6 or 7, it makes going up to a level 10 at the slightest mishap extremely likely. Once the crises is over we may drop back down to a 7, leaving us vulnerable to any little problem that may then occur in our life.

Self-awareness is key to recognizing when our moods are creeping up in intensity. Keeping a mood diary allows us to monitor our moods daily and also begin to see any patterns emerging. After every crisis, we should write down where we were, what time it was, who we were with, what happened, how we reacted, and so on. By doing this regularly we may discover certain triggers that tend to push us over the edge, whether it's a person, a certain time of day, or something else. Once we are aware of our triggers, we can then focus on either dealing with or avoiding them.

We may also start to become aware of the slight shifts in mood by looking at our behaviors. Perhaps we are a person who likes a tidy home but suddenly stops bothering to do housework. Maybe we are a person who sees their friends regularly but has started to isolate more. Little changes in our regular behaviors could very well be warning signs that there has been a shift in our mood. Remember, the sooner we recognize mood changes the sooner we can take action and potentially avoid our mood intensity increasing to the point of no return.

## *Mindfulness*

Practicing mindfulness can be helpful when we are experiencing a strong emotion, but it is also a useful skill to practice daily, regardless of the intensity of our emotions. By incorporating this skill into our daily lives, we become much more aware of our thoughts and feelings, thus enabling us to spot triggers and shifts in our moods.

Mindfulness also allows us to ride out any strong emotions rather than holding on to them. When we experience an emotion, we usually continue to feed the emotion with our thoughts rather than simply allowing it to come and go. An emotion lasts ninety seconds and yet we manage to hold on to them for so much longer than that, causing ourselves immeasurable suffering.

To practice mindfulness when experiencing a strong mood, we should find somewhere quiet to sit and take a few deep breaths in. Notice any physical sensations in our body. Are our hands sweating or shaking? How does our tummy feel? We should continue to take deep breaths in and slow breaths out. We often find that our intrusive thoughts will butt in, causing us to momentarily go off in a daydream. This is perfectly normal. But rather than thinking, "I can't do this properly," we should just notice that our mind has wandered and bring it back to focus on how we feel. When practicing mindfulness and being aware of everything in the here and now, we should do so without any judgments. No "I don't like this" or "this is amazing." We are just noticing things—nothing is neither good nor bad—it just is. When being mindful of an emotion, we will often find we can feel it intensifying but rather than fighting it, we just allow it to intensify and eventually it will lessen and lessen and then it will pass—we have let it go.

How to practice mindfulness is discussed in greater detail in chapter 5, Fear of Abandonment, in the skills section.

## *Talking*

There is much to be said about the power of talk therapy. Just being able to sit with someone and let out all of the things that we have been holding in is extremely therapeutic. The person does not even need to be a professional, just someone who will listen to what we have to say. It may be a friend, a family member, or a stranger on a helpline. Often, we do not need advice, only the means of expressing how we feel. For many of us, once we have been able to release all that we have been holding in, we feel lighter, as if a weight has been lifted.

When considering someone to talk to, we should look for someone who we know will listen to us nonjudgmentally. We may even say to the person beforehand that we only need to be heard, we do not need any advice. There may be times when we feel we do need some outside advice, and that is okay too. There is nothing wrong with asking other people their perspective. We must be aware, however, that we may not always like what we hear. We must remind ourselves that everyone is entitled to their own opinion, and just because they may not agree with what we have to say, it does not make them right, just as it doesn't make us necessarily right. We should try to listen to another person's views nonjudgmentally also. There are times when we may benefit from their advice greatly and other times when we would do good to simply dismiss it.

## Doing the Opposite

When experiencing an intense mood, the thought of doing the opposite of how we feel seems absurd, and yet it is an extremely effective skill to use. By taking opposite action we can successfully either change the way we feel or at least lessen the intensity of the emotion.

When we feel a strong emotion we often have the urge to do either nothing or something that will heighten the already powerful feeling. By forcing ourselves to take opposite action we are able to channel that intense emotion into something positive.

If we find we are in a rage at someone and have the urge to confront them, the opposite action would be to walk away. If we are anxious and feel like isolating on our own at home, the opposite action would be to get outside and surround ourselves with people. If we are sad, one opposite action would be to put on a film that will make us laugh. If we feel manic and want to do something crazy, the opposite action would be to do something calming such as meditating or reading a book. If we feel lonely, we should be around people, whether in a coffee shop or a park.

To conquer fear by taking opposite action, we must do exactly what it is that we fear. The more we do this the quicker the fear will fade away. When trying to work out what the opposite action is that we need to take, we should ask ourselves, *What is the thing I would least like to do right now?* The answer will very likely be the opposite action that we need to take.

## Skills Checklist
- Making healthy choices
- Becoming self-aware
- Mindfulness
- Talking
- Doing the opposite

Chapter 11

# CHRONIC FEELINGS
# OF EMPTINESS

*"I feel nothing or I feel everything.
I don't know which is worse".*
—Unknown

**What Are Chronic Feelings of Emptiness?**

There are times in our lives when we will go from feeling absolutely every tiny thing to suddenly feeling completely empty inside. Some of us feel as if we have a void within that nothing can fill, no matter how much we try.

This chronic feeling of emptiness can last days, weeks, even months, thus the word "chronic," meaning an illness that either persists for a long time or is constantly reoccurring.

Of course, the word "emptiness" can actually be misleading, as not everyone with BPD would describe this trait in this way. Each of us may experience this trait differently; one shoe doesn't fit all. Some of us may characterize chronic feelings of emptiness as persistent boredom—when in fact it's trait seven of BPD as listed in the DSM-IV-TR.

At a glance, this trait can seem very similar to depression. While many of us with BPD also suffer with depression, this trait is different. Our chronic feelings of emptiness are our own built-in defense mechanism. It is put in place, unconsciously, to protect us from the pain of our intense emotions. Unfortunately, while it does temporarily give us relief, it tends to not disappear immediately, rather staying there and blocking us from all of our emotions. The problem with this is that our emotions have not actually gone away; they are there in the background building up. When we do not face our emotions head on and deal with them as they arise, they will eventually build until they explode out of us.

## Our Thoughts

When we first begin to feel this emptiness inside, it can actually come as a relief to us, especially if we have just been through a period of extreme instability and mood swings. As time goes on, however, life starts to become more difficult. We think to ourselves, "Is this it? Is this all life has to offer?" We start questioning both the meaning of life and our purpose in it. Our thoughts can become extremely negative; we start asking ourselves, *What is the point?* Negative self-talk does not help our situation and yet we seem unable to stop it. We tell ourselves that we are nothing, we are worthless.

When suffering with chronic feelings of emptiness we can become confused as to what has happened to us. Sometimes we fear that it is the calm before the storm and begin to catastrophize about the future. We may find that our thoughts are racing and yet they have no effect whatsoever on our emotions, which is extremely unusual for us. So often our thoughts impact our feelings and yet with this trait it isn't necessarily the case, as our feelings are "under sedation."

## Our Feelings

There are times when we feel entirely cut off from our emotions. It can feel as if we are not ourselves. If we feel detached from our feelings we begin to detach from reality, much like dissociation. Life can be particularly lonely when we feel so disconnected to the outside world and to those around us.

There are those of us who feel so emotionally numb—almost dead inside—that we are desperate to have the chaos and intensity of our feelings back. We feel as if we are sinking deeper and deeper into a black hole and have no way of escape.

We feel unfulfilled and life feels boring. We are longing for something and yet we do not know what it is that we are yearning for. Our lack of emotion and inability to express our feelings can lead others to suspect that we are suffering with depression.

We may find that we become particularly irritable with those around us, snapping at them for the tiniest thing. This happens because our emotions haven't actually disappeared, they are merely being suppressed.

## Our Behaviors

When our mind detaches from our emotions and we are emotionally numb, it becomes extremely difficult for us to describe what we are going through to those around us. How can we describe a feeling that we are unable to identify ourselves? Is "nothing" even a feeling? Our inability to communicate with our loved ones can affect any connections that we previously had. We feel disconnected, and dissociation is common among those of us who suffer with this trait. We not only sever any connections to those around us but to ourselves as well.

We may feel lonely, even when in the company of others, and eventually begin to isolate ourselves. Once alone and left with only the company of our own mind, we start desperately thinking of a way out, a way to feel something, a way to fill the void.

We do not recognize that our emptiness comes from within; instead we look for external things to fulfill us. Out of sheer desperation we act impulsively, drinking alcohol, using drugs, having sex, gambling, shopping...doing anything that we believe may alleviate the feeling of nothingness. We may jump into a relationship, believing that our new partner can be the one to make us feel whole again. Of course, none of these things can relieve us from our numbed state and instead tend to only exacerbate our feelings of emptiness.

There are those of us who, rather than trying to fill the void, take a different tactic: try to trigger an emotional response in ourselves. This may include baiting someone: trying to provoke an angry response from another person and hoping that, by doing so, we too will feel something.

When we feel emotionally numb we can feel as if we are separated from the body in which we inhabit. When in this state we may self-harm, believing that if we can feel something physically that too may trigger us to feel things emotionally.

While living like a robot, we can start to believe that our once-loving feelings for someone have disappeared. We do not recognize that the feelings are being suppressed and instead think we no longer care about our loved one. Due to this misconception on our part, we may decide to end a relationship, only later on realizing that we made a mistake in doing so.

Many of us also find that, after going through a phase of chronic feelings of emptiness, we have no real memory of doing so. We can look back on this time and it all seems like a dream, not real or as if it never happened.

Our lack of emotions can also cause us to disengage—not only with others but also with any hobbies we may have had. Things that once brought us joy no longer interest us. Everything seems boring and pointless, and we therefore refuse to participate any more.

## What Is Happening in Our Brain?

Our brain is a marvelous thing, helping us survive in this big, bad world. When we sense a threat, our brain helps us to avoid it. If we feel pain, our brain enables us to get through it. When our emotions are unbearably painful, our brain helps us through the difficult times. Chronic feelings of emptiness happen when our brain has said, "Enough is enough! I'm stopping these feelings!"

As mentioned previously, those of us with borderline personality disorder have a fight-or-flight response that is easily triggered. Our fight response helps us fight a threat. The flight response helps us to run or avoid it. Fight or flight is not, however, our only response. We have another called "freeze." The freeze response is when we do not believe we have it in us to either fight or escape the threat, so our mind shuts down, numbing any feelings, so that we can avoid the pain.

As children, we were pretty helpless. If we suffered abuse or trauma, we undoubtedly could not fight or flee it, so our mind did the next best thing: it dissociated from the situation. When, in adulthood, a threat appears or our emotions are out of control, our mind knows it can help us by doing what it has done before: the freeze response is triggered.

## Where Does This Trait Come From?

With the intensity and ever-shifting moods that we suffer, it makes sense that, over time, we would develop coping mechanisms to help relieve us from our emotional turmoil and pain.

Chronic feelings of emptiness appear when our mind shuts out external stimuli to help ease our suffering. We do not do this consciously, of course, and this is why we are often confused and panicked when it happens.

Many of us find that when we first start therapy we go through this phase of emotion suppression. A lot of intense feelings can be triggered and, therefore, our mind protects us by putting up a "shield" that can block our emotions.

## How Does It Affect Those Around Us?

Depending on our behaviors, this trait can affect those around us accordingly. To begin with, they, like us, may find some relief from the chaos of our ever-changing moods. It is unlikely, however, that the feelings of relief will stay.

When we cut off from our loved ones, they may feel we have stopped caring about and loving them. They find that we have become distant and cold and no longer want to connect with them. If they reach out to help us, we distance ourselves further, which can leave them feeling both hurt and helpless.

Our impulsive behaviors, including self-harming, can also leave them feeling powerless. This is scary for them, as they do not understand why we are behaving in this way. It seems as if we are in self-destruct mode and we no longer care about either ourselves or them.

To our loved ones we come across as if we have given up and no longer have any fight left in us. They do not realize that our mind is simply protecting us from ourselves.

Loved ones can become frustrated and angry at us, particularly when we are snappy with them for no reason. When we purposefully taunt them to get an angry response, they may fall into our trap and react in the way we are hoping they will react: with anger and aggression. We know how to push people's buttons, and when we are trying to provoke them we will go to any lengths—name calling and verbally and physically attacking them. It is only natural that they would defend themselves, and, in doing so, we have achieved our goal: we have gotten a reaction.

There are family members who are wise to us and realize that we are baiting them simply to get a response; instead of giving us the response we are looking for, they walk away and do not engage in our games. When this happens, we can be left feeling frustrated, as our attempts at getting a reaction have failed.

## Skills for Dealing with Chronic Feelings of Emptiness

### Keeping Busy

The last thing we want to do when we feel empty inside is to keep busy with mundane, everyday tasks. We either want to sink deeper into a depression and isolate, or we try desperately to fill the void inside with anything that gives us immediate but temporary relief, such as drugs, drink, sex, or self-harm.

Rather than just trying to replace these behaviors, we should instead aim to fill up our days with healthy duties. This may include doing household chores, visiting friends or family members, catching up on correspondence, food shopping, exercising, engaging in hobbies, and participating in an organization. While all these things may seem either too boring or too arduous, by including them in our day we are accomplishing a number of things. First, we are taking up time that would usually be spent either moping about or acting impulsively. Second, we are taking opposite action, which can help alter the way that we feel. Third, we are doing something that positively impacts our self-esteem. At the end of each day we are able to look back, realizing that we have accomplished something, no matter how seemingly small.

When living with a chronic feeling of emptiness, it is all too easy for us to feel as if we are drowning in the void. Having structure in our days is comparable to having a lifeboat. The void is still there to begin with but we are floating safely above it, heading toward safety.

### Doing the Opposite

The various ways in which we try to fill the emptiness within us only leaves us feeling emptier in the long run. Once we can admit this and realize that our attempts at filling the void have been unsuccessful, we are able to be more open-minded to trying something new. Taking the opposite action of what we feel inclined to do is a valuable technique to use. If we want to act impulsively, we must stop and consider what we will do next, acting in a calm and controlled manner. If we are inclined to do absolutely nothing, refusing even to get out of bed, we should not only get up and get showered and dressed but also get out of the house, going for a walk or visiting friends. We find that we must push ourselves into action, and once we have done so we are left feeling less hollow. The more we do this, the more we realize that life itself is meaningful and that we have a purpose in it. In time, the feelings of emptiness fade away and we begin to feel whole again.

### Self-Care

The word "chronic" is defined as having something for either a long time or something that is constantly recurring. While we may all have "bad days" during which we may overeat or drink too much alcohol, if these behaviors become long term they begin to pose their own problems. Due to our feelings of emptiness being of the "chronic" nature, we can very easily get caught in the trap of neglecting ourselves for long periods of time. This lack of self-care eventually impacts us physically and mentally as well. We cannot expect to mistreat our bodies with absolutely no implications.

In chapter 10, Extreme Mood Swings, there is a section called "Healthy Choices" in the skills section. It is these healthy habits that we want to start including in our lives. Self-care can also include balance and routine, and these are discussed in greater detail in chapter 25, The Power of Balance and Routine.

When thinking of ways in which we can "care" for ourselves, we should focus on both caring for our physical selves as well as our mental selves. Both our physical and mental well-being interweave with one another, so to neglect one is to neglect both, just as to take care of one takes care of both.

Taking care of our mental health can include spirituality, mindfulness, meditation, relaxation, time-outs, and talking about or expressing our feelings through art. We must not forget, however, that skills focusing on our physical health also benefit our minds.

### Doing Something Meaningful

For many of us who suffer with chronic feelings of emptiness, we can go through life feeling lost. We may feel that we have no purpose in life and question whether there is a meaning to the painful life that we are living. What we then tend to do is fill our lives with meaningless things that therefore seem to confirm that life is indeed meaningless.

The truth is that we each have a meaning in life, a purpose, but discovering what that is is individual to each of us. One way that we can gain or regain our purpose is to do something meaningful for another person. By carrying out a random act of kindness on another person, we learn that we can make a difference in someone else's life. We have the power within us to bring joy to others, if we so choose. Not only do we realize that our kindness to others brings them happiness, we too gain pleasure from their joy. Random acts of kindness do not have to be huge gestures of helpfulness. Listed here are some ideas:

- Smile at someone
- Compliment someone
- Hold open a door for someone
- Bake a cake for a neighbor
- Offer to do grocery shopping for someone
- Write someone a letter
- Volunteer at a hospital, homeless shelter, or the like

We can also begin to add purpose to our life by doing things that bring us joy. Maybe we like to paint or draw or write or garden. Whatever we find pleasure in doing should be included in our schedule. Most of our days are spent either engaging in unhealthy things or in nothing at all, which is as equally unhealthy. Life is not supposed to be spent feeling as if we are stuck in Groundhog Day, with nothing to look forward to and nothing that makes us smile. Our life matters and it is what we make it. Take time to enjoy the small things in life, because when we look back we will see that they were actually big things.

## *Spirituality*

Spirituality is another way of trying to find meaning in life. For people who already follow a religion, spirituality is already a part of that. Going to church, synagogue, temple, mosque, or any other place of worship is helpful. But not all of us are religious or wish to be. So what should we do? Spirituality, while part of most religions, is not itself a religion, nor do we have to be religious to be spiritual. Spirituality can be described as:

- Believing there is something out there that is bigger than us (we do not need to know what it is)
- Believing that there is more to life than physical things or our physical self—we have a spirit
- Being kind
- Love
- Being nonjudgmental
- Accepting others and accepting ourselves, faults and all
- Recognizing when we have done wrong and trying to learn from it

There are many various definitions of what spirituality is, and being spiritual can be unique to each of us—we can develop our own path at our own pace. Reading literature on spirituality, meditating, spending time alone, connecting with others who are trying to lead a spiritual life, mindful breathing, spending time in nature, practicing the art of gratitude, kindness to others, self-reflection, and being open to signs from the universe are all ways in which we can begin to live a spiritual life.

**Skills Checklist**
- Keeping busy
- Doing the opposite
- Self-care
- Doing something meaningful
- Spirituality

Chapter 12

# EXPLOSIVE ANGER

*"Holding on to anger is like drinking poison*
*and waiting for the other person to die."*
—Buddha

**What Is Explosive Anger?**

Everybody and anybody can feel angry; it is a normal and healthy emotion. That is, except when it isn't. Explosive anger in those of us with BPD is certainly not a normal or healthy response. The reason it isn't "normal" is that it can be triggered by the slightest event, something that wouldn't cause someone without BPD to think twice about. Anger also tends not to be our primary emotion, even though we so often believe that it is; many a time fear is our primary emotion and anger is secondary, but due to how quickly our anger shows itself, we are unable to recognize that it was actually fear that came first, although fleeting, leading to our angry outburst. The reason it is not "healthy" is the way in which we express it, or at times do not express it, instead leaving it to churn away inside, consuming us.

Anger can be measured on a scale, with slight anger appearing as irritability and restlessness. The anger that shows itself in those of us with BPD tends to be at the other end of the scale: explosive. All of our emotions are intense, and our anger is certainly no different.

It is our explosive anger that can have a profound effect on those around us; we push our loved ones away and can treat them with such hatred that they decide to cut themselves off from us. This is not surprising, as our anger is often not justified, at least not the sheer force of it, although at the time we are adamant that it is. When we are in a rage, we often target those closest to us, even if they are not the cause of the anger. It may not be their fault, but we blame them nevertheless.

## Our Thoughts

When our anger surfaces we do not think rationally. Like a three-year-old throwing a tantrum, we are unstoppable and cannot be reasoned with. Our thoughts during an angry outburst are entirely irrational and we will say anything that we can in order to win the argument.

When we are angry we believe 100 percent that we are right in our thinking and in our judgment, and we will go to any lengths to prove that our thinking is correct. Perhaps we are angry because a partner is late home from work. Prior to our outburst, our mind starts thinking up all the reasons why our partner could possibly be late. Fear of abandonment is a core trait of BPD, and it is this trait that can guide our thinking. We automatically assume that our partner is going to abandon us, and our thinking follows this line of thought. We feed our thoughts with "evidence" that we make up in our head to prove that we are indeed correct in our judgment. The more we sit with these unhealthy thoughts the angrier we become until we reach explosive levels.

A lot of our thoughts are blame-based; we think that someone has or will do us a wrong turn. We are very adept at catastrophizing and working out future problems before they arise. Of course we cannot tell the future, but we so often believe that we can.

Our anger (or rather, hurt or fear) may not arise out of what someone has done but what they have not done. And when we think that someone does not care about us, due to either lack of attention or a lack of response, our fear of abandonment can be converted into anger. Here's a story that exemplifies this.

One night, I was lying in bed next to a partner and I decided to "test" their love for me. My thinking at the time was particularly warped: I decided that I would "play dead" to see how they responded. We must bear in mind that my partner was actually fast asleep and snoring at the time. I lay very still next to him and held my breath for as long as I could. Surely he would notice that I had stopped breathing? Nope. I got no response, he just carried on snoring, completely oblivious to the fact that his girlfriend had stopped breathing. I decided to step things up a notch.

I began breathing really fast and loud. This would surely get a response, as I was making a noise now. Still nothing. I could feel myself getting really annoyed. I could be having a massive asthma attack, and he was still in the world of nod. I had to think of a new plan. I decided to carry on with the fast breathing, but this time I would make my body shake as well; surely with both the noise and the movement he would wake up startled and desperately try to save my life? So I lay there, breathing quickly and loudly, while also making my body convulse. This absurd behavior went on for a few minutes before I decided it was pointless—he clearly didn't give a shit about me. I rolled over, went to sleep, and ignored him all the next day.

Resentments are events from the past that we store in our mind and think about over and over, again and again, each time refeeling how we did when it first happened—except that our "memory" of events changes slightly each time we remember it and our feelings become stronger and more intense. We hold on to any harms that people have caused us and replay them in our minds, focusing only on the parts that we choose to. An example of this is when we have an argument with a loved one. We shout and call them names, and they retaliate by calling us names and shouting back at us before storming out. The next time we replay an event like this, we only replay the part when they are shouting at us. We eliminate from our mind the part we played in the altercation and focus solely on what they did to us. In fact, we even begin to alter what they said or did, making it worse than what truly happened. After replaying this resentment over in our minds often enough, we start to believe our "memory" of this event to be true rather than our own distorted recollection of events. When we finally erupt in a fit of rage, we are adamant that our reasons for our rage are justified.

**Our Feelings**

What many of us do not realize is that in the days or week prior to our explosive episode, we may have been suppressing our emotions, causing them to build under the surface. When this happens, the pressure inside of us is bound to eventually explode.

Our fear of abandonment, although a trait of its own, must not be overlooked when it comes to our explosive anger. We are people who live in fear of being abandoned, and, by turning our fear and anxiety into anger, we feel as if we have some kind of control of the situation. We feel as if we are being proactive rather than sitting in fear and doing nothing. We fail to differentiate between real and imagined abandonment and therefore react inappropriately.

Many a time we feel vilified, indignant, hurt, abandoned, and fearful—and yet although these are how we feel unconsciously, they manifest as anger and rage. We are unaware that the anger we feel is being driven by a completely different emotion.

Our anger pulsates through our whole body, consuming us, and we are seemingly unable to control it. There are times when it isn't directed at others but instead at ourselves. We are people who have low self-esteem and talk negatively to ourselves on a regular basis.

We are often aware of the effect that we have on others, and this frustrates us, as we don't purposefully set out to hurt others, it just seems to happen. Our lack of control of our emotions irritates us and we feel helpless. Many of us feel that we have an uncontrollable beast that lives inside of us. We do not choose to have this beast, and we never know when it is going to show itself. We live in fear of it as much as our loved ones do. We get to a point when we start to believe that we are "bad" people. This can lead to us turning our anger on ourselves, hating who we are and how we behave, and angry that we are unable to control ourselves.

After directing our anger toward another person, we are often consumed with guilt, shame, and remorse for what we have done. Those of us with BPD are empathetic, and although we hurt people we too feel the hurt that we have caused and live with the regret of causing it. It is common for the shame and guilt that we feel to turn into anger, which is then aimed at ourselves. We want to punish ourselves for hurting those we care about, as we believe we deserve it.

## Our Behaviors

When angry, we are both uncontrollable and unstoppable. The rage explodes out of us with such force that it can even leave us shocked at our own behavior. Screaming and shouting are not uncommon when the rage hits us. We lash out violently, at times with absolutely no provocation. It is our violet outbursts that often have the most devastating effect on our loved ones, causing them to avoid us at all costs.

When our anger is aimed at a loved one, it isn't always expressed as an eruption, however. It can be far more subtle, passive aggressive, such that our loved ones do not know for sure whether we are angry at them. We may come across as slightly snappy or irritable, we may use sarcasm. We may give a loved one the silent treatment, withdraw from people, cutting them out due to the anger that we feel toward them. Other behaviors include blackmail, intimidation, and even doing something on purpose to spite whoever our anger is aimed at. These behaviors, however, are done impulsively rather than being calculated and thought through.

We also have anger that we turn inward; we may self-harm as a way of punishing ourselves. We may also act impulsively, doing something that puts us at risk, such as speeding in our car, crossing roads without looking, and generally going into self-destruct mode.

## What Is Happening in Our Brain?

When we experience a fit of rage, our prefrontal cortex, the rational part of our brain, shuts down. We are running entirely on emotion, and no matter how hard someone tries to reason with us, they will be unable to do so until we have calmed enough to allow our rational brain to start working.

As soon as we detect a threat, our fight-or-flight response is triggered and we get a rush of adrenaline. Our prefrontal cortex shuts down, and we are unable to look ahead at the consequences of our actions. The same thing happens in a toddler's brain when they are throwing a tantrum. While it isn't nice to see a three-year-old having a full-blown tantrum, to see a fully grown adult having one is absolutely petrifying.

## Where Does This Trait Come From?

Anger can be a learned behavior. If as children we were brought up in a home in which our caregivers showed their anger in huge outbursts, we may have adopted this method of expressing our anger, as we believe it to be perfectly normal.

Not all of us "learned" how to express our anger, though. Perhaps as a child we were taught to not show our anger and instead to suppress it. The problem with this is that the anger will build and build, and we are more likely to eventually either erupt or turn the anger inward on ourselves.

There are those of us who had a decent childhood but still grew into teenagers or adults who have explosive anger. This may be due to the borderline personality disorder itself. Studies have shown that we have a fight-or-flight response that is easily triggered (Redmayne 2015). Getting angry is the "fight" part and it is certainly necessary—if our survival is at stake. Unfortunately, our fight-or-flight response is triggered even when a situation is not a life-threatening. The intensity of our reaction would have outsiders believe that our survival is at risk, however. With our intense emotions, fear of abandonment, and unstable relationships it makes sense that we would also suffer with extreme anger, as we perceive everything around us to be a threat.

## How Does It Affect Those Around Us?

To those around us, our fits of rage can be terrifying. We may violently attack people physically or so violently with our words that our loved ones are sure we will get physical. We must realize that our anger explodes out of us with such force that it is bound to intimidate or frighten those around us. Our loved ones exposed to our eruptions don't understand that when we are in this state there is no reasoning with us. They struggle to understand how we can't see sense. Again and again they try to reason with us; when unsuccessful, they are left feeling completely powerless, not knowing why they can't get through to us.

If our angry outbursts are a regular occurrence, our loved ones begin to feel that they are walking on eggshells around us; they may even start avoiding us all together.

Due to how nasty we can become when we lose our temper, people can become fed up with us and dislike us immensely. We lash out so viciously and with such malice that we cause people great hurt; our anger often provokes them to retaliate, and they become angry back at us.

We act impulsively and at times without provocation, at least not from an outsider's point of view. Although we may have been triggered by something, to those around us there appears to be no trigger.

Once we calm down, we hope that those around us will be forgiving and understanding. We must, however, recognize the fact that our actions can have a hugely detrimental effect on our loved ones. We cannot take back all the mean and hurtful things that we have said, nor can we make someone forget the awful things that we have said. There are consequences for our actions, even though we do not think about them before acting out.

Our loved ones may choose to cut us out of their lives, they may not speak to us for a few days, and they may feel both angry and fearful of us. These are our consequences, and, although we may feel guilt and shame at our behavior afterward, we must accept that we have caused harms. We must understand that how our loved ones react to us afterward is beyond our power.

## Skills for Explosive Anger

### Counting to Ten (or One Hundred) and Breathing

When we feel a flood of anger sweep through our bodies, all too often we just react. The way in which we react only fuels our anger (and the other person's), causing the feelings to escalate to colossal levels; once at those levels, it is very difficult to come back down. If we are able to make ourselves stop and count to ten before reacting, we are less likely to say things that we will later regret. This is important, as the way we respond has an effect on how the other person responds. If we immediately respond with more anger, the person is likely to retaliate with heightened anger as well. This only enrages us further, and we become far less likely to implement our ten-second rule once a two-way argument has begun.

To use this skill effectively, the moment we feel that rage building inside of us we must consciously make ourselves stop before we react. We should then take in a long, slow breath and let out an equally long and slow breath. Once we have completed the exhalation we can say "one." We then repeat and say "two," "three," "four," and so on until "ten."

This technique works in two ways: First, the deep breathing helps to calm our fight-or-flight response by slowing down our oxygen. Once our fight-or-flight response has been calmed, the rational part of our brain can begin to work. Second, by concentrating solely on each breath and counting, we are temporarily distracting ourselves from thinking about what has made us angry in the first place. Depending on how angry we are, we may find that ten seconds is all we need to calm ourselves and prevent us from making a situation worse. If after ten seconds we still find that we are enraged, we should simply continue to breathe slowly and count.

### Taking a Time-Out

There are times when we are so infuriated that we actually need to be taken out of a situation in order for us to be able to calm down. Now, if we are alone with the person that we are angry with, there is nobody who can take us out of the situation except ourselves. But even if there is another person there, chances are good that if they tried to remove us we would not take kindly to it, and then they too would become a source of our anger. Therefore, it is crucial that we alone learn to recognize when we are better off removing ourselves.

When we feel our anger bubbling and are on the verge of either lashing out physically or verbally, it is probably a good time to remove ourselves from the situation as quickly as possible. We should walk away and take ourselves to a place where we can calm down. Some of us find that we need a quiet space to be in, and others may find it easier to go for a walk. Once removed from the situation, we should refrain from thinking over what it is that made us angry in the first place. Instead, we should focus on our breathing to help calm us. Once in a calmer state of mind, we are able to think things through rationally. We are often thankful that we didn't react in the way that we initially would have done had we not removed ourselves from the situation.

### Dealing with Resentments as They Arise

Because we tend to explode in a fit of rage, we typically believe that this is what anger is: a huge atomic explosion of pure undiluted fury. Anger, however, comes in many forms, and often what seems like an unpredictable, frenzied eruption is often something that could have quite easily been predicted, as we have been carrying it around with us for days, maybe even weeks. Minor irritations, small annoyances, and, most important, resentments, are all forms of anger.

In *The Big Book of Alcoholics Anonymous*, resentments are listed as one of the biggest causes of relapse. Why? Well, resentments literally eat us up inside. The word "resentment" comes from the Latin word "sentire," meaning to "feel." The "re" in resentment means "again," so to have a resentment is to "feel again." So, if someone has done something that has caused us indignation, upset, or annoyance, and we replay it in our minds again and again, refeeling how we felt when it first happened, we have built a resentment.

For those of us with BPD, resentments are easily formed due to our high sensitivity and our perception of events. Here is what happened to me one time:

I was in my car waiting for someone to pull out of a space so that I could take it. After a couple of minutes, the driver reversed out of the space, and I was momentarily blocked from pulling in. And in that time

191

a car that had just pulled up quickly nipped into the space! I felt rage wash over me. I couldn't believe the audacity of the driver. I felt like rolling down my window and hurling abuse at the couple in the car. Instead, I drove off, still raging, considering how I should get my revenge. I could follow them into the shop and confront them. I could scrape my key down the side of their car or I could wish them bad luck for the rest of the day.

After five minutes I found another parking space. I entered the shop and noticed the couple in there. I made sure that I stood blocking their way while pretending to look at groceries. I heard the lady say, "Excuse me," and I pretended not to hear. All of a sudden, I realized that if I didn't do something about this, it would become a full-blown resentment that I might hold on to for weeks! So I continued my shopping. When I next walked passed the man and lady, I gave them a warm smile...and they smiled back! This was all it took for my anger to go away. I didn't hate them anymore, in fact, maybe they just hadn't seen me and it wasn't a personal attack on me after all.

The above example illustrates the damaging effect a resentment can have on us. While those who we resent go about their days completely oblivious, we are consumed with anger. The quote at the beginning of this chapter sums it up perfectly: "Holding on to anger [resentment] is like drinking poison and waiting for the other person to die."

Of course, smaller resentments, similar to the one above, tend to be easier to rid ourselves of, but they are also easier to pick up. We often find we are carrying around a number of resentments at any one time. If we want to let go of any resentments we may be holding on to, we must first become aware of them. We can do this by writing a list of anyone who we feel angry at and why. Below is a made-up example:

| Resentment | Reason for Resentment |
| --- | --- |
| Ex-partner | Breaking up with me |
| Police | Arresting me |
| My old school | Not protecting me from bullies |
| Bullies | Bullying me |

| Partner | Forgetting my birthday |
| Friend | Being too busy with work to see me |
| Social services | Thinking I am a bad mum or dad |
| Neighbor | Asking me to turn my music down |
| Landlord | Asking me to leave |
| God | Not answering my prayers |
| A stranger | Driving too fast |

When we start writing our list, we find that it is a lot longer than we first imagined it would be. All of these events from our past are still negatively affecting us today. If we continue holding on to them, they will continue to negatively impact our future. We have to ask ourselves, *Is it worth it?*

We can also look at our list and ask ourselves if perhaps a current resentment actually stems from older, forgotten, or unconscious hurts. For example, resenting a friend for working too much may actually stem from a childhood hurt, when a parent spent all their time at work. Maybe the resentment of social services stems from always being told as a child that we were no good. If this is the case, chances are we have actually perceived these current events based on past experiences. Social services may not actually believe that we are a bad parent, and our friend may actually have plenty of time for us usually, just not at the moment we need them. If we can recognize that our resentment stems from something in our past, we can then let it go relatively easily.

If we are able to free ourselves of our resentments, we find that we are less likely to anger so quickly. There a few ways in which we can work through our resentments:

1. Understand that we cannot change the past and that we are powerless over other people. We are not powerless over how we let them affect us.
2. Repeat out loud to ourselves daily the phrase "I forgive them." In time, we come to find we have truly forgiven them.
3. Recognize that we had a part to play in what happened. It's not likely that we were 100 percent innocent. Did we contribute to

the altercation in some way? Taking responsibility for our own part can allow us to see it from the other person's perspective.

4. Realize that our memory of events may not be completely accurate.

5. Write down our resentments and ask ourselves, *What purpose does this resentment have, other than to make me miserable?*

6. Understand that we are all human—people make mistakes, it doesn't mean they shouldn't be forgiven. Try to focus on the person as opposed to what they did.

7. Show others compassion, as we would like others to show us.

When we have cleared up resentments from our past, we can then, at the end of each day, ask ourselves, *Have I built a resentment today?* It is a lot easier to let a resentment go immediately rather than allowing it to grow.

Although letting go of resentments doesn't prevent us from ever getting angry, it does prevent unresolved anger from building up beneath the surface. This can lessen the number of angry outbursts that we experience.

### Getting Physical

Anger is one of the harder emotions to control, as it is a primal instinct, there to protect us from dangerous situations. When we detect a threat and our fight-or-flight response is triggered, we get a rush of adrenaline. This happens to give us a large amount of energy in a short span of time so that we can protect ourselves.

The skill of taking time to slowly breathe and count is one way of counteracting the surge of energy. Getting physical is almost the opposite. We are not fighting against the rush of adrenaline, but going with it … except in a nondestructive way. When we feel that rush of adrenaline we need to release it in a healthy way—we might go for a run, punch or scream into pillows—anything that releases all that energy but without slugging someone in the face.

Once we have calmed down we find that we are then able to rationalize, something we couldn't do when in attack mode.

## *Communication*

The way in which we communicate when we feel angry determines the outcome. We cannot expect to hurl abuse at someone or physically attack them and have no consequences. Of course, in the heat of the moment we are not going to consider the consequences, but that is exactly why we need to think about the way in which we communicate prior to an outburst.

If we find that we tend to get angry at the same person repeatedly, we must ask ourselves, *Why is this?* What do we believe they do that makes us so angry? Once we know the answer to this we can learn to preempt it. We can imagine a situation in which they anger us, and we can visualize how we could deal with the situation differently. By running through some made-up dialogue, we can come up with some nonaggressive statements that we can then use the next time we feel ourselves getting angry at that person.

When thinking of statements to make, we should refrain from starting them with "You," as this tends to make people defensive. We can use statements such as "I feel ... when you ..." If we have practiced saying different statements to ourselves prior to an angry outburst, we are far more likely to use them in the next argument that we have.

If, however, we feel as if the argument is escalating, we are probably best to stop all communication and walk away for the time being. We can always regather our thoughts and return later on, once we are calmer and feeling more in control of our actions.

When dealing with intense anger, one way of decreasing the amount of explosive episodes that we have is to communicate with others often. If someone has upset us, we shouldn't leave it unresolved, no matter how minor we think it is. If we do just leave it, the next time something upsets or annoys us, we are likely to feel it more intensely. Let's imagine we are an empty bottle with a lid on top; every time someone does something to upset us, we fill up a little bit. Eventually we become full, and all it takes is one small thing to cause us to blow our lid and explode. By communicating often about how we feel, we can let off steam gradually rather than in one almighty explosion.

Learning to be assertive is another communication technique that is very beneficial. Those of us who are unable to stand up for ourselves or able to say no to people often find that we become frustrated and angry with ourselves. Assertiveness allows us to stand up for ourselves and be heard (in a healthy way), rather than continuing to feel like a doormat.

Before talking assertively with someone, we should first consider what it is we expect from them. It may be that we want to ask someone to stop doing something, or maybe we want to discuss how something has made us feel. When having the conversation, we need to stick to the point that we wish to make, keeping it simple and without long explanations. We should make eye contact and talk in a calm voice. It is possible for us to be polite while also being firm. Assertiveness is a skill that takes a bit of practice but, once achieved, can help us feel as if we have some control over how we are treated by others.

**Skills Checklist**
- Counting to ten (or one hundred) and breathing
- Taking a time-out
- Dealing with resentments as they arise
- Getting physical
- Communication

# Chapter 13

# FEELING SUSPICIOUS OR OUT OF TOUCH WITH REALITY

*"Suspicion is a heavy armor and with its weight
it impedes more than it protects."*
—Robert Burns

**What Is Meant by Feeling Suspicious or Out of Touch with Reality?**

Those of us with BPD can spend a lot of time feeling suspicious or paranoid about other people's motives. We have serious trust issues with those we care about and believe that people are going to either leave or betray us (that's our fear of abandonment showing up again). Our abandonment issues are so severe that we struggle to build trust in relationships because we think that everyone is out to get us.

Becoming out of touch with reality, or dissociating, is usually triggered by a painful or traumatic event. We dissociate as a way of protecting ourselves from what is happening around us. Dissociation is also known as emotional numbing.

I first experienced dissociation when I was about eight years old. A teacher shouted at me in front of the whole class. I felt humiliated, angry, and indignant as I was being shouted at for talking, even though it had been the girl next to me who had been talking. I remember all of a sudden feeling as if I had stepped outside my body and standing to one side, watching my body react.

I flung my desk forward and stormed out of the classroom. The teacher followed, and I punched her in the stomach. I vaguely remember the teacher then trying to throw me down the stairs, although I am not sure if this is a figment of my imagination. I do not remember anything beyond this point.

I tried explaining to my mum what had happened to me; she assumed I was having blackouts and took me to the doctor, who sent me for all kinds of brain scans. Obviously nothing showed up, as it wasn't blackouts that I was having but moments of dissociation. As a child, I had no way of explaining it properly; it wasn't until I was an adult that I looked back and went "Aha!"

Dissociation is different from psychosis in the fact that we are detaching from reality as opposed to losing reality.

There are different ways we can dissociate. First, we can dissociate by detaching ourselves from our body—everything feels like a dream, as if it is not real life. Second, we can dissociate by disconnecting from who we are—we become someone new, maybe with a new hometown, a new life, and new friends, often forgetting a lot of our past. Third, we may experience memory loss. There are those of us who have big gaps in our memories, completely forgetting certain past events. Our mind blocks these memories as a way of protecting us. After a dissociative state, we may find that there is much of it that we cannot remember. There are some of us who dissociate for a few hours and others who dissociate for weeks or even months at a time.

If as a child we experienced ongoing abuse, we may have taught ourselves to use our imagination to help us escape the trauma. By using our imagination we could imagine that we were somewhere else, somewhere safe, away from the abuse.

## Our Thoughts

When we dissociate our mind is basically saying, "I can't deal with this," although it is unconscious and we are not aware of this. Once we dissociate, it can feel very strange—we start questioning what is real and what is not.

Feeling suspicious can have a huge influence on our mood. We find that we have intrusive and upsetting thoughts that we are unable to push away. Our intrusive thoughts make us feel as if our own mind is out to get us. This has happened to me numerous times.

For example, I would constantly have thoughts that my partner was going to cheat on me. At first, the thoughts were just suspicious, questioning "What is he up to right now?" They would soon change, however, to facts. I would tell myself, "He's with someone right now. You need to catch him out." Then the images would start coming. I would make up scenarios in my head and they would feel so real that I would start to believe them.

Our severe distrust of others is worsened by our thoughts. We are able to think up the worst scenarios for everything, and our imaginations can get so carried away that we struggle to distinguish between what is true and what is false. The same goes for when we catastrophize; we can get so caught up in our own thoughts that we struggle to see the reality of the situation.

Catastrophizing is something I'm not stranger to. I used to panic every time my kids went on a car journey, thinking the car was going to crash and they would all be killed. I would then start to panic that someone else in my family was about to die a painful death. One thought would lead to another and another, each time progressing in severity.

Our thoughts are nonstop, and we seem unable to stop them from taking over our mind. We have a battle going on in our head that we can't seem to win.

## Our Feelings

When dissociating from situations, we feel emotionally numb. Everything around us can seem to be happening in slow motion or as if in a dream. We are detached from the situation; it's as if we are watching something happening to another person rather than to ourselves. We can feel spaced out and even experience the feeling of floating up and watching our body from above.

In my past, there were times when I seemed to be in a constant daydream. I was only half aware of what was going on around me, and the other half of me was away with the fairies. I could spend weeks in this state and never realized that this was a form of dissociation.

The good thing about dissociating is that we do not feel the intensely painful emotions that we would feel if we did not dissociate. The bad thing about it is that we are not actually dealing with the situation.

Our feelings, when it comes to our paranoid and intrusive thoughts, are not numbed and are all consuming. Due to our nonstop and unhelpful thinking, we can feel as if we are drowning in our emotions, with no way of saving ourselves.

Our thoughts feel as if they are real, even if they are imagined and our body reacts accordingly. We may feel physically sick, shaking with nerves, or burning up with rage. Emotionally we are a wreck, with intense emotions coursing through our body, leaving us inconsolable and despairing.

When our emotions are of this magnitude, we are left in a very vulnerable position. We think that either people are out to hurt us or that something bad is going to happen; emotionally we feel scared and anxious. Our fight-or-flight response is triggered, and we believe we must do something to stop whatever it is that we believe is going to happen.

## Our Behaviors

When we dissociate, those around us are not always aware of it. If we take on different personalities or we feel as if we have detached from our bodies, it is all happening in our mind and is therefore not something that can be seen by others. What can be noticed by others is our behaviors once we have dissociated. We may start to behave differently than normal and seem to be out of character. We must be careful when we act while in a dissociative state, as we are far more likely to put our safety at risk, as our numbed emotions can cause us to feel as if we are untouchable.

There are those of us who desperately try to rid ourselves of the dissociation by physically harming ourselves so that we can feel something.

Our paranoia and intrusive thoughts can also drive us to act impulsively. Our thoughts and feelings become so all-consuming that we are forced to take action as we desperately try to stop them. Turning up unannounced at a loved one's work and causing a scene, phoning or texting someone nonstop, stalking, demanding we search someone's phone or emails, casting blame, and locking ourselves in the house and closing all the curtains are all behaviors caused by our paranoia and intrusive thoughts.

When we are taking action, we are distracting ourselves from our constant intrusive thoughts. We feel as if we are being proactive, unable to see that our behaviors are only further damaging us and our relationships. Our behaviors seem perfectly justified to us, as we believe our thoughts to be facts. The intensity of our feelings fuels our behaviors; we are unable to calm down or to rationalize at this point. Instead, we steam forward, trying frantically to prove that our suspicions are correct rather than questioning our thinking and looking for evidence to prove that our mistrusts are unfounded. In fact, any information that suggests that we may be wrong is dismissed swiftly. We carry on with our mission to prove that we are right.

I am certainly guilty of being on a mission to prove how right I am. One time, I was convinced my partner was cheating on me. I had absolutely no evidence to suggest this was the case, but once the thought was in my mind it just kept growing until it reached a point when I felt 100 percent sure I was correct. If I phoned him and he was on another call, I told myself he was on the phone with another woman. If he said he needed to go to the store, I told myself he was meeting up with someone.

One day, I completely lost it and demanded he let me look through his phone, which he did. I couldn't find anything that I was looking for, but rather than thinking that perhaps I was wrong, I came to the conclusion that he had a secret phone hidden somewhere. I spent the next week searching high and low for this phone, which never turned up. I decided he must leave his secret phone at work.

Our paranoia and catastrophizing can lead us to isolate ourselves from the outside world. While in isolation, with nobody there for distraction, we find that our paranoia worsens. We may close all the curtains in the house, lock all the doors, and sit in darkness. Sitting in the silence and darkness, our mind may start playing tricks on us. We begin hearing and seeing things that are not actually there. When this happens, we start peeping through a gap in the curtains or through the letterbox.

## What Is Happening in Our Brain?

### Dissociation

There haven't been enough studies done relating to BPD, dissociation, and the brain. It seems clear, however, that when we dissociate, our brain has gone on the defense to protect us. If, as a child, we suffered some type of trauma in which we had no way of escaping, our brain allowed us to detach mentally so that we could get through it. Whenever we then go through a stressful event, our mind is able to detach from the reality of the situation. The problem with this is that this defense mode kicks in even when the traumatic event has long passed.

In the face of danger, our brain gears us up to either flee danger or fight it. For people who are unable to do this, such as children, the brain can respond by "freezing." This enables the person going through the trauma to shut off from what is happening to them. The brain either releases chemicals that can "numb" the body, causing us to go stiff and rigid, or shuts off the "thinking" part of itself, which can cause us to act a bit like a zombie, doing things but not being consciously aware of our actions.

### Intrusive Thoughts

It is believed that a region of our prefrontal cortex is responsible for defending our brain from intrusive thoughts. Unfortunately, it is not always successful at doing so, and this dysregulation of this area may be the reason for various mental health disorders.

A more recent study has shown that a neurotransmitter called GABA can affect whether we can suppress unwanted thoughts. The study found that people who were successful at preventing the intrusive thoughts had higher concentrations of GABA in their hippocampus than those who were unable to suppress the intrusive thoughts (Schmitz, TW et al. 2017).

### Where Does This Trait Come From?

Dissociation often develops in childhood or at a time in our lives when we are going through a traumatic event. Our mind goes into a protective mode to help us deal with the situation. As we grow older, whenever we go through a difficult time, our mind will dissociate as a coping mechanism.

Paranoia among us may stem from our fear of abandonment and unclear self-image. We do not believe that we are lovable, so we doubt other people's motives. We already believe that those who love us are going to abandon us, and our mind is constantly looking out for threats of this happening. This, in turn, leads to our paranoia worsening.

Hallucinations may come about due to isolation and a mind that is both paranoid and catastrophizing. While I was in rehab the owner, Lorraine, told us, "Your mind is like a bad part of town, do *not* go there on your own."

### How Does It Affect Those Around Us?

When we dissociate, people around us may notice that we are acting strangely, or they may think we are just choosing not to listen to them. The absolute ferocity in which our suspicions are thrown at those around us can lead them to feeling confused. After all, most of the time our suspicions are unfounded and unjust. A loved one may try to convince us that we are barking up the wrong tree but then quickly realize that there is no reasoning with us. No matter how much a loved one tells us that they love us and wouldn't betray us, we remain determined to prove them wrong. They feel as if they are fighting a losing battle with us, which they are.

When we start behaving out of character and isolating, those around us are yet again left feeling powerless to help us. They may try to reach out to us, but we push them away. In the end, people stop reaching out to us, thinking we mustn't want the help. Unfortunately, this is not the case. It is not that we don't want the help; we simply don't always recognize that we need help, at least not straightaway. It is usually when we hit rock bottom that we recognize we need help and that we cannot do it alone. But by this point we may have pushed everyone so far away that we no longer have the support that we need.

## Skills for Dealing with Dissociation

### Recognizing Our Triggers

For most of us, dissociation does not just happen, even if it feels like it. There tends to be triggers that cause us to dissociate. To begin recognizing what our triggers are, we may keep a diary that we fill in after every dissociative episode. Places, events, people, dates, and the like can all be triggers; it is up to us to work out which ones are triggers.

Once we know what our triggers are, we can aim to either avoid them or, if that's not possible, put a coping plan into place beforehand.

### Using Our Senses

Using our five senses is a way of grounding ourselves and bringing ourselves back to the present moment. We may use our senses to help us self-soothe, to shock our bodies back into the here and now, or coax ourselves back to reality gently.

Self-soothing with our senses may include having a warm bubble bath, cuddling a pet, massaging oil onto our skin, listening to relaxing music, eating a favorite meal, smelling a nice scent, or gently squeezing a stress ball.

To "shock" ourselves back to reality, we need to use something that feels strong to our senses. Ice cubes on our skin, dipping our face into cold water, having a cold shower, flicking an elastic band on our wrist, really slow and deep breathing, or intense exercise can all help.

Another way of using our senses to help bring us back to the present is to play the 5, 4, 3, 2, 1 game:

Name five things you can see in the room.

Name four things you can feel in the room.

Name three things you can hear in the room.

Name two things you can smell in the room.

Name one thing you can taste right now.

This game helps to both ground and distract us.

### Acceptance and Understanding

Understanding why we have this trait is helpful in learning to accept it rather than fighting it. When we become freaked out due to dissociating, we often find that it only makes the matter worse. We therefore need to accept dissociation for what it is: our brain trying to protect us. The more we berate ourselves over it, the less likely we will be able to overcome it.

We must also accept that while this defense mechanism served its purpose once upon a time, it no longer does. For most of us, the major traumatic event of our past is over, yet we still dissociate in times of stress, as it is our automatic coping mechanism. However, we now need to learn how to deal with a crisis without blocking it every time. We need to learn how to "feel" again. That is not to say that when we first start "feeling" it isn't painful. Of course it will be, but it is still a vital step on our road to recovery. This isn't something that needs to be rushed—we can go at our own pace, with no pressure. Self-soothing techniques can replace the dissociation; they can teach us that it is possible to "feel" while also coping with the pain, and in a healthier way.

### Trauma Therapy

It must never be overlooked that there are those of us with BPD that have suffered the worst abuse imaginable and often for a prolonged period of time, sometimes years. In cases of severe abuse, it is always worth working with a trauma specialist. A professional can help us come to terms with past events in a safe environment. Having trauma therapy can enable us to overcome flashbacks and dissociation. It is important to know that we can go at our own pace, and if talking ever becomes too painful, we can tell our therapist. If we find we are dissociating during therapy we can also tell our therapist.

A more recent form of trauma therapy is eye movement desensitization and reprocessing (EMDR). This form of therapy involves working with a specialist who can make hand movements that cause a patient's eyes to move in a certain way. Rather than focusing mainly on the traumatic event, it focuses on the symptoms and feelings caused by the event. At the moment, it is a controversial form of therapy, with some professionals saying it does not work. Other studies, however, have shown it to be incredibly effective (Shapiro 2014), successfully reducing negative feelings and memories associated with the traumatic event.

## Skills for Dealing with Intrusive Thoughts and Paranoia

### Checking the Facts: Past Fears vs. Reality

Intrusive thoughts are a form of anxiety—they come from our fears, often fears from our past. Once we recognize where this fear stems from, we can begin to separate it from our current fear. We can do this by checking the facts.

If we are having intrusive thoughts that someone we love is going to die, we first must ask ourselves, *Where does this fear comes from? Did I lose a loved one as a child?* If our intrusive thoughts are suspicious ones, thinking that someone is betraying our trust, we should ask ourselves if we have been betrayed before. The chances are highly likely that these intrusive thoughts are based on past facts as opposed to present ones.

We can write down what our intrusive thought is and question what facts we are basing our assumptions on. We can then look at the present moment and list the reasons why the thought is not based on reality.

When we look at the second column, we often find that they are based on past experiences or that they are very general, such as "everyone dies." When we then look at the third column, we can clearly see that our thoughts are not based on reality of the present moment.

### Mindfulness

Mindfulness is a wonderful skill for helping us stay in the here and now, but it is also helpful in enabling us to just notice our thoughts, without judgment. To do this, it is a good idea to sit somewhere quiet and take some slow, deep breaths to relax ourselves. We should begin to use our senses to notice what is going on around us. Maybe we can hear cars or birds outside, or we can notice how our body feels physically. As an intrusive thought enters our mind, we should imagine it as a bubble floating up into the air. We can notice the thought, without wishing it wasn't there or thinking that it is bad. We simply notice it and think "Oh, that's another thought floating up and away." Then we can bring our mind back to any physical sensations we are experiencing. No doubt another thought will pop up, and again we should imagine it as a bubble just floating by.

The problem with trying to forget a thought or push it away is that the more we try to do this, the more we end up thinking about the thought. The more we think about the thought, the more it will grow and consume our mind. When using mindfulness, we are not trying to stop our thoughts. We are doing the opposite, noticing them for what they are: just a thought.

### Distraction

It is impossible for us to have intrusive thoughts if our mind is focused on something else. Being able to distract our mind is therefore highly effective at cutting off our unwanted thoughts.

A good way to distract our minds is by focusing on problem-solving puzzles. We might play a game of sudoku, complete a crossword, or do math sums in our head. We can even invent our own games, such as the one below:

| Letter | Girls Name | Boys Name | Animal | Fruit or Veg | City |
|--------|------------|-----------|--------|--------------|------|
| A | Angela | Aaron | Aardvark | Apple | Amsterdam |
| B | Brenda | Barnaby | Baboon | Broccoli | Boston |
| C | Claire | Carl | Chimpanzee | Cauliflower | Chelsea |

We can try to fill in a row in thirty seconds and work our way through the alphabet. If we are with others, we can play this game with them, seeing who can complete a row the quickest. Doing mental tasks like this is a great way of blocking our intrusive thoughts. If out and about in our vehicle, playing games such as counting the number of red cars that we see is another way of distracting ourselves from our thoughts.

### Medication

If our intrusive thoughts get to a point when they start negatively impacting our life, it is time to seek professional help. Most people, at some time in their lives, experience intrusive thoughts that they're easily able to manage via implementing coping skills. For some of us, however, the intrusive thoughts become constant. When this happens, it can lead to depression and anxiety. If our thoughts are taking over our day-to-day lives, it is not practical to be spending our days distracting ourselves or meditating, as we will find we are unable to do anything else.

Medication, while definitely not a solution to all of our problems, can definitely help ease intrusive thoughts, freeing up our days so that we can also focus on our recovery, something that seems an impossibility when intrusive thoughts are devouring and exhausting us.

## Skills Checklist

### To Prevent Dissociation
- Recognizing our triggers
- Using our senses
- Acceptance and understanding
- Trauma therapy

### To Prevent Intrusive Thoughts and Paranoia
- Checking the facts: Past fears vs. reality
- Mindfulness
- Distraction
- Medication

# PART III

# RECOVERING

Chapter 14

# THE
# RECOVERY
# PROCESS

*"Even if you're on the right track,*
*you will get run over if you just sit there."*
—Will Rogers

Recovery can mean different things to different people. When thinking about recovery, we must ask ourselves, *What does it mean to me?* Each of us may have an entirely different idea of what we expect recovery to be, and that is okay. There is no right or wrong answer, only whatever answer feels right for us. Here are just a few ideas of what recovery could mean to us:

- To be free from the shackles that are our emotions
- To have healthy relationships
- To be able to work
- To be able to socialize free from anxiety
- To have less frequent and intense ups and downs
- To complete a college course
- To be independent
- To spend more time happy than unhappy
- To be able to understand my feelings more
- To build trust
- To not be on medication anymore
- To feel grown up

- To have higher self-esteem
- To not act impulsively
- To stop self-harming

We may find that we see recovery as all of these things, some of these things, or just one of these things—or something different altogether.

So how do we recover from this debilitating disorder? In chapter 17, different types of therapy are discussed in greater detail. However, not everyone is fortunate enough to be offered therapy, but that does not mean recovery is impossible. There are always skills that we can learn from the comfort of our own home, and we certainly should not lose hope if therapy is not an option for us.

Recovery does not mean that life will always be plain sailing. It does not mean that life will always be easy or that we will never again have a crisis. We are powerless against other people, places, or things. There are things that are beyond our control: deaths, breakups, the weather, job loss, sickness, and so on. What recovery does give us is the ability to face these life challenges without being destroyed by them.

## Recovery Is a Process

Recovery does not happen overnight or even over a few nights. It is a process that takes time, and the amount of time it takes is different for each individual. There are those of us who may find we notice changes after a few months and others that still see no change after a year of therapy. There are times when we begin to feel as if we are making progress, only to realize we have taken three steps backward. On the occasions when we feel we are going backward, we must remind ourselves that this is a perfectly normal part of the process—it certainly does not mean we have failed at recovery.

There are certain things that we must consider when first starting our journey of recovery that can make the process easier for us.

## Slow and Steady Wins the Race

Small steps are vital. We need to have patience and take cautious and gentle steps while walking the recovery path. If we dive right into the deep end and steam ahead with no caution, we are likely to become unstuck. That is not to say we shouldn't give recovery our all. If we only half-heartedly attempt recovery we are likely to fail. We have had our lives destroyed by this illness, and so we must grab recovery with both hands and just keep holding on. We can do this while also being cautious and patient.

When we first start therapy, it is unwise for us to think that we are now able to take on new responsibilities, such as starting a new job, a new relationship, or a college course. Putting too much pressure on ourselves early on can cause us to relapse and end up worse off than when we started. We need to accept that while these responsibilities are things we would like to aim for, right now all we need to do is focus on our recovery, without any other distractions and pressures.

## We Get Out What We Put In

To get the most benefit out of therapy, we need to put in the work. Recovery is not handed to us on a plate; it takes commitment, determination, and hard work. While this can sound daunting, we should remind ourselves that this could mean the difference between life and death. BPD is a serious disorder, and we must treat recovery seriously.

We will not benefit from therapy if we miss therapy sessions, don't complete assigned homework, and avoid practicing the new skills we are taught.

We must remind ourselves that, over the painful years of our lives, we have developed unhealthy coping mechanisms to get us through difficult times. Every time we use one of our unhelpful coping mechanisms, our brain strengthens that particular neural pathway. We need to now build new neural pathways in order to weaken the old ones. To build new neural pathways, we need to practice the skills as often as we can. The more we use a new skill, the stronger the new neural pathway becomes. The less we use our unhelpful coping mechanisms, the weaker those neural pathways become. This is important, because when we are in a crisis, our brain will send electricity shooting down the stronger neural pathway. We want the healthy coping mechanisms to be the ones that our brain automatically turns to when in a crisis. Practice makes this process perfect—or at least highly possible.

## Building a Support Network

Recovery is something that can be done alone, but it's easier when we have a support network in place. While other people cannot do our recovery for us, they can be there as support.

A support network can include as few or as many people as we want, but it should comprise of people we trust. Because we tend to struggle with trust, we need to think back to both bad and good times and ask ourselves, *Who had been there for us?* The people we include in our "circle of trust" or support network may vary considerably. Here are some people to consider.

- A family member
- A partner
- A community care nurse
- A social worker
- A counselor or therapist
- A friend
- Social services
- Someone from our child's school
- Someone from a local children's center
- A doctor
- A neighbor
- A midwife
- Someone from a drug and alcohol service
- People in 12-step fellowships
- A health visitor

The people in our support network are not there to help us only when we reach crisis point, nor are they there for us to dump on them. They are there to help us in our recovery. What they can do for us and how they can help will depend on who they are and our relationship with them.

When I first started my journey of recovery, I surrounded myself with people who were a good influence on me. Rather than just focusing on who was there for me when I was at my lowest, I looked for those who were there for me whenever I had been doing well, the people who truly wanted to see me happy. I had always believed that I had too many friends to count, but, upon closer inspection, I realized I could count my true friends on one hand. This came to light when I had been through rehab and started to get my life back together. The "friends" who had been there for me when I was drinking and using every day, when my life was a mess, stopped contacting me when I got my life back in order. It hurt, of course, but it was also an eye-opener.

My support network included a number of various people. I had my wonderful mum, my brother Carl, and my stepdad, Lee. My dad, stepmum, and brother Daniel live in Ireland, but I knew they were there if I ever needed to pick up the phone. I also had a handful of close friends, family members, a social worker from the children's center, my mental health nurse, my psychiatrist, the school counselor, my midwife, and a student midwife who all worked closely with me. And what about my partner, you ask? My partner was in recovery from addiction himself! Even now I look back in wonder at how we managed to get through this together—me completely crazy at times with the BPD and him struggling to maintain his sanity "in a world that was out to get him" (his words). Somehow we came out the other side, relationship still intact. The fact is, we could barely support ourselves, let alone one another, but by realizing this and each focusing solely on our own recoveries, we got through.

My support network helped me in a variety of ways: listening when I needed to talk, letting me explain what I had learned in therapy and helping me to reinforce it, helping me to stay positive, helping me to build my self-esteem, offering me help with the children, talking to me calmly when I was feeling anything but calm, and putting boundaries in place, which helped me start to take responsibility for my actions.

**Obstacles**

Nobody says that recovery is easy; hard work is involved, and even if we work our hardest, we will still have obstacles to overcome along the way. Life is life, and we have no way of guaranteeing an easy path ahead of us.

We may find that after a few months into recovery our relationship breaks down or a loved one passes away. We may relapse on drugs or alcohol, lose our children to social services, or get ill. The list of obstacles is endless, and all of them can cause us immense pain and threaten our recovery. I faced my own challenges during recovery.

When I first started recovery, I managed to put down the drink and drugs and started learning new coping skills. Then my dear grandad passed away, and I was absolutely devastated. The pain was so intense that I wanted to drink or use drugs to numb my feelings. But I was in recovery, I didn't want to reach for those things, and every single feeling was felt so deeply. I hadn't practiced any of the healthy coping skills enough to put them into practice. I remembered back to when my wonderful nana had passed away—I got ridiculously drunk and all I could think about was *my* loss. This time I changed my thinking; I didn't make it all about me and my feelings. I thought of my dad and uncles who had lost their father. I was determined to be there for them this time. The sadness of my grandad's passing didn't lessen, but I was able to deal with the situation in a more rational way. If I were to crumble, I would only be making things harder for myself and those around me, plus no amount of drinking or using would bring my grandad back. For the first time ever, I considered the consequences before I acted out.

- Remembering that we are powerless over other people and events is important. We must not only understand that we are powerless but also truly accept that we are.
- We must pause and remind ourselves of the consequences of wanting to act on our feelings. We mustn't let our emotional brain take over; we need to force our rational brain into action.
- When life events turn up and risk our recovery, we must try

not to mask our feelings or suppress them. It is important that we process our feelings in a healthy way, such as talking with a therapist, loved one, or friend.

- We need to be kind to ourselves and use positive and sensitive self-talk, reminding ourselves that we can get through this difficult time without succumbing to the BPD traits that risk our demise.

## Taking Responsibility

When we are in recovery, we start to become self-aware. While this is wonderful and necessary for our recovery, it also brings with it some brutal home truths. We discover that the way in which we have behaved has been most unpleasant, to say the very least. We have caused multiple harms along the way, often acting maliciously, without consideration or thought for the people we hurt.

While it is correct that our behaviors often stem from our intense feelings and inability to manage them, we cannot expect others to understand this. Neither can we expect forgiveness for our actions by continuing to blame the BPD. It is crucial for our recovery that we take responsibility for our actions rather than blaming the illness or others.

By taking responsibility we stop looking for excuses for our behaviors. This is vital, for if we carry on casting blame we are likely to continue with our old ways, never truly recovering.

Once we can recognize our shortcomings, we can start to identify all those who we have harmed. We may write a list of all those with whom we wish to make amends. When we have our list, we can then set out to apologize for the harms that we have caused. There may be some people who we have hurt so badly that they refuse to see us; in this instance, to continue to try and make contact with them when they do not wish for us to do so will only cause further harms, something we must avoid. We must accept that not everyone will be forgiving.

If we find it too difficult to sit with someone and apologize, we can consider writing a letter of apology. When making amends, we must be careful to not justify our previous actions in any way. People do not need or want to hear the reasons for our behaviors, as it will sound as if we are making excuses; a simple apology will suffice.

The amends process is a truly wonderful experience. We are able to undo some of the hurt that we have caused and rebuild old relationships, even those devastated by our illness. Although daunting to think about, once we have made amends we feel free—free from the guilt and shame that we carry around—and ready for a fresh new start. By recognizing our defects and taking responsibility for them, we stop making excuses and gain power over our behaviors, enabling us to be more aware of our actions in the future.

## What Families Need to Know

BPD is a family illness—it doesn't cause damage only to those of us with it but to our loved ones as well. It is not surprising then that recovery brings freedom and a new lease on life not just for us but for our family members and those around us too; when we recover, they too can recover.

Family members should be aware that recovery is a process; it does not happen overnight, and there is no actual time limit it takes for someone to get well. Often a family member will get excited to see their loved one with BPD doing so well with their therapy, only for them to take a few steps backward, leaving the family member distraught, thinking that the therapy has failed and their loved one is back to square one. Steps backward are a part of recovery; very few, if any, of us will get recovery straightaway with no setbacks. It is important that this is mentioned, as so often a family member's look of disappointment can leave us feeling as if we have failed, which then leaves us feeling ready to give up.

Putting pressure on us is also dangerous. We are as desperate to recover as much as our loved ones are eager for it. We already put too much pressure on ourselves; we certainly do not need added pressure from others.

Pressure can also come in the form of loved ones expecting too much too soon. It is wise for loved ones to have no expectations and to simply observe the small changes as they happen without comparisons of the past or hope for the future. Patience is key.

While positive affirmations seem wonderful, they can actually be as damaging as negative words to us. When we start therapy and first begin noticing small positive changes, our life can feel alien to us. We are used to chaos and being dependent on others. Chaos is familiar to us, so when things become calmer and we become less reliant on others, we can find that our fear of abandonment is triggered. We can start fearing independence and we miss people worrying about us. When our loved ones start taking a step back, we equate this lack of worrying to mean that they no longer care about us. When this happens, we may find that we sabotage our own recovery, either through drinking, using drugs, shouting, self-harming, and so on. When we do this, we are trying to convey to our loved ones that we still need them.

Boundaries are very important for ourselves and our loved ones. We will often try to push boundaries, and in doing so cause harm to our family, friends, and ourselves. Although to start with we may fight back against boundaries put in place, over time we all benefit from them.

There are times during therapy when we start getting excited about our future. We may want to enroll in a college course or apply for a dream job. Often, family members can get excited for us, and their excitement feeds our excitement even more. It is important that loved ones refrain from doing this. It is never a good idea for us to take on too much too soon, as we will be setting up ourselves to fail. Family members should remind us that while this is a wonderful idea for the future, we do not need to rush into anything new so early into recovery.

It is entirely normal for loved ones to be interested in our therapy, and it is good for them to be involved; however, there will be times when we don't want to discuss recovery or anything BPD related. BPD is our life, and sometimes we just want a break from it to discuss normal everyday things. If we do not want to discuss therapy, then it is important for loved ones to not push the subject; we will talk when we want to.

It is also vital that a loved one does not try to do our recovery for us—the work has to be ours and ours alone. If a family member starts telling us what we should be doing, we can become very defensive. If we are not willing to put in the work ourselves, we will not recover, whether or not loved ones do our work for us. For example, we may bring home worksheets that a loved one wants to help us with, and while we know they mean their best, homework is usually private and personal. We are more likely to be completely honest if left alone to do the work, without the worry that someone else is monitoring us.

Family members who get involved with our therapy do so because they love and care for us. Please be aware, however, that asking us daily, "Have you practiced your skills today?" is unlikely to help us. We do not do well under pressure. To us, a simple question like this can seem like pressure or a patronizing gesture. We are sensitive people who spend most of our time feeling less than and judged; being questioned about our recovery only exacerbates these feelings.

As mentioned previously, the recovery process is a family process—we all recover together. For this to happen it is imperative that family members look after themselves. Loved ones can spend so much time worrying about us that they entirely forget about their own self-care and love.

Family members might isolate from those around them, as they do not want to hear others speak badly of us. They can then be left feeling very alone, with no support. Life can become pretty miserable and the future can seem daunting. Loved ones have just as much right to the freedom and happiness that we want. For this to happen, loved ones must find their own path of recovery.

Recovery for loved ones includes talking to someone about their feelings openly. Counseling is always worth consideration, for although our loved ones do not necessarily have a personality disorder them-selves, it does not mean their mental health has not suffered due to the damage that we cause.

Constantly being in the company of someone with BPD can be extremely draining. So loved ones should set aside plenty of time and space for themselves. Time out is vital for their own well-being. A time-out does not mean loved ones should go away for two weeks but it can include taking a day for themselves once a week. Visiting friends for a weekend, spending an evening at the cinema, doing anything that is relaxing is helpful—don't spend this time worrying about us.

It is also worth noting that it is never acceptable for us to abuse a loved one physically or mentally. If our loved ones feel as if they are being intimidated by us, or that they aren't safe, they have every right to phone the police or our mental health team. No, we will not like this, but the safety of our loved ones is just as important as ours; loved ones must do all that they can to keep themselves safe.

## When We Refuse to Seek Help

There are those of us with borderline personality disorder who are completely unaware of our condition. Perhaps we are in denial or perhaps we have no self-awareness. Most of us will go through a stage where we do not believe the problem lies within us; we instead believe that everyone else is to blame. While this is problematic to start with, most of us, in time, come to realize that we are the problem, so we decide we need help in order to recover.

This is not always the case, however. There are times when we are completely unable to admit that we need help and instead carry on a path of destruction. Family members are left frantic with worry and not knowing what to do.

Unfortunately, while you can try to guide a loved one, there are times when we refuse any guidance. We cannot be forced into recovery. In order for recovery to work, we must be dedicated to it and want it for ourselves. The first step we must take is admitting there is a problem; unless this step is taken, recovery will not happen.

For many, it takes us hitting rock bottom to finally put our hands up and surrender, admitting that we need help. Hitting rock bottom is exceptionally painful—for those of us experiencing it and for our loved ones watching on helplessly. This painful experience is often needed to see the reality of our situation. It's our impetus to come back fighting for our survival.

There are family members and loved ones who desperately want to make life easier for us. They understand the pain we are in and try to do what they can to alleviate it. This may include allowing us to treat them like dirt and refusing to turn their backs on us. It may include giving us money in the hope of relieving our financial burdens, although we will often squander this money while acting impulsively. Family members must be aware that although they believe they are helping us, they are actually enabling us to carry on as we are, making no changes.

Whether we are in recovery or not, boundaries are important, as is self-care. It is vital that loved ones take care of themselves rather than allow us to take them down with us. Family members should build their own support network and take time for themselves. They should not become a doormat that we may wipe our feet on. If we are in recovery and have taken steps backward, there is little you can do. Likewise, if we point blank refuse any kind of help, loved ones should realize that there is nothing they can do for us at that point. Just because we choose not to recover does not mean that loved ones have to carry on suffering. Loved ones may decide to cut us out of their lives for the time being in order to protect themselves. When doing this, it is important that loved ones tell us why they are doing this. Loved ones can let us know that they will be there for us when we decide the time is right to accept help. What family members may find is that we hit rock bottom sooner than we would have, had they carried on as things were. This may prompt those with BPD to seek help.

This is not to say that every family member should just cut their BPD loved one out their life. We are sick people who live a life of pain and suffering, which in turn causes us to act out on our feelings in unhealthy ways. We do not choose to be this way, and many of us wish that we had a loving and supportive family. Family members need to realize that there is only so much they can do for us, though. Loved ones cannot fix us or make us better, we have to do that ourselves, although with a supportive family behind us it makes our recovery process easier than if we have to do it alone.

If loved ones believe that we are a risk to ourselves or others, it is vital that they inform someone of the situation. This may include the police, social services, or a mental health team. We may not thank our loved ones for it, but they may be saving our life.

Chapter 15

# THE UPSIDES
# OF HAVING BPD

*"Sensitive people suffer more,*
*but they also love and dream more."*
—Augusto Cury

So much information is available on the negatives of having this
disorder that many people fail to realize that there are also positives
that come with having BPD. It is important for us to recognize these
positive aspects, as they too make up who we are.

### Self-Aware

Many of us go through a phase in which we do not recognize the
BPD traits in ourselves. But after receiving our diagnosis, we usually
find that we are quickly able to identify where the traits pop up in our
lives. This self-awareness typically continues to grow until we reach a
point when we are more self-aware than the general population. We
begin to understand why we behave the way that we do and admit when
we have caused harm to others. It is through our self-awareness that we
can recover and begin to thrive.

### Spontaneous and Fun

Our impulsiveness is not always negative. Many of us are both fun
to be around and spontaneous. Our pure energy attracts people to us,
and we are often known to be the life and the soul of the party. We have
an energy that is unrivaled by others, and once we begin recovery, this
fun energy becomes more and more pronounced.

*Nonjudgmental*

Perhaps it is because we go through life feeling so judged all of the time that causes us to view people in a nonjudgmental way. We understand that although we come across as people who are out to harm others, we are in fact suffering inside. This insight allows us to not take people at face value and to never judge a book by its cover. Unless we have walked in another person's shoes, we do not know what they have been through, and because of this we typically do not cast judgment.

*Empathetic, Compassionate, and Kind*

We are extremely empathetic people. Having suffered both internally and externally, we are easily able to empathize with others who have struggles. We are hugely compassionate, particularly to our fellow borderlines, wishing them only the best and trying to help them in any way we can. Although often struggling with our own demons, we always try to support our fellows. When we learn something that helps us, we readily pass it on to others in our situation, in the hope that they too can recover.

*Intuitive and Sensitive to Others*

Our emotions are extreme and intense, and this possibly contributes to our super-sensitivity of other people's emotions. We can often sense how others are feeling without them having to tell us. Having this trait combined with a tendency to be empathetic makes us a good friend to have, always there as support and an ear to listen. When we sense that someone is feeling down, we go out of our way to try and cheer them up, even when we are not feeling so great ourselves.

*Passionate and Loving*

When we love we really love. We never love half-heartedly and always give all of ourselves to the object of our affection, often leaving ourselves open to getting hurt. When we are in a relationship, we let our loved one know how amazing they are and how they make us feel. We can make them feel on top of the world. Our relationships are filled with passion and are intense, at least until our BPD traits surface and start to cause us problems. It is not that we lose the passion and love, rather, our negative feelings overshadow the positive ones. The positives are still there, however, and with recovery we can let them flourish.

### Artistic, Creative, and Talented

Those of us with BPD tend to be incredibly artistic, whether it's through music, dance, drama, art, or writing. This could be related to the fact that our feelings are so intense and we are such passionate people. The sheer force of our emotions tends to erupt from us in unhealthy ways, but when we direct that energy into something artistic, we can really shine.

### Intelligent and Interesting

People are always fascinated by what we have to say. Maybe it is the way in which we describe things or the stories that we tell that make us so fascinating to be around. Friends and strangers alike hold on to our every word, interested in what we have to say. The intensity of our feelings and our tendency to have quite a colorful past may contribute to being interesting and intelligent.

### Parenting

Due to BPD, there are certainly times when we struggle with parenthood. There is so much negativity regarding borderline parents that the positives can be completely eclipsed. But the truth is, we can be amazing parents. With our love, compassion, kindness, and energy we have all the necessary ingredients to thrive at parenthood. It is unfortunate that we also happen to have a few nasty ingredients thrown in the pot also. Recovery enables us to eliminate these unwanted ingredients and be wonderful parents to our children.

### Resilience and Strength

We are strong. We are survivors. We are fighters. We are warriors. There are not many people who can go through what we do and survive. There are times when we feel anything but strong—but strong we are. It is often only after we emerge on the other side that we have that light bulb moment, after asking ourselves, *How did I get through that and survive?!* At last we realize our own true strength.

Chapter 16

# THE TEN STEPS
# OF RECOVERY

*"The journey of a thousand miles begins with one step."*
—Lao-tzu

A lcoholics Anonymous has long been centered around the twelve steps of recovery. I'd like to offer my own ten steps for recovery from BPD.

### Step 1. We admit there is a problem

We cannot expect to recover if we do not first admit that we have a problem. Whether we admit this to another person or only to ourselves does not matter, so long as we can recognize that something is not right and that we need to take action to resolve it. For most of us, admitting there is a problem comes after hitting rock bottom, when life becomes so unmanageable and painful that we can no longer deny it. The longer we live in denial the longer our pain shall continue.

### Step 2. We ask for help

As soon as we acknowledge that we have a problem, we need to ask for help. We cannot continue to struggle, thinking that circumstances will miraculously change for us. We mustn't let pride hold us back, as it may well be our downfall. There are those of us who seek professional help immediately and those of us who first talk of our problems with a close confidant. Once we have asked for help we may then begin building ourselves a support network, which may include both professionals and personal acquaintances.

### Step 3. We gather knowledge

Having asked for help and having started to build a small support network, it is time for us to arm ourselves with knowledge of this disorder. Information on borderline personality disorder is plentiful on the Internet. We must realize, however, that not all information is an accurate representation of the disorder; for all the helpful information online, there is an equal, if not larger, amount of unhelpful and damaging information. We must be careful, therefore, when gaining our knowledge. We should aim to look up information on reputable websites. If we come across information that is entirely negative and unconstructive, we should turn away from it.

There are an enormous amount of us with BPD that have our own websites or channels, give our own thoughts on the disorder. Our opinions may vary greatly and it is up to us, the viewer, to decide with whom we can relate. We must be aware that an opinion is just that: an opinion and not a fact. Through finding others with BPD and listening to their views, we can start to identify with them. We can also start to believe that we too can recover from this disorder. Hope is a powerful incentive to keep pushing us forward in our recovery.

### Step 4. We accept our disorder

Being able to identify with others similar to ourselves we are ready to reach another milestone in our recovery: acceptance of our disorder. Acceptance does not mean that we are happy about having it; it means simply acknowledging that we do have it. There are those among us who find step 4 a huge relief once taken. There are others who struggle with this step, just as we struggled with admitting we have a problem and asking for help. We may think that by accepting the disorder we are succumbing to it and giving in, however, by having acceptance we are freeing ourselves and taking back the power that we have lost. Rather than fearing the illness, with acceptance we are able to look at it logically and make a conscious decision to take steps to recover.

### Step 5. We consent to medication and commit to treatment

Once we have accepted our disorder, we are finally ready to start taking further action toward our recovery. There are multiple treatment options for borderline personality disorder. While there is no medication specifically proven to help with BPD, there are medications that can alleviate some of the symptoms, such as depression, anxiety, and intrusive thoughts. So although medication can help us, it should never be the only treatment method. When prescribed medication, we must be aware that drinking alcohol or drug use can hinder the effect. If we struggle with addiction, we should at this point begin to look at ways to recover from this also.

Treatment for BPD should include skills-based therapy and counseling. When engaging in therapy we must do so whole-heartedly. We take out of it that which we put in. Turning up to all appointments and not missing group sessions is vital. We must also set aside time of our own to practice any skills taught or to complete any homework allocated. Borderline personality disorder is a disorder that takes lives; we must never become complacent or lazy in regard to our recovery, remembering at all times when the skills that we are learning now can in fact save our life.

For those of us who cannot access professional help, we must start looking at self-help options rather than giving up. The Internet is abundant with self-help websites, and through these we can learn new skills that will help us on our journey.

### Step 6. We practice self-care

Self-care is something that we have usually failed to achieve over the years. We abuse our bodies with alcohol, drugs, sex, and food, to name just a few. How we treat our bodies has a massive impact on the state of our mind. When we reach this step, we need to take a look at how we treat ourselves physically and mentally. Do we eat too much sugar? Do we eat regular meals? Do we get enough sleep? Do we take our prescribed medication sensibly? Do we exercise? Do we drink too much alcohol or take illegal substances? Do we live in a clean and tidy home? Do we wash ourselves regularly? Do we have a balanced life? Our answers to these questions will determine our next course of action, whether it be creating a routine for ourselves, eating healthier, or cutting down on our alcohol intake. By taking better care of ourselves, recovery becomes both easier and more enjoyable. We are able to let go of the bad habits that risk hampering our recovery.

### Step 7. We practice self-help

We have taken steps to receive the help that we need, and self-awareness may have begun for some of us. It is now time for us to up our game and start to help ourselves. Self-help is necessary, as it is only we who can do our recovery—others cannot do it for us.

Self-help does not only include making sure that we complete therapy-related homework and practice our skills outside of group. When taking this step, we are dedicating ourselves to our own recovery. Self-help books, blogs, and videos are all included in this step. Not every self-help book will work for every person with BPD, so it is up to us to try new things and see what we find helpful.

### Step 8. We develop self-awareness and make amends

With therapy and self help, we start to become self-aware. This is absolutely imperative for our recovery, for if we fail to recognize our behaviors as they surface, we will be unable to make changes, believing there is nothing that we need to change.

Self-awareness brings with it eye-opening truths about ourselves: behaviors that hurt those around us and cause self-destruction. The truth can be hard to swallow, and there are those of us who are overcome with guilt and remorse for our previous actions. Now is not a time to wallow in self-pity, as this can be yet another downfall in our recovery.

Making amends where possible brings us freedom and allows us to move forward. There are times when making amends is not possible: we may not have contact information for someone anymore, or to make contact with someone may cause further harm, and so on. In these cases, it is enough if we truly believe that we would make amends to that person if it were possible. When making amends to someone we must do so with no expectations; some loved ones will not be ready to hear that we are sorry, or they may not accept our apology due to the severe hurt that we have caused them. If this happens we mustn't let it destroy us; we should know that at least we made the attempt, freeing ourselves from any guilt.

The amends process is one that can take many years, and we do not need to stay on this step until all amends are made. We must consider those who have been hurt by us and take responsibility for the harms that we have caused. At this point, we must stop blaming others and take a look at ourselves; there will always be others who may cause us harm, but this step is not about pointing the finger. Instead we must only look at our part—if we have done wrong, we must promptly admit it.

Once we are able to recognize our shortcomings as and when they appear, we are ready to make changes. To do this we continue engaging in therapy and move on to the next step.

### Step 9. We practice spirituality

Spirituality is different to religion, and it can mean many different things to different people. Those who follow a religion can be spiritual, but people can also be spiritual without being religious. Many of us suffering with BPD have found spirituality to have a profound effect on our mental health and well-being.

Those of us who follow a religion may visit a place of worship or pray. Those of us who are spiritual and not religious tend to find comfort in such things as meditation, yoga, and quiet reflection.

As human beings, we love to question the world around us, looking for the meaning of life or trying to connect to a higher power, whether that be God, nature, art, our inner-self, or the Universe. Spirituality allows us time to contemplate these things and find peace within ourselves.

### Step 10. We look after our tribe

Just as one alcoholic can help another alcoholic or one drug addict can help another addict, we must realize the power of one person with BPD helping another person with BPD. We are people who understand each other and can look at one another nonjudgmentally, for only we understand the true pain that we've experienced. By reaching out to others who are in the same situation that we were once in, we are able to share our own recovery experience with them, offering them hope while ensuring we continue on our own path of recovery.

It is when we reach step 10 and start helping others with BPD that are further behind in their recovery than we are that we can appreciate just how far we have come and just how much we have accomplished along the way. Our journey may have been a difficult one with many setbacks along the way, but we can look back and say to ourselves, "I have made it!" By sharing our individual and challenging journeys with others, people can see that recovery is possible, no matter what obstacles appear along the way. Those of us with BPD are true warriors; we can look out for our tribe like no one else can, allowing them to believe in themselves when no one else does and offering them hope when they feel all hope is lost.

Chapter 17

# TREATMENT

*"If you always do what you've always done,*
*you'll always get what you always got."*
—Jessie Potter

There are multiple treatment options for those of us with borderline personality disorder. Unfortunately, not all of the options are available to everyone, due to finances, location, waiting lists, and lack of professionals trained in this area. While professional treatment is ideal, it does not mean that recovery is out of bounds for those of us who cannot access professional help.

Within this chapter are brief descriptions of the various treatment options available, as well as information for those of us who must rely on self-help.

### Dialectical Behavior Therapy (DBT)

DBT was designed by Marsha Linehan specifically for the treatment of borderline personality disorder. DBT is based on cognitive behavioral therapy (CBT), but, rather than just focusing on "change," it also incorporates acceptance and draws on Buddhist principles.

There are four modules to complete, including mindfulness (which is at the very core of DBT), distress tolerance, emotion regulation, and interpersonal effectiveness.

DBT therapy includes group therapy, individual counseling, and phone consultations.

*Cognitive Behavioral Therapy (CBT)*

CBT is a talking therapy whereby we look at our thoughts and beliefs and see how they affect our feelings and behaviors. Rather than looking back on past problems, we focus on current ones. While working with a therapist, we will learn to identify and question negative beliefs and thoughts. By learning to change how we think or perceive certain events, we are able to change our feelings and behaviors toward them.

*Schema-Focused Therapy*

Long-term patterns of thoughts or behaviors, often originating in childhood, are known as schemas. As we grow up, we develop certain schemas—often maladaptive ones that cause us problems in our day-to-day lives. Schema-focused therapy includes identifying which maladaptive schemas we have, recognizing when they appear in our life, and learning to replace them with more-helpful behaviors.

*Systems Training for Emotional Predictability and Problem Solving (STEPPS)*

STEPPS therapy includes CBT skills training and looking at early schemas. The training is done in three steps: awareness of illness, emotion management skills training, and behavior management skills training. STEPPS differs from other approaches, as it includes family members and friends. Loved ones become "reinforcers" of the skills and learn to understand BPD, therefore helping break the stigma attached to it.

*Mentalization-Based Therapy (MBT)*

The belief behind this therapy is that those of us with BPD, at least most of us, developed attachment issues when we were very young, therefore causing us problems in our relationships as adults. MBT is aimed at helping us understand both our feelings and the feelings of others, as well as recognizing the impact of our behaviors toward others.

*General Psychiatric Help*

Many of us will have a psychologist or a member of a mental health team working with us. This may include a psychiatric nurse who comes out and visits us at home or a crisis team who we can turn to in times of crisis.

It is usually our mental health team who will refer us for further therapy for our BPD. Unfortunately, due to different circumstances, not all of us can access therapy. If this is the case, we need to make the most out of the help we do receive from our mental health team. We must turn up to every appointment on time and be completely honest about how we are feeling. If different forms of group therapy are offered, we should at least try out a few to see if we find it helpful or not.

## Medication

Medication, while in no way a cure, can bring great relief to those of us with BPD. There is currently no proof that medication can help with the BPD itself, but, as we are aware, those of us with this disorder often find that we have other disorders, such as anxiety, depression, and so forth. Medication can help relieve some of the symptoms of these other disorders and help "take the edge off." This is particularly useful when it comes to us engaging in therapy. Many of us find that we are too depressed to take part in therapy or that we are too anxious to walk into a room full of complete strangers. This can seriously hinder our recovery, but, with the help of certain medications, we can be relieved, to a certain extent, of some of these issues and are therefore able to turn up to therapy sessions and engage fully in them.

No medication is guaranteed to work, and it is very much about trial and error. One medicine may be a life-saver for someone with BPD and yet the same medicine may cause someone else with BPD to feel much worse. Medicines frequently used for those of us with BPD include antidepressants, mood stabilizers, and antipsychotics.

## Self-Help

There are those of us who, due to either finances or location, are simply unable to access the professional treatment that we so desperately need. Lack of professional treatment does not mean that recovery is not possible for us. Whether we participate in professional treatment or we do not, self-help is vital. We cannot expect to attend a weekly therapy session while putting in absolutely no work at home and still recover. Self-help is essential for any of us who want to recover from this disorder.

For those of us who are participating in therapy groups, we will usually be assigned homework that we must complete at home. For those of us who do not receive professional therapy, we must assign ourselves homework.

There is so much information online regarding different self-help methods, and we do not need to be confined to only BPD self-help. We may read books on conquering our fears, overcoming grief, and so much more. Not all books will help all people, but unless we set out to discover what helps us, we will never know.

Due to the lack of professional therapy available, more and more people are choosing to sign up for online courses. The BPD Tribe, founded by myself and Megan Hunter, is a place where those with BPD can feel safe, a place where we belong and feel we are at home. There is a wealth of information on this site, as well as the option to sign up and become a member of our tribe or to enroll in courses. We also have a family section specifically aimed at family members and loved ones.

For anyone wanting to recover, a great self-help task is to work through the ten steps listed in this book. These steps can be taken by anyone, from the newly diagnosed and the not yet diagnosed to those already in recovery.

### 12-Step Fellowships

Although first developed to help alcoholics, the 12 steps are a spiritual program that anyone can benefit from. Rather than a program that we do once and put down, it is a set of principles that we can live our life by. If we happen to also suffer with an addiction of some kind, be it shopping or drugs, the 12 steps can help free us from them.

### *Group Therapy (Formal and Informal)*

Most mental health teams will know of group therapies that you can apply to participate in. The subject matter of the therapy can vary greatly, from specific CBT courses to groups aimed at single sexes, discussing any mental health problems we may have. Some groups teach skills while others are more discussion oriented. Attending a group can seem daunting, especially if we also suffer with anxiety, but if we can force ourselves to attend that first meeting, we often find it extremely beneficial. We are among others like ourselves and can feel accepted.

PART IV

# BPD AND...

Chapter 18

# BPD AND PARENTING

*"You can be a mess and still be a good Mom.*
*We are allowed to be both".*
—Unknown

Being a parent is one of the most difficult jobs in the world. As parents, we are responsible for this little person, and it is our job to help them have a wonderful childhood and grow into a healthy, emotionally stable young person. Quite a responsibility.

When we bring BPD into the equation, that huge responsibility can feel a million times larger, as if it is simply not a possibility at all. How can we possibly be responsible for another human being when we can barely take care of ourselves?

Those of us with children have an intense love for them. It's not our lack of love for them that is the issue, rather it's the BPD and how it makes us behave. We struggle with our intense emotions—good and bad—unable to regulate them or consider the consequences of our actions. Our BPD causes us to feel and behave as if we are a child—not a good combination when we are, in fact, parents with a child of our own.

Of course, there are those who question whether those of us with BPD should be parents at all, believing that we damage our children, leading to the BPD cycle continuing for generations. While it is true that those of us who are unaware of our BPD or are unwilling to change can damage our children, for most of us this is simply not the case. We are people who love our children more than words can describe and desperately want to change the way we are, learning how to control the BPD and be the best parents we can possibly be.

I've experienced my own tumultuous journey as a parent of young children. When I would feel my mood drop or I could feel a rage inside of me dying to erupt, it didn't matter that my children were there. I would just explode and start shouting, wanting to smash up the TV (but never actually doing it), or wanting to walk out (but never actually leaving them). For young children, this behavior can be terrifying; they're unable to understand that Mummy is struggling with her emotions and they think that they are the cause of the eruption.

I have always made a point of discussing my BPD in an age-appropriate way with my children. I've explained the difference between mental health and physical health, and what BPD is in a simplified way. I discuss feelings with them, and we talk about ways of expressing our feelings in a healthy way. I have never showed my young children my self-harm scars or explained that self-harm is a BPD trait. They know that Mummy can feel normal healthy feelings but in a much more intense way, often causing me to act in a way that isn't necessarily helpful, such as shouting or not talking at all. My children know that they are *never* the cause of these "moments" and that I will talk to them about it once I am calm. Following episodes when I have been extremely bad tempered or moody, I will sit on my kids' beds at story time and talk to them, apologizing for being so moody, explaining again about the BPD and how it is not their fault and that I love them very much.

I am fortunate that I have come a long way in recovery, that I am now able to manage my BPD, although that is not to say I don't have bad days. My bad days are nowhere near how they used to be, but I still take the time to talk things through with my children so that they are never left feeling confused or blaming themselves for my bad mood.

I have always been upfront about my BPD; I've made a point of sitting with my children's teachers and school counselors to discuss the disorder. In this way, I ensure my children get extra support and that they have someone watching out for them. Although I try my best to monitor my children's well-being, I am biased—there is always the chance that I don't see something is wrong when it clearly is. Having school staff look out for my kids also gives me the added peace of mind that, if a problem should arise, I can deal with it straightaway.

Being a parent with BPD is scary and downright overwhelming at times. So often we struggle and yet are too scared to ask for help, thinking that we will have our children taken from us if we are honest. The problem with this belief is that, if we do not ask for help, nothing will change and we risk causing emotional damage to our children.

## Putting Our Recovery First So Those We Love Do Not Come Last

If we want to truly be the best parent that we can be, it is vital that we put our recovery first. That means our recovery must come before even our children. To the outside world this may sound harsh, yet it is the brutal truth.

So what is meant by putting our recovery first? It means making sure we go to all appointments and group therapy sessions, practice our skills at home, and take care of ourselves physically and mentally. We need to find a balance in our lives and not believe that our children alone can be the ones to save us from BPD. No matter how much we love our children, unless we take our recovery 100 percent seriously we will not recover.

Putting our recovery first, ahead of our children, can be a tremendous struggle. Four years ago, while I was attending 12-step meetings to help with my drug addiction, I felt this strain firsthand. I was trying to find balance in my life: seeing friends, working on my recovery, working on my family life, being healthy and fit, and sorting my finances, to name a few.

There were days when my kids would beg me not to go to a meeting, wanting me to stay at home and read to them instead. Seeing their little faces looking up at me, begging me to stay, was horrendous. I felt so torn. It would have been so easy for me to just stay at home with them, but I knew that if I didn't attend my meeting I risked relapse and therefore the destruction of my family. So I would go to the meeting, putting my recovery first and ensuring that my children would not end up coming last.

## Building a Support Network

We cannot expect to find recovery and be a parent without someone to help support us. Building a support network enables us to focus on both our recovery and being a parent. Who we include in our support network is very much up to us. We may have close family and friends who can watch our children while we attend meetings relevant to our recovery, spend an hour at the gym, or go for a coffee with a friend. These same people may be able to help us in our times of need; if we feel we are close to hitting crisis point, we can call on someone who can watch the children for us, protecting them from witnessing our outburst and giving us some much-needed time and space to calm down.

## Creating a Routine

With our ever-changing moods, everything in our life can feel chaotic. While a routine won't prevent our shifts in moods, it can certainly help give us some stability. When we have a routine, we know where we are at and what we are doing at any given time.

We can get ourselves very worked up over all the things that we need to accomplish in a day, from cleaning our home to feeding our children. We can easily become overwhelmed, rendering ourselves unable to complete even the simplest of tasks. There may be times when even the thought of what to cook the kids for dinner causes our brain to feel overloaded.

Once we put a routine in place, even if it is really basic, life becomes a bit less complicated. When thinking about starting a routine, keep in mind that a routine can be flexible and does not need to be rigid. That way, if we plan lunch for noon and we lose track of time or something happens, lunch at 12:30 or 1 is going to be okay; we don't panic and instead simply alter our routine ever so slightly.

When first writing out a routine, start with the very basics. For example: Breakfast at 7:30 am, lunch at noon, dinner at 4:30 pm, kids' bedtime at 7 pm.

It is important to know that children thrive on a routine, so by adopting one we are not only helping ourselves but our little ones too.

We should try out our new routine and get familiar with it for a week or two, then add to it. Perhaps we can set a time on a Sunday when we sit and plan out our week ahead, including times of any appointments, shopping trips, coffees with friends, parents' evenings, and so on. We may also consider planning our meals at the beginning of the week so we know what we will be having each day. No longer will we panic over what we should cook for dinner when we have already planned ahead.

## Carving Out Me Time

Every parent craves some time to ourselves, although very few of us ensure that we get it. Life takes over—we can get so wrapped up in doing mundane daily chores that, day after day, like Groundhog Day, we never get any time for ourselves.

Me time is incredibly important in recovery. It is time when we can do something for ourselves, something that we enjoy. If we do not take any time for ourselves, we can easily become resentful and unfulfilled. It is not that our children do not fulfill us, it's more of a case everyone needing balance in their lives, and those of us with BPD are no different.

Making time for myself is something I need to schedule—or it won't happen. My whole life revolves around my children. While I am okay with that, there comes a time when I recognize that I need to think about myself as well. If I am happy, my children are happy. If I am miserable, that too will affect how my children feel. I make sure my children are all in bed and asleep by 8 pm. That gives me a couple of hours to myself before I go to bed. Sometimes I'll read a magazine, sometimes I will watch a film. It is just nice to have time to wind down and relax.

Whether we take some time each day or we take some time to ourselves a few times a week does not matter, so long as we know that we have some time to ourselves coming up. We may go out with friends or we may just sit in a park and read a book—whatever makes us feel good about ourselves—so that our focus is solely on ourselves.

## Having a Time-Out Rule

Taking a time-out is not a form of punishment; it's a tool that can be used to help someone calm down, whether it be us or our children. Young children are known for their temper tantrums (which are, in fact, very similar to our own). Having a time-out rule can be extremely helpful.

When first introducing this family rule, it is important to let everyone know that it is not a form of punishment. It is simply some time allotted to whoever needs it to calm down. The place someone goes to calm down does not matter, so long as it is a quiet space. A bedroom, the kitchen, the lounge, somewhere they can sit in peace for five, ten, or fifteen minutes, however long they need to calm down. A child may find that sitting quietly for two minutes is all they need. There is no time limit, and the person taking a time-out is entirely in control.

Children may find it helpful to have a cuddly toy that they bring with them on time-out to help calm them down.

As adults, we can put ourselves in a time-out. We may walk around the garden for a few minutes or go to our bedroom. There will be days when we keep needing to put ourselves in time-out. We should pay attention to this—perhaps when this happens it is time to call someone in our support network to watch over our children so that we can take a bit longer to soothe ourselves.

## Having Fun

So much of our time is spent running around doing daily chores or suffering with our intense mood swings that life can become pretty miserable. It is therefore important to tackle this with opposite action. We should set aside some time each week when we have fun with our children. We may take them to a park and kick a ball about, have a movie night together, or play games with them. The whole point of this time is that everyone has fun and laughs together. By laughing with our children we are able to momentarily forget our problems; spending quality time with them is beneficial for all of us.

## Talking to Our Children About BPD

There are some of us who do not feel it is acceptable to discuss our mental health with our children. We fail to realize that, by not discussing it with them, we are actually leaving them open to blame themselves for our behavior. Little children perceive things differently than an adult. They do not understand that we can be in a bad mood and that it has nothing to do with them. We therefore have a responsibility to help them understand.

Of course, we cannot explain drug addiction or self-harm to them, as this would be extremely traumatic for them to hear. We can, however, discuss things in a simplified and age-appropriate way. It is vital that we let our children know just how much we love them and how they are not to blame in any way for the way we behave.

## Wondering If Our Child Will Grow Up to Have BPD

Only those of us who suffer with this disorder can truly understand how difficult it is just to get through one day at a time. Those of us with BPD wouldn't wish it on our worst enemy, and therefore the thought of one of our children developing it is one of our biggest fears. We know that genetics plays a part in this disorder, and so if our children develop it, it wouldn't come as a surprise, although it is still devastating to contemplate.

We must realize that if we are learning to manage our disorder, we are in fact the best parent we can be for our BPD child. We will understand them like no one else will. We will also have skills that we have learned along the way that we can pass on to them, hopefully teaching them to manage the disorder before it gets out of hand. We can lead them on the path to recovery, holding their hand the whole way and leading them out the other side.

There is no way to know whether our children will definitely develop the disorder. We cannot predict the future or prevent what is going to happen from happening. We are powerless over these things, and we must accept it rather than spending every day worrying about what will or will not be or feeling guilty that we have passed on this disorder.

What we are able to do is monitor our children and hopefully recognize any warning signs early on, dealing with them as and when they arise. We need to give our children as much support as we can and guide them on their own journey.

## When Our Child Has Been Taken from Us

There are those of us who, due to our lack of recovery, have had the awful experience of losing our children. They may be taken from us to live with a foster family, to be put in the care of family members, or to be given up for adoption. For this to happen to a parent is completely devastating; it can leave us at rock bottom, not wanting to go on, feeling as if our world has ended and completely succumbing to the disorder.

We must realize that, although we are devastated and in immense pain, life must go on and we must not give up now. Surely this experience shows us the true destruction this disorder has upon our lives.

If social services is involved, it is always advised that we work with them rather than against them. Instead of thinking that they are out to get us, we must change our mindset and realize that they are there to protect our children. Our children and what is best for them must always come first, no matter how much pain it causes us.

By engaging in services and putting our recovery first, we are able to show those involved in the care of our children that we are trying our best. As we begin to recover, we become stronger and are better able to think rationally about our circumstances. Through our hard work and unselfishness, there are those of us who are fortunate enough to eventually have our children returned to our care. There is not a time limit on when this may happen, so we must remain both patient and committed to our recovery in the meantime.

If the time comes for us to be reunited with our children, and we have worked tirelessly on our recovery, the future for both ourselves and our children will be a brighter one.

Chapter 19

# BPD AND WORK

*"You can't stop the waves, but you can learn to surf."*
—Jon Kabat-Zinn

M any of us go through periods when work is an impossibility, due to either our BPD symptoms or our co-occurring disorders, such as depression. When we do work, we find that we never spend long at one workplace before either getting the sack or walking out.

Workplace problems arise commonly due to our inability to have healthy relationships with others. Perhaps we become too clingy with a colleague and they rebuff us, causing us to feel hurt and express it with anger. Other times we may perceive the actions of others inaccurately; someone doesn't say good morning to us and we take that to mean they have a problem with us. If a supervisor tells us we have done something wrong, we may take that to mean they think our work is rubbish and we can be left feeling humiliated.

I have had my own troubles at work. No matter where I worked, I always felt that other women were bitchy to me. They would exclude me from everything, all going to lunch together but not inviting me, or making tea for each other but not for me.

Of course, over the years there was the odd female who was lovely, but the majority always seemed to have real issues with me, no matter how nice I tried to be to them. It made work life miserable, and I would never spend long in one place.

Looking back, I can see that I always got on with the men, not in a sexual way, just as friends, but maybe other females didn't like this about me, maybe they saw me as a threat.

Working while struggling with BPD can make life immeasurably difficult for us, although not to work is often not an option; we may have a family to support and a home to run and our paycheck is not something that we can afford to lose. It is therefore essential that we take steps to try and alleviate some of the problems that arise with working.

## Taking Care of Ourselves Physically and Mentally

Of course, we cannot just make the BPD suddenly disappear, yet we can try to help ourselves as much as possible. Self-care is vital if we want life to become that little bit easier for us. We cannot expect to drink copious amounts of alcohol one evening and wake up feeling refreshed in the morning. Lack of sleep and poor diet, among many other things, can affect the way we feel. Our physical and mental health are closely entwined, and it is essential that we take care of both.

We should ensure that we take time to relax and wind down after a stressful day. Many of us struggle with disturbed sleep or an inability to fall asleep when we plan to. Lack of sleep can cause us a multitude of problems and will interfere with our day-to-day lives, making it essential that we deal with this problem immediately.

There were times when I suffered from lack of sleep. When I struggled with cocaine addiction, I would spend most nights snorting cocaine and not getting any sleep. I would roll into work late and high as a kite. Sometimes I brought more cocaine into work with me, other times I was unable to do so and would then suffer the comedown at work, snapping at colleagues and sometimes just walking out.

We must not abuse our body. Cutting out the drink and drugs, eating well, and getting sleep are so important.

## Being Open About Our Diagnosis

We can be open about our diagnosis of BPD while also being cautious. Unfortunately, BPD carries a huge stigma, and for this reason we would be foolish to discuss our having it with any Tom, Dick, or Harry, for we are then leaving ourselves open to be hurt.

When working for somebody, however, it would be beneficial to have someone who understands a bit about us and our disorder. If nobody knows how we feel, how can we expect anyone to understand what we are dealing with? Perhaps we have a human resources department where we can confide with someone about our disorder, or maybe we have a boss who we feel we can talk to. None of us truly want to openly disclose our mental health issues, but to not disclose them with anyone can actually cause us even more problems.

We must be selective when deciding in whom to confide; choosing someone with some authority is smart, because if the time comes when we are struggling, they are in a position to offer us help and guidance. When selecting someone, we need to be sure that what we tell them remains private and confidential.

We must then decide exactly what information we wish to disclose. We do not need to tell them our life story or anything that we do not feel comfortable disclosing. We should explain what the disorder is and how it affects us when it comes to our work. After all, we are having this discussion in regard to our work life, not our personal life.

It is important to point out however, that due to the stigma attached to this disorder and mental health in general, you should exercise caution before jumping in and disclosing this information to your work.

It is unfortunate that due to businesses being required to place any employee that discloses a serious mental illness in a 'protected' class (at least in certain countries), they would rather look for excuses to let their employee go, whether it be finding 'fault' in their work or phasing out the position.

It is therefore vital that you consider your options carefully before making any decisions. In an ideal world, we could be open and honest about our disorder and receive the relevant support, but we do not live in an ideal world and instead of the support we are looking for we may receive only negative consequences.

When considering whether to disclose this information to your employer, you may ask yourself the following questions:

1. Can I juggle work and recovery?
2. How much is my mental health affecting my work?
3. How much is my work affecting my mental health?
4. How do I think my work will react if I were to disclose this information?
5. If I do not disclose this information, am I likely to lose my job anyway due to my mental health?
6. What are the positives of disclosing this information vs the negatives.

If you decide that it is in your best interest to talk with your employer about your mental health then you may find the following letter useful. You may want to copy it and give it to someone at your workplace to help them understand Borderline Personality Disorder, or you may like to edit it so that it is more personal. You may want to show it first to a member of your mental health team, a trusted friend or family member.

To Whom It May Concern:

I am giving you this letter to try and explain what I am suffering with. I have been diagnosed with a severe mental health issue, called borderline personality disorder (BPD).

The reason I am handing you this letter rather than explaining it to you is that it is a very complex disorder. Many people with it struggle to explain exactly what it is and how it affects them.

BPD is characterized by extreme emotions. Something that may seem minor to yourself has the power to devastate someone with this disorder. Not only are the emotions extremely intense, they are also un-regulated, meaning they can change rapidly from one minute to the next. The sufferer often feels as if they are on an emotional roller coaster, unable to get off. Due to this, BPD has a huge impact on every aspect of my life, from how I relate to other people to how I feel about myself.

There are days when I may feel okay, followed by days of not wanting to get out of bed. Severe depression and anxiety often go hand in hand with BPD, as do other mental health disorders.

Explosive anger, unclear self-image, unstable relationships, self-harm and suicide, fear of abandonment, being out of touch with reality, chronic feelings of emptiness, extreme mood swings, and impulsive reckless behaviors are all BPD traits.

I am trying to learn to manage the symptoms of BPD, as there is no cure. Recovery, however, takes time and does not happen overnight. It is not uncommon for someone to take two steps forward followed by three steps backward.

Thank you for taking the time to read this, to better understand this disorder, and to hopefully offer me the relevant help and support.

## Putting Recovery First

If we could all afford to give up our jobs to work solely on our recovery, then most of us would. Unfortunately, this simply isn't an option for the majority of us, and instead we are forced to balance our work life and recovery. This is not always ideal, but it certainly can be done.

If we have discussed our disorder with someone at work, we can then discuss having leave from work each week to participate in therapy. This may mean having three hours off, one day per week. Therapy is vital for our recovery, and if we have the chance to enroll in a therapy group, we must grab it with both hands.

In our spare time, we must ensure that we practice the skills we have been taught, ensuring they become ingrained in us.

If we are fortunate enough to have the option to stop work to focus solely on our recovery, this too is something we should do. Once we have learned everything we need to and we finally have the BPD under control, we are better able to hold down a job in the future. If we have the opportunity to put recovery first, we must always do so. Recovery will bring us freedom, happiness, and the ability to live fulfilling lives.

## BPD and Co-Occurring Disorders

Very rarely does someone have BPD alone. We often find that other disorders also contribute to our inability to work. These could be depression, anxiety, or addiction, to name but a few. As with putting our BPD recovery first, it is imperative that we deal with these disorders also. Whether we need medication to help alleviate the anxiety or depressive symptoms, or we join a 12-step fellowship to help with our addiction, it is vital that we do not overlook these other disorders, as they too can impact our work life. I'll say more about co-occurring disorders in chapter 24.

Chapter 20

# BPD AND MEN

*"Your illness doesn't define you.*
*Your strength and courage does."*
—Unknown

While it is more common for females to be diagnosed with BPD, more and more evidence suggests it is much more prevalent among men than first believed. So why do fewer men receive the diagnosis of BPD? There are a number of reasons why this may be, and, in order to understand them, we must first look at both the similarities and the differences between male and females with BPD (or undiagnosed BPD).

*Similarities*
- Males and females with BPD have equal levels of emotional distress.
- Males and females self-harm equally.
- Males and females with BPD attempt suicide.

*Differences*
- Substance use disorders are more common in males with BPD, whereas females are more likely to suffer with eating, anxiety, mood, or post-traumatic stress disorders.
- Males are more likely to exhibit the symptoms of explosive anger and impulsive, self-destructive behaviors.

This is not to say that females do not suffer with explosive anger or substance misuse, or that males with BPD do not suffer with eating disorders or anxiety. These are merely general similarities and differences noted between the sexes.

Looking at the differences between the two sexes, we can begin to have an insight into why females are more commonly diagnosed than males. A female with an eating, anxiety, or mood disorder is far more likely to be referred by their doctor to a mental health team, where they can then be assessed and diagnosed. If a male presents with signs of extreme rage, impulsive behaviors, and/or substance misuse, he is more likely to be diagnosed with antisocial personality disorder and either referred to a rehab facility or, worse, arrested for his actions. It is unfair and yet it is the harsh truth. Females are far more likely to be guided on to the correct path of recovery, whereas men travel the path to injunctions, rehab, and prison.

We know that BPD is highly stigmatized; perhaps due to this, clinicians are far more likely to diagnose a female exhibiting some of the traits, rather than diagnosing a male who presents with the same traits, due to gender bias.

Whether it is due to cultural issues, upbringing, or stigma, men are far less likely to seek professional help, at least not in the form of psychotherapy. Whereas females will seek help from a mental health team, males are more inclined to seek help through a rehabilitation center for their drug misuse. That is, if they seek help at all. It is a sad fact that many men choose to suffer in silence rather than seeking the help they so desperately need and deserve. Men are often stereotyped as "tough," so their suffering with self-esteem issues and insecurities often goes unnoticed. The problem is exacerbated when they do seek help and are unfairly misdiagnosed, and therefore miss out on relevant treatment.

As we know from the similarities, males suffer with the same emotional distress as females, and yet the support for them seems to be lacking. All-male therapy groups are an option, and yet with so few diagnosed men, compared to women, there may not be enough participants for an all-male group to take place.

Men with BPD need a safe place where they can talk freely among themselves with other men with BPD, allowing them to realize they are not alone and enabling them to open up without feeling judged. My site, bpdtribe.com holds groups specifically for men, allowing them the privacy to open up about themselves in a safe environment with others similar to themselves.

While recovery is the same for both males and females, tips for men would include not keeping the disorder to yourselves. Speak to a close friend or a family member. All too often men carry on, suffering in silence, when they really do not need to. More and more men are being diagnosed with BPD, and it is important that they reach out to one another. The more men who stand up and say, "I have BPD," the quicker people will stop seeing this as a female disorder. BPD is not something to be ashamed of and neither is suffering with our mental health. There are so many men out there suffering, feeling as if they are on their own, when this just isn't the case.

So how does BPD present in a man? Of course, every man is different and so there is no one answer to this. However, there are some commonalities that tend to show up in men with BPD. If you are a man with BPD and you think, "I don't do that," I apologize. Not every man with BPD behaves in the same way, but there are some red flags that can indicate that a man is suffering with BPD:

- Numerous relationships, often in quick succession of one another and sometimes crossing over
- Black-and white thinking—blowing hot and cold in a relationship
- Relationships tend to be short and often end due to either their hot tempers or aggressiveness (verbally and physically)
- An inability to communicate when they have a problem. A partner or loved one is often left wondering what they have done wrong. Later on the BPD male then carries on as if nothing has happened, leaving loved ones confused
- Can become very defensive if they feel criticized
- Irrational jealousy. They may make accusations and explode with

anger only to apologize profusely later on

- Can be very critical and controlling in relationships
- Full of self-hatred and very self-critical—even if they are incredibly successful. Nothing is ever good enough.
- Can easily cut people out of their lives and are known for holding grudges
- Can detach from their emotions
- Can appear as narcissistic and shock people with extreme attention-grabbing behaviors, which are due to deep insecurities
- Can be sent into an intense rage or a depression from the smallest frustration
- May drink a lot and be very moody
- Seek out sex when feeling insecure
- Tend to not discuss their childhoods in great detail
- Believe that people can never live up to their expectations
- Very distrusting of others
- Incredibly charming when first in a relationship, but this never lasts very long
- Avoiding relationships completely, as they do not believe women can be trusted

Just like women with BPD, men want to be loved. This can cause them much internal pain, but, rather than expressing it, the pain is often suppressed; to the outside world they come across as hostile.

Due to anger issues, men often find that they are more commonly sent for anger management. It invariably never works, as there is more to BPD than just anger issues. This is why getting the correct diagnosis is imperative. The treatment for both men and women is the same, but unless a man gets correctly diagnosed, he will miss out on the right treatment.

If you are a male and you suspect you have BPD, it is worth discussing this with a medical professional. If you feel that you are being misdiagnosed with something else due to you being a male, discuss this with them also. Ask why they do not think you have BPD. What are the reasons? Perhaps they haven't even considered diagnosing BPD due to the fact that you are male. By having this conversation with them, you may open their eyes to something they hadn't previously contemplated.

## Paternal Postpartum Depression

Postpartum depression is something that many people believe only affects women but it is now known that this illness is not limited to only females.

Having a baby brings many changes, sleepless nights, more responsibility and pressures, and less independence, for both the mother and the father. While maternal postpartum depression is more well-known, paternal postpartum depression is certainly not uncommon. Many new fathers may find they have a few weeks where they feel low in their mood. If this low mood continues past week 3, it is probably worth considering PPPD.

Symptoms of Paternal Postpartum Depression
- Feelings of frustration or irritability
- Self-medicating with drugs or alcohol
- Increased anger
- Significant weight gain or loss
- Risky behavior
- Fatigue
- Loss of interest in hobbies, sex, work
- Overwhelming sadness
- Problems with concentration
- Forgetfulness
- Becoming stressed easily
- Feelings of guilt
- Anxiety, panic attacks
- Increase in physical aches and pains
- Uncontrollable crying
- Feelings of worthlessness and shame
- Isolating
- Thoughts of suicide

If you believe you may be suffering with PPPD, please know that you are not alone and help is out there. Do not suffer in silence, hoping that these feelings will disappear on their own, because they won't. You may feel as if there is no way out, but there is, you just need to ask for help.

**What You Need To Do**

- Speak to your doctor
- Stay connected to friends and explain how you are feeling
- Take care of your physical health—eat well, exercise
- Relaxation—meditation, acupuncture, yoga
- Counseling and/or medication
- Join an online support group specifically for men suffering with PPPD

You may feel at times as if things will never improve, but they will. Just as your feelings are temporary, so is PPPD. You will get through this.

Chapter 21

# BPD AND WOMEN

*"Empowered women empower women."*
—Unknown

A separate chapter is needed for women due to the fact that women have experiences that men with BPD do not have. Namely, pregnancy and menstruation, both of which can cause our BPD symptoms to skyrocket.

While both males and females have hormones, it is women whose hormones tend to fluctuate greatly month to month and during pregnancy.

## Monthly Cycle

Women who suffer absolutely no mental health issues can find that once a month, seven to ten days before their period, they change into a different person: irritable, angry, and depressed, to name just a few symptoms. The intensity of the change varies from woman to woman. There are those who suffer with a slight shift in mood and others who seem unrecognizable to the woman they usually are. Then we add BPD to the mix and the intensity shifts up a notch. Not every woman with BPD does have this problem, but it seems that many do.

Estrogen and progesterone are the main hormones involved when it comes to our menstrual cycle and pregnancy. Both of these hormones have the power to alter our mood and emotions, and therefore our behaviors. When we consider that those of us with BPD are also extremely sensitive and struggle to regulate our moods most of the time, it makes sense that when we also have hormones affecting our emotions, everything is exacerbated.

The fact that menstruating can also cause us physical pain just adds to our emotional pain. Lack of sleep, constantly feeling hungry, and being bloated can all add to our misery. We may try various forms of contraceptives to help with these symptoms, but considering that most of the contraceptives also include progesterone or estrogen, many of us find that we are no better off—in fact, sometimes it only makes matters worse.

In my case, once a month for about two to three days, I would become like a woman possessed. The anger that I felt was off the scale—and it would come from nowhere, with no trigger. I would wake up with rage and feel like smashing the house up. I would snap at anyone I spoke to and would walk around feeling as if my blood was boiling. Two days later, the chocolate cravings would kick in and my anger would slowly subside.

For some women, this surge of hormones can cause them to feel as if there is nothing left to live for; they can they can even feel suicidal and therefore are particularly vulnerable at this time.

There is no quick fix to this problem, but there are steps we can take to help us alleviate some of the symptoms and understand what is going on with our bodies.

**Keeping a Diary**

By keeping a diary, we can begin to predict when our mood may drop. Each month we should look out for any physical and/or emotional changes that suggest it may be menstrual. Are we craving junk food? Are we getting tummy pains? When does our mood change? When do we get our period? By doing this, we can eventually begin to preempt changes from happening.

We can also tell ourselves, "I am feeling this way, as I have a surge of hormones rushing through my body." This certainly does not invalidate how we are feeling, but it can help us to recognize one of the causes of our intense emotions. We can remind ourselves that we only need to get through the next few days before our hormones will stabilize again.

By keeping a diary, we can also take steps to help alleviate our symptoms of PMS. Exercise, although one of the things we probably least like to do, is actually beneficial in making us feel better. Exercise cannot only lift our mood, it can also help with the physical pains of menstruation. Yoga is a form of exercise that also calms the mind and helps us to relax; if we practice yoga, we get multiple benefits physically and mentally.

Watching what we eat is also important. Yes, we may crave every bit of junk food we can get our hands on, but inevitably the food can make us feel a whole lot worse. Of course, if we want a piece of chocolate, we should have a piece of chocolate—just not ten bars of it. Anything high in sugar, fat, caffeine, or alcohol can affect our brain chemicals, making us feel worse in the long run.

If we know the date we are likely to start experiencing premenstrual symptoms, we can start taking care of ourselves a little bit more beforehand. We can also talk to a close friend or loved one and explain just how we feel prior to our period. Rather than isolating for days, we can plan to have a movie night in with a loved one or friend, or go for a brisk walk. No, it is not what we want to do, but once we do it we feel better. We learn ways in which we can get through this time each month in one piece.

If we find that nothing seems to work for us, we must speak with a professional and let them know how bad things are. This way we are protecting ourselves at this vulnerable time. A professional can direct us to a crisis team; if things seem to be worsening, we can contact someone in an emergency.

## Pregnancy

While getting pregnant is supposed to be the most wonderful thing in the world, getting pregnant while suffering with BPD can be anything but wonderful. Yet again, as with our monthly cycle, no two women are the same. Some women with BPD are fortunate enough to go through pregnancy unscathed. Unfortunately, many of us find that pregnancy aggravates our BPD. This isn't surprising, as pregnancy has a massive impact on our hormones.

We must also consider that many of us go off our medications during pregnancy. Our doctor will weigh the pros and cons of stopping our medication, and although some medicines are a definite no-no in pregnancy, there are others that are deemed slightly safer to use. Of course, with all medications there is no conclusive evidence that there are absolutely no risks; due to this, many of us decide to stop the medication to be on the safe side. This can wreak havoc on our mental health.

I experienced utter pandemonium during my first pregnancy. I decided to stop all my medication without first consulting with my doctor. Within weeks of stopping, I was overcome with intrusive thoughts, paranoia, depression, and angry outbursts. I felt completely overwhelmed and absolutely terrified. I was terrified I would lose the baby, terrified of the birth, terrified of being a mum. My list of fears was enormous and I felt powerless to stop them.

**Pregnancy brings with it many challenges:**
- Every little tummy pain can cause us to freak out, thinking that something is wrong
- Hormones, and therefore mood, can change rapidly
- Tiredness that is so extreme only a woman who has been pregnant can understand it
- Sore boobs
- Morning sickness
- Increased sex drive or no sex drive
- Backaches
- Indigestion and heartburn
- Itchy skin
- Needing the toilet constantly, even in the night
- Bleeding gums
- Varicose veins
- Swollen feet
- Pelvic pain

For someone with BPD, these challenges can have a detrimental effect on how we think and feel; therefore, it is a priority to ensure we receive the right support. Many studies have shown that women who already suffer with mental health have increased chances that pregnancy will cause her mental health to suffer more—either before the birth or after it.

It's also important that when we do get support we get enough of it. During my first two pregnancies, the support I got was minimal. In the background I had my mental health team and a wonderful care-nurse, Yolanda, but I was under the direct care of midwives who didn't understand mental health and who I hardly ever saw. The appointments with my mental health team did not increase due to pregnancy so my appointments tended to be months apart. During the few midwife appointments, she only dealt with the physical aspects of pregnancy rather than what I was having problems with—my mental health.

When I moved to Bournemouth, I was fortunate to be referred to a team of midwives called The Sunshine Team. These midwives are specially trained to deal with vulnerable women—women who suffer domestic abuse, are young, have drug or alcohol problems, or suffer with mental health.

There are very few of these teams dotted around the country, which is such a shame, as the support I received from them was immeasurably helpful. I was also still under the care of a mental health team, and during my third pregnancy I also received help from a specialist perinatal mental health team.

Support in pregnancy can make all the difference, but it is not always readily available. Those of us who suffer with BPD and become pregnant must seek out as much help as we can. There are times when we have to shout to be heard. We should not have to struggle through pregnancy on our own.

Being our own advocate is crucial when dealing with doctors, nurses, and others. In addition, we need to be aware that the stigma of having BPD exists even in the medical and social services fields, as hard as that is to believe. During my third pregnancy, I was no longer taking drugs, but social services was involved, as I had self-harmed. My social worker seemed to really focus on the fact that I had been a drug addict rather than on my mental health.

When I gave birth, my social worker came to the hospital to talk with the midwives on duty. Then, without my knowledge or consent, my son was drug tested, as was I. I stayed in the hospital for four or five days, and the midwives on the ward were anything but nice. I was made to feel like a terrible mother and looked down upon.

The day I got home, my social worker turned up to tell me that my drug test had come back positive for opiates! Luckily, my partner pointed out that, on the day I gave birth, the doctor had given me dihydrocodeine—an opioid. My social worker disagreed, saying the midwives on the ward said that medication hadn't been administered. I was left distraught with worry for four days before they realized they had made a mistake. There was never an apology.

Luckily, I had my midwife from The Sunshine Team for support. This experience really opened my eyes to the way that those of us with mental health issues can be treated. My midwife suggested I make a complaint to the hospital, but because I started suffering with postpartum depression, I never did.

More medical professionals need to be educated on mental health. Until this happens, however, we must understand that not everyone we deal with will understand what we are going though or be sympathetic.

There are a few things we can do to help us during pregnancy however:

- Practice coping skills daily, as they can be a vital tool to help us during pregnancy.
- Take care of ourselves physically—a healthy body equals a healthy mind.
- Relax and unwind. We are growing a baby inside of us, and this takes a toll on our bodies. We should rest wherever possible.
- Talk about how we are feeling. This enables us to let it out. Or

we can keep a diary and write down how we are feeling.

- Ask for help. Speak to a doctor or midwife and let them know that we need extra support. There are times when we have to keep asking before any action is taken, but we shouldn't give up—we deserve to be heard.
- Don't judge ourselves. Pregnancy can be difficult, and if we need to go back on our medication then we should, without feeling like a failure.
- Stay in the present moment. Pregnancy can cause us to feel incredibly anxious and fearful of the future. The more we focus on this, the worse it gets. Instead we should try and focus on the here and now, practicing mindfulness or meditation to help us. Worrying about what the future holds will not help.
- Understand that it is perfectly natural for our bodies to change and that it is only temporary. Pregnancy is a beautiful thing and we should try to embrace it.

## Postpartum Period

Having survived pregnancy, there are those of us who find that our troubles start after our baby is born. Again, if someone has suffered with their mental health prior to pregnancy, it is far more likely they will also suffer with it after pregnancy (National Health Service, 2018).

Postpartum Depression (PPD) can cause us to feel consumed by sadness, anger, anxiety, and even psychosis. We may even feel as if we haven't bonded with our baby. We can feel so alone and believe we are a bad person for having the thoughts that we have. If any of us feel this way, it is imperative we speak to someone about how we are feeling.

I suffered with the baby blues in the first few days after giving birth to my daughter. Unfortunately, these feelings of sadness did not disappear within the first week but instead carried on for many months. I refused to leave my bedroom and instead took to my bed with my little girl where I stayed, cut off from the outside world.

I can remember one night staring at her beautiful little face and becoming convinced that she was possessed by the devil. I was ashamed of my thoughts and was unable to verbalize them to anyone due to this shame. Instead, I kept my thoughts to myself but they only seemed to get worse. I was sure that the only way to *save* my child was to have her exorcized.

Eventually I got to the point where I opened up with my mental health team and I was put on medication. My symptoms improved but did not altogether disappear. Although I no longer felt my baby was possessed, I was still suffering severe anxiety, positive that something bad would happen to her. What if someone took her? What if she died? These thoughts consumed me and turned me into a nervous wreck.

Having suffered with my self-esteem most of my life, having a baby did not help matters at all. My body had changed, I was so tired and any form of personal hygiene went out the window. Sex scared the hell out of me; What if he doesn't find me attractive anymore? I also started to see sex as something dirty, certainly not something I should be doing now I was a Mother.

I had spent most of my life wishing that I would one day be a Mom and now that I was one I felt desperately lost and fearful. I would spend day after day just staring at my baby, sometimes crying, sometimes feeling just so inadequate – how on Earth was I supposed to be responsible for this little Human Being when I could barely take care of myself?

Having a baby can bring so many changes; social changes, body changes, financial changes and interpersonal changes. We can struggle with our lack of independency, our sex drive, negative thoughts and anxiety.

Postpartum depression can be mild and happen slowly over time or it can be severe and happen suddenly. Nor does it necessarily happen immediately after birth; it can appear many months later. Other symptoms of postpartum depression can include panic attacks, lack of concentration and forgetfulness.

**It is important to know that:**

- We are not alone—postpartum depression affects many women.
- Feeling the way we do does not mean we are bad.
- It is okay to ask for help—in fact, it is crucial that we do.
- Our feelings are temporary, as is postpartum depression.
- Bonding with our baby does not always happen immediately – it is something that takes time.
- We can get through this.

If you feel as if this is something that you are struggling with, communication is key, as is understanding through learning about PPD. You might check with your local hospital to see if they have any support for women struggling with PPD, as many do offer help. Speak with your child health nurse, your mental health team, your doctor or a professional counselor. Medication may also help, as will practicing stress management skills such as meditation or exercise.

There are also online support groups for women with PPD; connecting with other women in a similar situation to yourself is also worthwhile.

Chapter 22

# BPD AND SEX

*"The opposite of loneliness, it's not togetherness.*
*It is intimacy."*
—Richard Bach

S ex is an important part of relationships, and yet for those of us with BPD it can be the bane of our life. Many of us have some sort of issue when it comes to sex, whether it's fixing on it constantly, or avoiding any kind of intimacy at all costs. In this chapter, we will look at the various issues we may experience and the reasons for them.

### Sexual Masochism

Although not every person with BPD has suffered abuse in their past, many of us have, and this is possibly a major cause of our sex issues. There has been a link between people, particularly women with BPD and sexual masochism (Frías Á, et al 2017). Sexual masochism can be a healthy part of a relationship, but for those of us with BPD it is often a self-injurious behavior brought on by our emotional distress in regard to past traumatic events.

Rough sex can cause us to feel victimized—something that feels familiar to us, and perhaps subconsciously we associate the physical pain we experience during sex with love. Of course, the physical pain also releases endorphins, causing us to feel a momentary high, which can become addictive.

### Reckless Sex

We may find that we are prone to sexual promiscuity, always on the hunt for a new sexual partner and acting impulsively, even if we are in a committed relationship. We suffer with chronic feelings of emptiness, and we are often under the illusion that sex with another person can fill this void. We may equate sex with love—we feel wanted and admired, even if it is temporary. By seducing another person we feel both in control and powerful.

Sex is a primal instinct, so it may feel like the most natural thing in the world to us; we don't consider the consequences of having random and unprotected sex. We run with our primal instinct, and it isn't until afterward that we regret our actions.

**Intimacy**

Although we suffer with a fear of abandonment, most of us crave connection and acceptance from others. Our relationships often begin intensely and full of passion. Having someone want us sexually causes us to feel as if we have found the love we have being searching for. As our relationship grows, however, fear begins to creep in and we may become emotionally distant, causing us to lose interest in sex altogether. While sex without emotion is something we can usually do quite easily, as soon as we feel someone is getting psychologically close to us, we tend to back off.

This behavioral pattern is something I used to struggle with. When I was first with a partner, the sex would be amazing and I would do everything to please them. As soon as we became emotionally attached, however, I would get to a point where I didn't want to have sex with them at all. If they touched me I would cringe and feel like screaming, "Get off me!"

My first relationship was when I was fourteen and the boy was eighteen. He talked me into having sex with him only a week into the relationship. I was so scared of losing him that I went along with it. My first time was rushed and painful, nothing I imagined it would be.

A couple of months into the relationship I came down with the flu. I was so sick that I couldn't get out of bed. My mum had to work but was happy that I had my boyfriend there to keep an eye on me. She never considered the possibility that our relationship was a sexual one, for if she had there was no way she would have left us alone in the house to-gether. That week, my boyfriend would climb on top of me to have sex, knowing how ill I was and with me crying beneath him begging him to stop. After that, the thought of sex turned my stomach. I felt it was dirty and disgusting, and I believe I have carried these feelings with me all these years. Strangely, for many years I had completely forgotten about this experience. One day, years later, it hit me like a ton of bricks—I couldn't believe that my mind had forgotten such a traumatic event.

When first in a relationship, many of us find that we can wear a mask and be whoever we think the other person wants us to be. When having sex, we can pretend to be an actor playing a part in an erotic film. We may spend huge amounts of time refining our external image, en-suring that we are perfect, at least outwardly. Of course, the longer our relationship goes on, the more we begin to show our true selves and are unable to simply play a part anymore.

### Pressured into Having Sex

If we are in a relationship, we may find that sex no longer interests us—we may even detest it. Our partner, however, still has needs and will often let us know of them. When this happens we feel torn. We do not want to have sex, and yet we are scared they will get it elsewhere if we don't "fulfill their needs." We begrudgingly have sex, feeling angry at our partner and frustrated at ourselves. This only further increases our negative feelings toward sex, and the vicious cycle continues. If we were to talk openly with our partner about our issues, we would often find that they are willing to take things at our pace, but very rarely will we let our guard down and show our insecurities.

### Sex as a Weapon

When we learn that sex brings with it power, we may begin to use it as a weapon, either offering it as a reward or holding it back as pun-ishment. While this seems callous, we do this because we desperately need to feel in control. This need for control often stems from our child-hoods and lack of control in them. When we wield sex as a weapon, our partners are left feeling like an object and not respected, which is understandable. Just as we want to be treated correctly, we must also learn what is acceptable and unacceptable in a relationship. When we start to use sex as a power play in a relationship, we are both disrespecting our partner and ourselves. We can use sex as a weapon without even being conscious of doing so, but we need to become aware of it so that we can take action to stop this behavior.

## Fixing on Porn

Some of us struggle to truly enjoy sex. We find it impossible to let ourselves go and take pleasure from it; instead we prefer to stay in "character" and focus solely on the needs of the other person. Part of this is due to our desperate need of acceptance and wanting the other person to think we are the best thing that has ever happened to them, and part of it is due to being afraid to be ourselves, fearing we will not be liked.

We still have needs, however, and some of us find that masturbation is a way of getting instant gratification without having to worry about intimacy. It's our way of getting our needs met. Watching porn can become addictive, with us turning to it more and more, and shying away from actual physical contact with someone. Porn can initially seem like the answer to our problems. Due to our low self-esteem, however, watching porn has serious adverse effects. We can begin comparing ourselves to the people in the porn film and feeling as if we always fall short. This invariably causes us to feel even more insecure when we do have sex, distancing ourselves further from any physical intimacy.

When it comes to our partner watching porn, we find that we are overcome with jealousy. This feeds into our insecurities, and we may blame our partner for preferring porn to us or think that they only watch porn because they find us so repulsive. We feel as if we have been cheated on, unable to comprehend that our partner watching porn has nothing to do with us. It does not mean they do not fancy us, neither does it mean they prefer porn to having sex with us.

## Avoiding Sex

There are those of us who outright avoid sex altogether. Again, due to childhood trauma, bad experiences, or lack of trust, we can have negative emotions when it comes to sex. Disgust, fear, anger, and anxiety are all feelings that we may associate with sex, therefore avoiding it seems the better option. By shunning sex, we feel both in control and able to protect ourselves from the hurt we believe sex can cause.

The problem with avoiding sex altogether is that we miss out on the chance to build intimate relationships.

Whether it is our fear of abandonment, chronic feelings of emptiness, unstable self-image, or past trauma that is behind our sexual issues, they are something that eventually need to be looked at in order for us to recover in all areas of our life. We mustn't put pressure on ourselves though; we must understand that this is a sensitive subject, one that cannot be forced or rushed.

Counseling can be beneficial for us, as can building our self-esteem. Depending on what issues we have, the solutions can vary greatly. It is wise to first tackle the BPD itself, with some of us finding that our sexual issues seem to disappear with time and recovery. There are some of us who may need further help with overcoming our issues, and we must accept that we might not be able to do it on our own. This does not mean we are failures—in fact, recognizing when we need some extra help takes both strength and courage.

Chapter 23

# BPD AND TEENAGERS

*"Difficult roads often lead to*
*beautiful destinations."*
—Zig Ziglar

The teenage years can be particularly painful for both the teenager and the parents. A teenager is no longer a child (at least not in their eyes) and not yet an adult (as much as they feel as if they are), yet they are trying to find their place in the world, attempting to fit in. The average teenager will suffer with moodiness, an unstable sense of self, impulsivity, and tense relationships. Many parents would struggle to differentiate between a typical teenager and a teen with BPD, but there are differences and it is important to know what they are.

The signs of my own BPD were present when I was a teenager. My mum believed that I was just a hormonal teen and that my mood swings, extreme emotions, and recklessness would pass as I grew up. How wrong she was. I deteriorated until I ended up on a mental health ward after multiple suicide attempts. I didn't get diagnosed with BPD until I was twenty-one. The signs had been there for many years, though, and had I been diagnosed sooner perhaps things wouldn't have gotten as bad as they did.

I often get messages from young teens looking for advice. They watch my videos on YouTube and believe that they too have BPD. The stories are very similar: their parents think that they are just hormonal teens, and nobody will take them seriously. These youngsters are crying out for help and yet they aren't being heard.

For parents, coming to terms with a possible BPD diagnosis is difficult—not only does borderline personality disorder have a stigma attached to it, many people diagnosed with it have suffered some form of loss, trauma, or abuse. Any parent that learns of this is likely to go on the defensive. They might say, "How can my child have BPD? They had a decent childhood. I wasn't abusive." Parents may also feel that, if their child is diagnosed with this disorder, the professionals will judge them for this very same reason. Nobody wants to be judged, especially if they don't believe they have done anything wrong. If a parent is willing to take their child's mental health seriously, then they should not be judged, as clearly they care about their child and wish only to support them.

What parents need to know is that 70 percent of people with BPD make at least one suicide attempt, and 10 percent of people with BPD actually commit suicide (Skodol et al. 2002) and therefore is not something that should be dismissed as simply "hormones."

A big problem that numerous teenagers face is the fact that many professionals still refuse to diagnose someone with BPD before the age of eighteen. There are different reasons for this, one being that professionals, like parents, can believe it is too difficult to distinguish between typical teenage behaviors and BPD traits. Another reason is that some professionals do not think it wise to diagnose a personality disorder when a teen's personality is still forming. Teenagers also risk (as do adults) being misdiagnosed. Bipolar, teen anxiety, substance use disorder, depression, or PTSD is common misdiagnosis of BPD. Luckily, more therapists are being trained to help treat teenagers with BPD, so improvements are being made all the time. There is also more and more evidence pointing towards early intervention and prevention (Paris et al. 2013).

So how does BPD appear in teenagers? Often it presents in a very similar way to adults with BPD: extreme emotional reactions that seem really out of proportion to the event that triggered them, a distorted self-image, fear of abandonment, rapid mood changes, and impulsivity.

282

The best way to differentiate a typical teen from one with something else going on is that, for a teen with BPD, everything is more intense and more frequent, especially their moods and behaviors.

Another trait that seems to appear more commonly in teens is narcissism. The teenager seems unable to feel empathy toward others and can appear to be loud or big-headed, as they desperately want to be noticed and validated by other people. Of course, this "narcissism" is actually a defense mechanism that helps them deal with their fear of abandonment, a core trait of BPD.

Questions parents can ask themselves when considering if their teenager may be suffering with BPD may include:

- Do they partake in impulsive and risky behaviors? This may include acting out sexually or abusing drugs or alcohol. Are they taking risks on a regular basis that may jeopardize their safety or the safety of others?
- Do they tend to see everything or everyone in black and white— all good or all bad?
- Can their mood change suddenly with seemingly no trigger? Are their mood swings often—up and down multiple times in a day sometimes?
- Are they self-harming, having thoughts of suicide, or engaging in suicidal behavior?
- Do their relationships with others tend to be incredibly unstable?
- Do they suffer with extreme anger issues? Do they lash out at the slightest thing?
- Do they tend to be extremely dependent on others? If someone has to go somewhere, can it leave them devastated?
- Do they seem overly anxious—even when there doesn't seem to be anything for them to be anxious over?
- Are they incapable of noticing how others feel? Do they lack empathy?
- During a meltdown, is it extremely hard to calm them down?

- Do they tend to act like a chameleon, constantly changing to fit in with whoever they are with?
- Are they unable to change the way they behave, no matter how guilty they feel after an event?
- How do they react after an argument with parents? If they shout and slam doors, they may be your typical teenager. If they punch a hole in the door, smash a glass on the floor, attack family members, or run away, they're not a typical teen.
- When they are sad do they lean on their friends for support? This is what a typical teen would do. If, however, they isolate and self-harm, or sink into a deep depression with suicidal thoughts or behaviors, it's time to get them seen by a doctor.

If parents can answer yes to even a few of these questions, then perhaps it is worth seeking help from an expert. The first step would be to see a doctor. Parents can then ask to be referred to a mental health team, which can carry out a proper assessment. When assessing a teenager, the professional will be looking for five or more of the nine traits listed in the DSM-IV-TR, and the teen must have had these traits for at least one year.

The good news is that the earlier treatment begins, the better the final outcome. The recovery process for teenagers is the same as with adults: group therapy, learning new skills, counseling, and so on. Experiential therapies may also prove helpful for teenagers, perhaps more so than talking therapy alone. These sorts of therapies include:

- Music therapy
- Art therapy
- Creative writing
- Equine therapy
- Adventure therapy
- Animal-assisted therapy
- Recreation therapy
- Dance

- Psychodrama
- Wilderness therapy

Rather than talking about certain events, teens are able to experience them through role play, art, dance, or any of the activities above. A therapist will work with them while they take part. Teenagers can find it a lot less daunting to express their feelings and work through events in this therapeutic way than simply sitting and discussing them face to face with a therapist.

Other things that can be helpful in recovery are taking part in mindfulness groups and yoga. Teenagers might even like to join their parents in doing a group like this. This can be a wonderful way to bond and for parents to show their teen that they are there for them.

Parent-child relationships can become incredibly strained during the teenage years, and parents can seem to do no right. Please understand, though, that when a teenager is having a meltdown of epic proportions, the reasoning part of their brain has shut down—they will not be able to rationalize with anyone. Parents may want to scream and shout at them, but if a teen has BPD, this will get parents nowhere. It is always best to wait and talk to them once they have calmed down. Also, know that just because a child may behave as if they hate their parents, it is in fact themself that they hate, and through pure frustration and anger they lash out at those closest to them.

Growing up in a world feeling misunderstood, judged, and different is scary for any teenager, whether they tell their parents this or not. Parents can offer them something that they so desperately want: love, acceptance, and support.

Chapter 24

# BPD AND OTHER DISORDERS

*"Remember you were given life because you are*
*strong enough to live it."*
—Unknown

It is uncommon for those of us diagnosed with BPD to only suffer with *this* disorder. Borderline personality disorder often comes hand in hand with other disorders, whether that is because we are vulnerable due to our mental health and therefore easily able to develop other disorders or perhaps due to these disorders being "part of" BPD instead of being separate from it.

The danger with having more than one disorder is that other disorders, such as depression or anxiety, may get diagnosed while BPD goes unnoticed. When this happens, the BPD remains untreated, causing us to carry on suffering until the correct diagnosis is made and the correct psychotherapy is offered.

This chapter looks at the most common comorbid disorders of BPD and ways to tackle them.

**Depression**

One of the most common comorbid disorders of BPD is depression. It's not surprising considering our extreme highs and lows and the destruction that BPD has on our lives. Many of us with borderline personality disorder struggle with depression, often severe, for months at a time, unable to take care of ourselves and losing all interest in things that we once found joy in.

Depression is certainly something I have struggled with. When I was depressed, I very rarely realized I was depressed until after the fog had lifted. During my lowest points I would feel constantly tired, unable to get out of bed, unable or not wanting to answer my phone for anyone. I wouldn't wash or eat properly, and I would sleep for hours on end just wishing the days away.

One of the traits of BPD is chronic feelings of emptiness, which can feel like depression. The difference is that no amount of antidepressants can cure us of that chronic feeling of emptiness. Antidepressants can, however, lift the fog and increase our mood slightly. While this certainly has no effect on the BPD, it can increase our willingness to engage in therapy, which, in turn, can help with the BPD.

As well as taking antidepressants, we can take action to help relieve us of our depression. The problem, however, lies in the fact that all the things that can help with depression are all the things we are least likely to want to do when we are depressed. We must force ourselves into action, constantly reminding ourselves that we will feel better afterward. We just need to take that first step—and we can do it, no matter how much we tell ourselves that we can't.

### Stop Isolating

When we feel at our lowest, the last thing we want to do is connect with anyone around us, preferring to stay inside our little bubble of misery and cutting off from the outside world. This, however, will only makes matters worse for us. We need to connect to others—it is vital that we reach out. Talking is such a powerful recovery tool, and sometimes all it takes is for us to let everything out for us to feel slightly better, as if a weight has been lifted.

### Self-care

Self-care tends to come lowest on our list of priorities when we feel depressed, and yet once we start to take care of ourselves physically we start to improve mentally. Eat, sleep, drink water, and exercise are all things we neglect to do, but they can have a massively positive impact on the way we feel.

## Get Outside

Hibernating indoors will only deplete our vitamin D. The sunshine helps increase our serotonin levels, which can then lift our mood. We do not need to spend hours outdoors—only twenty minutes a day can do the trick. Getting back to nature also has a positive effect on us; we can take a nice walk in the local park, go and feed some ducks (animals also have a positive effect on our mental health), or do some yoga on the beach.

## Exercise

Exercise falls under self-care, but it is important to also know that energy energizes. If we lie around all day doing nothing, we will have less energy than if we go out for a brisk walk. Exercise also releases feel-good chemicals in our brain, which can help alleviate depression.

## Start Doing Things We Used to Enjoy

Is there a book we love to read, a favorite film we like to watch, or a hobby that used to get us excited? If so, we need to re-spark our interest in these things. It is not that we no longer like them; it is the depression that has taken over. We need to get excited again—and it is possible for this to happen—but we must take the first step. We cannot expect for our old happy feelings to return immediately, and, more often than not, we won't feel any different to begin with, but we must persevere.

## Anxiety

Anxiety is also prevalent among those of us with BPD and can have an adverse effect on our recovery. Many treatment options for BPD include group therapy, and anxiety can interfere with us wanting to participate in such activities; the thought of walking into a room full of strangers is terrifying, and we will often avoid doing so at all costs.

Anxiety can leave us immobilized, unable to venture outside the "safe haven" that is our home. Anxiety around other people as well as anxiety around events and circumstances can cause us to isolate and cut ourselves off from the outside world.

As with all the disorders, anxiety disorder is on a spectrum, ranging from minor anxiety to severe anxiety, for which panic attacks are a common occurrence. No matter where we are on the spectrum, this disorder can hinder our recovery if not dealt with correctly.

My own anxiety was so severe that I could have a panic attack just from walking into a supermarket. I was so full of fear all of the time that eventually I just stopped going out.

One day I had a few drinks at home and realized that this reduced my anxiety; I was able to go out and not worry about people staring at me (which is what I thought people did). I felt as if I had found a "cure" for my anxiety. So I began drinking alcohol daily, from the moment I woke up until the moment I went to sleep or, rather, passed out.

I couldn't see it at the time, but all I had done was substitute one problem for another problem. I had never actually relieved myself of the anxiety but just masked it temporarily. If I didn't drink alcohol, the anxiety would still be there. Drinking alcohol daily caused me a whole host of other problems, and my life started spiraling out of control. In fact, after having a few drinks, I started using more and more cocaine, causing my anxiety to skyrocket and leaving me with even more problems than I had to begin with.

Treatment for anxiety can include medication and therapy, as well as self-help and alternative therapies.

Those of us with BPD have a fear of abandonment and an unclear self-image, which can cause us to feel anxious. We also have a fight-or-flight response that is easily triggered, plus a hypersensitive amygdala, all possible causes of our anxiety. While it is interesting to know the reasons we experience anxiety, it does not actually help us when it comes to alleviating the symptoms.

### *Take Care of Our Physical Well-Being*

Taking care of ourselves physically is essential, as things such as lack of sleep and diet can all lead to anxiety. Caffeine, alcohol, high-sugared foods, and drugs can cause anxiety to worsen.

## Keep a Diary

Any of us who suffer with anxiety understand that it can feel as if our mind is racing, and we can be easily overcome by a barrage of negative thoughts. Keeping a diary of these thoughts can prove beneficial, enabling us to take control of them and let them out in a helpful and non-destructive manner.

We should write down any worries that are playing in our mind. Later we can set aside time to read through them. This way, we are not avoiding them but dealing with them as they arise. We're able to look at them more rationally than if we hold them in and play them over and over in our minds.

By jotting down information, such as what happened prior to feeling anxious, the date and time, and our thoughts, we may be able to find a pattern, enabling us to recognize triggers and thus avoid them.

We should also keep note of any positive aspects of our lives; all too often we get so wrapped up in the negatives that we actually feed our anxiety and fail to acknowledge that there are any positives in our lives. By writing them down and reading them back, we can identify and appreciate them.

## Breathing

The physical effects of anxiety on our body include heart palpitations, rapid breathing, trembling hands, and sweating, just to name a few. By slowing down our breathing, we are able to decrease our heart rate and begin to stabilize our body. We do not necessarily need to breathe deeply, just more slowly and steadily. Focusing on our breathing while counting can also help distract us from our incessant thoughts.

## Medication

Many antianxiety medicines can actually exacerbate BPD traits. For example, Valium, while helpful for those without BPD, can actually cause those of us with BPD to easily become addicted to the medication or to act impulsively and recklessly. We must discuss with our mental health caregiver what other medications can be used to treat anxiety in those of us with BPD.

## *Yoga, Massage, Reflexology, Aromatherapy, Hypnotherapy, and Meditation*

Alternative therapies such as these can also prove effective when dealing with anxiety. While something may work for one person, it may not necessarily work for another, so it is worth trying out the different therapies to discover what works for us.

### *Acceptance*

Those of us with BPD often have low self-esteem and are constantly worried that people will not like us. We need to accept that we are powerless over what other people think or do. We cannot control others or life events, and, by letting go of the need to do so, we can help free ourselves of the anxiety that we have regarding this.

## Bipolar Disorder (BD)

One of the symptoms of BPD is extreme mood swings so it is not surprising that those of us with BPD can be misdiagnosed with bipolar, a mood disorder. Although the two disorders have overlapping symptoms and can seem similar, they are in fact two very different disorders.

It is not uncommon, however, to be diagnosed with both disorders. In fact, as many as 96 percent of people with BPD also get diagnosed with a mood disorder in their lifetime (McGlashan et al. 2000).

### *Medication*

Medication used to treat someone with BPD can have a negative effect on someone with BD: it can exacerbate their symptoms. Medication is something that would need to be discussed with our mental health team. There are medications that have proven to be successful at treating these disorders when they are comorbid with one another.

### *Therapy*

Whether we have BPD on its own or comorbid with BD, we need to have therapy that can teach us skills to live our lives. Participating in therapies such as DBT, MBT, and the like can prove helpful. There are ongoing studies to determine the effects that these therapies have on bipolar disorder.

## Post-Traumatic Stress Disorder (PTSD)

Considering that both BPD and PTSD commonly develop from experiencing traumatic events, it is not surprising that the two disorders often overlap.

Those of us with BPD tend to live life impulsively and are therefore more likely to also suffer from trauma of some sort along the way, whether it's sexual, physical, or drink or drug related.

### Eye movement desensitizing and reprocessing (EMDR)

This therapy includes making side-to-side eye movements while going over the traumatic event in our mind. Trained therapists are then able to make the brain work in a different way to deal with the painful memories.

### Trauma-focused CBT

This psychological treatment includes teaching techniques that help us come to terms with the traumatic event.

### Group Therapy

Discussing our situation with others who have experienced similar things can be helpful. Not only are we among others who understand what we are going through, we can share methods of managing our symptoms and learn from one another.

## Addiction

The fourth symptom of BPD, as listed in the DSM-IV-TR, is impulsive, reckless behavior. This commonly involves the improper use of illegal substances, prescription medication, or alcohol.

Living with BPD is extremely painful, and many of us turn to drugs or alcohol as a way of easing our pain. Unfortunately, this often spirals into an addiction and leaves us much worse off. We initially believe that we have found a solution to our problems, only for the addiction to become a problem of its own.

It is not only drugs and alcohol that we may become addicted to. Any behavior that temporarily makes us feel better can lead to an addiction. This includes sex, gambling, shopping, and social media. These behaviors give us a buzz and temporarily mask how we really feel. Unfortunately, with every high that we experience there is the come down, making us feel worse than we did previously and causing us to repeat the destructive behavior and, in doing so, continuing the vicious cycle.

The longer the addiction continues the more destruction it causes in our lives, from physical health problems and debt to losing our family or our homes. Our addiction leaves a path of ruin behind us and can severely hamper our recovery. The reason is that our addiction blocks us from forming healthy coping habits. This happened in my own life. I was enrolled in STEPPS for BPD, hoping that at last I had found something that could help ease my symptoms. But the meds that had been subscribed didn't seem to help at all, and I was getting more and more desperate.

I turned up to every session but refused to confide in anyone that I was drinking alcohol and using drugs daily. In fact, I was turning up under the influence, and very little information went in. I was able to successfully pass the drug tests because I had a stash of my own clean pee. I had spent time in the hospital following an overdose, and I had saved a cup of pee during the couple of weeks that I got clean.

So every week I would bring this cup with me to the hospital. Sure enough, every time they dipped in the strip that would detect drugs it would come back as clear. I did this for months, before one day owning up to what I had been doing.

I explained that I had to use drink and drugs, as nothing else seemed to help me. My wonderful therapist, Yolanda, pointed out that nothing else would work *because* of the drink and drugs; they were interfering with both my medication and my therapy.

Our addiction becomes our coping mechanism, and in order to overcome it we need to replace it with healthy coping mechanisms. But in order to learn healthy coping mechanisms, we need to overcome our addiction; it is a catch-22.

When dealing with addiction alongside BPD it is important not to solely focus on the addiction. There are people who do not have BPD and suffer with substance misuse or another addictive behavior, and in these instances the addiction alone can be treated. For those of us who have BPD and struggle with addiction, the method of treating it needs to incorporate the fact that the BPD is more than likely to be the driving force behind the addiction. Removing the addictive behaviors without treating the BPD does not solve the underlying problem and leaves us open to relapse. The addiction is a coping mechanism for us, and if we have it removed it is vital that we have new and healthy coping mechanisms in place.

### Rehab

There are those of us who need time away from our daily lives to be able to get enough clean time to beat the addiction. When considering a rehabilitation center, we must look for one that understands mental health, especially BPD, and is used to dealing with dual-diagnosis rather than addiction alone.

We all know it can be dangerous to mix drugs for comorbid disorders, but it can be just as dangerous to suddenly stop medication of one issue to treat another. I discovered this the hard way. I entered my first rehab with the intention of getting clean from alcohol and cocaine. On my first day, they stopped all of the medications that had been prescribed by my mental health team.

I felt out of control and as if I were going crazy. My mood dropped in an environment that I was not used to and surrounded by strangers. I started acting out of character. I was desperate to make friends and have people like me so I made up gossip about myself and about other people. My behavior landed me in trouble and I got kicked out of treatment.

They gave me an hour's notice to pack my bags and catch a four-hour train to home. I was hysterical, screaming and crying. I felt like the biggest failure and wanted to die. I decided that if I were put on that train I would kill myself. I couldn't think clearly or rationally. Luckily, my mum and stepdad spoke to the rehab staff. They were frantic with worry and explained that it wasn't safe to put me on a train. My stepdad picked me up.

Once home, my mental health was completely erratic. I made a suicide attempt that landed me on the mental health ward yet again. Finally back under my mental health team, I was put back on all of my medications—but at an even higher dosage. My mental health team couldn't believe how negligent the rehab center had been in withdrawing the medication that I had been on for years and had been prescribed for a very valid reason. They managed to get me into a different rehab facility, one that understood mental health problems and certainly wouldn't take me off my meds.

Once at this new rehab, I thrived and lasted the six weeks of treatment. I then went on to complete five months of secondary treatment at a different rehab. In this secondary rehab, I was fortunate to have two wonderful therapists. Maria specialized in eating disorders and Sue in addiction. I used to follow Sue about like a little lost puppy. At the time, I really felt as if I were well! Only with hindsight do I realize that the BPD symptoms were in full swing. I threw tantrums there, felt lost if Sue wasn't around, and "fixed" myself by spending money on things that I didn't need on our daily trip into town.

Looking back I can understand, based on my behaviors, why the first rehab dismissed me. But I also feel incredibly angry because their negligence put my life at risk. Had I not been taken off all of my meds, I wouldn't have behaved the way I did, and I wouldn't have been kicked out in the first place.

When considering a rehab facility, it is vital that we discuss the BPD with them prior to attending. If they do not understand it, they may not be able to offer us the care that we need and deserve.

Rehabs are a way for us to get some clean time, but they are not a cure. Once we have completed treatment, it is imperative that we continue to work on our recovery, for if we do not, it is highly likely that we will go back to our old ways. This is the time when we need to start implementing new and healthy coping skills that can replace the old and destructive ones of our past.

## *12-Step Fellowships*

Alcoholics Anonymous was the first 12-step fellowship and due to the success of it, numerous other 12-step fellowships have come about, including Cocaine Anonymous, Narcotics Anonymous, and Gamblers Anonymous.

The 12 steps are a spiritual way to live life, looking at ourselves and our behaviors, making changes where possible and helping others. The wonderful thing about these fellowships is that they are free and they are anonymous. When we enter into a fellowship we are surrounded by others who struggle with addiction just as we do. Spirituality can have a positive effect on both the borderline personality disorder and addiction. We must again realize, however, that we are not simply dealing with addiction. The addiction and the BPD must both be treated.

It must be added that just as some rehab facilities do not understand BPD, nor does everyone in the fellowships. There are those of us who have met people who claim that we should not be on medication, as addiction is our problem and any form of medication is a mind-altering drug; they allege that this means, technically, we are still using. This is not the case when it comes to borderline personality disorder. If a medical professional has prescribed us medication, then we should carry on taking it as they have instructed us to do so. To stop taking our medication without our doctor's say so is irresponsible, dangerous, and poses a risk to our recovery.

## *Detox*

Depending on what we are addicted to and the amount that we have been taking, we may need to detox first. Alcohol is the most dangerous detox and must be done under medical supervision. Some of us may need a one, two, or even six-week detox just to get the drugs out of our system before we fully engage in therapy for the BPD and addiction.

## Eating Disorders

With our low self-esteem and unstable or unclear self-image, eating disorders are prevalent among us. We are crippled with self-doubt and loathing, and many of us can develop eating disorders as either a way to change ourselves or to feel in control of something. There are those of us who also use our eating as a way to self-harm.

Eating disorders come in many different forms. Anorexia, bulimia, emotional overeating, binge eating, night-eating syndrome, and purging disorder are all forms of eating disorders that can affect us. I myself struggled with an eating disorder.

My bulimia started when I was sixteen years old. I decided that I needed to take drastic measures to lose weight quickly, as I hated my appearance and felt self-conscious about my belly, thinking I had to wear baggy clothes to cover it up. My negative thoughts about myself first appeared when I was fourteen and my boyfriend would repeatedly tell me that I was fat.

I can remember talking openly to a lady about bulimia when I was eighteen years old. She explained that she had suffered with it until she reached thirty years old. I thought, "I will never still be making myself sick when I'm that old." How wrong I was. My bulimia continued with me into my thirties and was the most difficult thing to rid myself of, even harder than the drugs and alcohol.

I don't know if, in the end, I would just make myself sick out of habit, because even as my confidence grew and my self-loathing dissipated the bulimia continued. I did notice that if I ever felt a strong negative emotion, perhaps after an argument with a loved one, I would immediately go and make myself sick. Was this a way of harming myself or was I subconsciously thinking, "Look what they made me do"?

Eating disorders, just like drugs and alcohol, can seriously impact both our mental and physical well-being and therefore need to be treated.

### Hospitalization

In the most severe cases of the disorder, a few of us may find ourselves as an inpatient.

### Eating Disorders Clinic

Having weekly or fortnightly appointments with a trained eating disorders specialist is an option for many of us. It is extremely difficult to overcome an eating disorder without some outside help. The first step would be for us to talk with our GP and see if they can refer us to the relevant people.

### Keep a Food Diary

This includes writing down the times we eat, what we eat, and how we feel before and after eating, followed by what action we took. By doing this we can look for patterns and start trying to implement new routines into our eating habits.

### Eat a Little and Often

If we immediately start trying to eat three big meals a day, we are likely to experience difficulties. Instead, we should try to eat six small meals a day, as this is often a lot more manageable for us to do.

### Get Busy

Immediately after meals tends to be a difficult time for us, so it's worth using distraction techniques, such as going for a walk after eating. While this may be difficult to do straightaway, the more we do it the easier it becomes.

### Learn About Nutrition

By reading up about nutrition and learning what is good and what is bad for our bodies, we start to view food differently. Over time we begin to see the benefits of eating healthily and giving our bodies the right fuel. Rather than seeing food as the enemy, we start to have a healthier relationship with it.

### Build Self-Esteem

Taking steps to increase our self-esteem will also have a positive effect on our eating habits. We should start trying to focus on our positives, writing them down or repeating positive affirmations to ourselves in the mirror. We may not feel as if we are being truthful to begin with, but we can fake it to make it. As time goes by we start to believe what it is that we are saying or writing about ourselves.

## Limit Social Media

Social media is wonderful in some respects, but in others it is incredibly damaging. Photos of fit young men and women become something we begin to compare ourselves to and aim to be like. We fail to appreciate that everyone is unique and that the photos we are seeing aren't necessarily a true representation of the person in them. With numerous filters and photo editing, we often start comparing ourselves to something that is simply not real. If suffering with low self-esteem, we would be wise to avoid social media as much as possible and not let it take over our lives and destroy the little confidence that we may have.

## Other Personality Disorders

There are ten recognized personality disorders that are grouped into three clusters. Cluster A includes the "paranoid" personality disorders. Cluster B includes the "dramatic" personality disorders. Cluster C includes the "anxious" personality disorders. Borderline personality disorder is in Cluster B.

While there are those of us with BPD that can also have a personality disorder that is in clusters A and C, it is more common for us to have a dual diagnosis with another cluster B personality disorder.

The cluster B's include antisocial personality disorder, histrionic personality disorder, and narcissistic personality disorder.

Those of us who fall in the cluster B's find it hard to deal with our emotions and can be seen as unpredictable and erratic in our behaviors.

## Medication

Medication can be used to treat some of the symptoms, whether they be depression, anxiety, or psychotic episodes, but should not be the only treatment used.

## Talking Therapy

Talking with a therapist regularly is a treatment method used for all of the personality disorders. Having someone listen to us and offer valuable feedback can be incredibly helpful. We are often too embarrassed to have this kind of conversation with someone outside of the medical profession, and yet talking is a vital part of our recovery. Being able to talk to a therapist without feeling judged is extremely beneficial.

### Group Therapy

Being among those similar to ourselves can help us feel less alone and more understood. So many of us go through life feeling both alone and judged, believing that there is nobody out there like ourselves. This is simply not the case, and we are definitely not alone, no matter what personality disorders we may suffer from. By participating in group therapy we can acknowledge this and gain support from our fellows.

### Skills-Based Therapy

It isn't only those of us with BPD who can benefit from learning new coping skills. Skills-based therapy can help with many of the personality disorders. Although DBT was initially developed to help those of us with BPD, we find many mental health organizations and clinics using it to also help those with other personality disorders and mental health issues. The cluster B's are known for having problems linked to emotion dysregulation; learning how to regulate our emotions is an important part of our recovery.

# PART V

# FROM SURVIVING TO THRIVING

Chapter 25

# THE POWER OF BALANCE AND ROUTINE

*"Balance is not something you find—*
*it's something you create."*
—Jana Kingsford

O ur lives are chaotic, and we struggle through each day with an all-or-nothing, black-or-white attitude. We do not do things by halves, and every day is a whirlwind, full of surprises and with no way to predict how it will end. Balance and routine can seem boring and mundane, and as much as we crave it we also fear it.

Balance and routine are the polar opposite of how we live our life, and yet they are incredibly powerful things for us to put in place. They enable us to start living a more manageable life, and, once in place, the positive effects they have on our mental health is numerous.

The chaos I had in my life definitely could have benefited from a regular, healthy routine. Daily life for me was a huge struggle. Simple things, like what I should make the kids for lunch, seemed like a monumental obstacle. I woke up every morning with a feeling of dread, no plan for the day ahead, and never knowing whether I was coming or going. From morning to night I would be praying for the day to be over. Not only was there absolutely no hint of a routine, I had the most imbalanced life imaginable. There were times when I would spend the whole day in the pub downing bottles of wine and who knows what else, and other times when I wouldn't budge off the sofa. I only saw friends if

I was out drinking, so sometimes I would go months of not seeing them followed by months of seeing them daily. I didn't work, I could barely look after my children, all my money went to drink or drugs (or occasionally plants for the garden if my new fixation was making the garden look amazing, which I would do while drinking bottles of wine), I didn't know what spirituality was, my health and fitness was nonexistent, and me time consisted of me snorting cocaine off a grubby pub toilet.

Routine and balance can free us from the chaos in which we live. If we have a basic routine in place, life becomes easier, with less surprises and more manageability. We find that we are much better able to face each day head on without the fear of what lies ahead.

Establishing a routine as early on as possible is suggested. We each have different priorities, and no two routines are the same. To ease ourselves into this new way of living, it is wise to start off small and simple. This helps us avoid the downfall of too much too soon. Starting with a wake-up time and a setting a bedtime is a start. This also helps enable us to have a decent night's sleep, as opposed to sitting up until 3 am and sleeping past midday, which has a negative effect on our internal body clock.

Once we have adjusted to a very basic routine, we can then start adding to it: breakfast, lunch, and dinner at a set time would be the next step. By setting mealtimes, we are ensuring that we are eating regularly, which is beneficial for our physical and mental well-being. We can continue with this process, adding things until we feel that we have a good, solid daily routine in place.

We must also consider how balanced our life is. In order to do this, we must look at the different areas that should be included in our life: family time, social life, health and fitness, work, money, relaxation, spirituality, fun, and, of course, recovery. When looking at these different areas can we honestly say we include all of them in our week in equal proportion? Most of us cannot. If we want to live a fulfilled life in which we are both content and happy, it is vital that we create some kind of balance.

Once a week, for thirty minutes, we should take the time to sit and plan out our week ahead. We can immediately start on Monday and work our way through to Sunday simply adding in what we wish to include in our daily routine: waking up, mealtimes, and bedtime. We then add in the school drop-off and pickup (if we do it), a weekly shop, housework, work, and so on, working our way through the week. We then start back on Monday and begin to fill in any appointments or errands we have for the week ahead. Once completed, we then have a weekly plan of everything that *needs* to be done. We can then focus on adding in things that help us to have more balance in our life.

A coffee with a friend, taking the children to the park, going for a walk in the country, practicing our recovery skills, enjoying a swim, catching up on our emails, meditating, sorting out paperwork—these are all things that can be added into our weekly planner. We do not need to cram them all into one day, but we can spread them out over the week. When looking at our planner we can then ask ourselves, *Does my week look balanced?* If every day we have added in going to the gym, but have missed out seeing friends or having time to our self, then maybe we need to make some changes.

It is very easy for us to fall into the trap of all work and no play. But as the saying goes, that only makes Jack a dull boy. The whole point of recovery is to have a life worth living; to do that, we need to ensure our life is not taken up with one thing but instead a variety of things.

We find that once we have an established routine in place and our life is more balanced, we can finally sense the peace and calm that we so desperately desire. We also find that life is far from boring when our days are diverse. Once we get to this place, we are then ready to start setting ourselves goals.

## Setting Goals

Having goals to aim for helps us to focus, and when we achieve the set goals our self-esteem is boosted and we feel wonderful.

When setting goals we should start small and make them achievable, as the last thing we want to do is set ourselves up for failure. Small goals may include:

- Going for a fifteen-minute jog three times a week
- Saving $5 a week
- Getting our finances in order
- Starting to write a book
- Phoning a longtime friend who we haven't been in contact with for a while
- Drinking a liter of water a day
- Getting eight to nine hours of sleep a night
- Signing up for an online recovery course

These small goals are all things we can start aiming for today. And they don't take an exceptionally long time to complete. Once we have chosen a small goal, we can then think about how we are going to achieve it. We need to make sure our goal is SMART.

S **Specific**—Is it clearly written? Is the goal specific to what we want to achieve?

M **Measurable**—Does the goal include how much, how often, or how many?

A **Achievable**—Is the goal realistic? Can we access the support we need to achieve the goal? Do we have the right resources to complete the goal?

R **Relevant**—Is this goal going to have a positive impact on our lives, no matter how small?

T **Time-bound**—Have we specified a date when we would like to have completed the goal?

To help us reach our target, we can draw up a plan. On a blank piece of paper or in a journal, we can answer these questions:

- What is my goal?
- How will this goal benefit me?
- What steps can I take to achieve my goal?
- What obstacles may get in my way? How will I overcome them?

How will I feel once we've reached our goal, we need to be sure to celebrate and reward ourselves.

## Rewarding Ourselves

Everyone likes rewards and why shouldn't we? Rewards make us feel good, they confirm that we have done something well. Unfortunately, very few of us actually receive rewards, especially for the smaller things in life that we manage to do. Yet for those of us with BPD, the small things are actually huge things, and we certainly deserve to be rewarded for them.

If we know that there is a reward in sight when we accomplish something, it can actually help drive us to achieve what needs to be done. Rewarding ourselves is something that we should all do. We are not talking large sums of money or a new car, although they would be nice. Rewards need to be something that will make us feel good about ourselves without causing us any harm. For example, if we reward ourselves with an expensive pair of shoes that leaves us short of money, the reward is actually causing a harm, which negates the point.

Ideas of what may merit a reward and what the rewards could be are listed here.

## What May Merit a Reward?

- Completing a skills module in therapy
- Achieving our SMART goal
- Accomplishing a routine
- Achieving a balanced life
- Passing a test
- Keeping on top of the housework
- Eating healthily
- Practicing new skills each day
- Reading a book
- Losing or putting on some weight
- Establishing a healthy sleep pattern
- Just because we feel we deserve it!
- Waking up at a set time each day

## Rewards Given to Self

- A new haircut
- A new DVD
- An inexpensive (under $5) gift to selves
- A night off to relax
- Going to the cinema
- Takeout
- A new book
- A pamper day at home (face mask, relaxing bath, etc.)
- Lunch or coffee with a friend
- Allocating time to start streaming a series

The rewards that we give to ourselves do not need to cost money. They are symbolic of a pat on the back and acknowledgement for our hard work.

Chapter 26

# LIVING LIFE
# SUCCESSFULLY
# WITH BPD

*"Remember—progress not perfection."*
—Unknown

Just because we have borderline personality disorder does not mean that we cannot lead a happy and successful life. We know that when our BPD is unmanaged life becomes painful and difficult, but we also know that this disorder *can* be managed.

If we follow the ten steps laid out in chapter 16, we will be well on our way to having the successful life that we rightly deserve. Throughout this book are numerous skills that we can start putting into practice today. We will eventually get to the point in which we look back, only then realizing just how far we have come. When the light bulb moment happens, it can awaken us to how strong we truly are. Recovery from BPD is ongoing, and, although we can finally reach the point in which we feel we have fully "recovered," there are still things we can carry on doing to ensure that (1) we keep moving forward in our recovery, and (2) we live a successful life.

**Gratitude**

So many of us go through life taking the smallest things for granted. Those of us with BPD have often spent years of our lives just existing. When at last we come out the other side, we are so overwhelmed with joy that we can't wait to finally start living our life, which is what we do—living life to the fullest yet sometimes forgetting the importance of being grateful.

The benefits from practicing the art of gratitude are numerous.

- Increases optimism
- Reduces materialism
- Increases spiritualism
- Reduces self-centeredness
- Boosts self-esteem
- Improves sleep
- Makes us happier
- Boosts our immune system
- Increases energy levels
- Reduces feelings of envy
- Makes our memories happier
- Deepens friendships
- Increases productivity
- Makes us friendlier
- Improves our decision making
- Helps us relax

Considering that these are only a few of the benefits, it is surprising how few of us practice being grateful on a daily basis. The good news is that it is never too late to start—and it is easy to do.

- We can keep a journal and write down what we are grateful for every day. We should try and list three to five things, at least, and be specific. Writing "I'm thankful for my mum" is great, but we need to think about *why* we are thankful for her.
- As we write down what we are grateful for we need to try and "feel" it.
- We should think of new things to be grateful for every day, rather than filling our journals with the same things over and over.
- We do not only need to focus on the big stuff but also the teeny-tiny things that usually go unnoticed by us.
- We do not only need to be grateful for "things" but also for

other people: the person serving us in our local shop, the bus driver, the teachers at our kid's school, the person who smiled at us in the street.

- We can practice other ways to be grateful beyond a journal. Other ideas are:
  1. Having a gratitude stone in our pocket, and every time we touch it we think of something to be grateful for
  2. Writing a group message on our phone to share our gratitude with our close friends (when doing this we must be careful not to get carried away with our ego and start writing things that we think our friends will think are good!)
  3. Sending someone a thank-you card or letter
  4. Writing a thank-you letter that we don't send
  5. Keeping a gratitude box that we add to every time we feel grateful for something
  6. Spending ten minutes sitting quietly each day thinking and feeling the things we are grateful for
  7. Setting an alarm each day to remind us to practice being grateful

## Embracing Our Qualities

Having lived with borderline personality disorder, we find that we are incredibly proficient when it comes to looking at our faults, and yet we fail to acknowledge any of our good qualities. As we come into recovery, our self-esteem builds and we are less likely to feed the negative thoughts that we have about ourselves, instead pushing them away as they arise. We still often forget, however, to start focusing on our individual positive qualities.

Each of us is unique and we all have different qualities that make up who we are. Many of us spend much of our time comparing ourselves to others and then are left feeling less than, when instead we should be embracing who we are and what makes us wonderful. This includes qualities about ourselves that we do not necessarily see as positive.

In chapter 15 we looked at the positives of having BPD. Now it is time for us to look at how those positives manifest in ourselves. Rather than scrutinizing our looks and picking out everything that we hate about ourselves, we need to move our focus to what we like about ourselves. It may be our hair color, our eyes, our knees, or our nails! We may have a laugh that people say they love, maybe we are great listeners or we are kind, funny, or hardworking. No matter how small or irrelevant they seem, these are the things that we need to concentrate on, as these are what make us who we are. By continuing to embrace our qualities, our self-esteem will grow and our self-hate will dissipate.

How often do we do things that we don't particularly want to do but still go ahead and do just because we want to fit in and be accepted? Yet we are not truly accepting ourselves when we do this. We need to start doing what makes us happy. Do we like to spend a Friday night in reading a book but find we get dragged out to a pub or club? Why do we do this? Often it is due to peer pressure, fear of missing out, or fear that we will be left out if we do not go. Do we feel the need to post selfies constantly, as that seems to get more likes than when we post pictures of our new kitten? We live in a world in which we tend to do what we think others want us to do rather than focusing on doing what makes us happy.

For so long we have lived our lives fearing that we will be abandoned, insecure, and people-pleasing wherever we go. The years we have wasted wishing we were thinner, bigger, funnier, smarter, taller, or shorter are not far behind us. We have worked so hard for our recovery and we need to make changes, for if nothing changes, nothing changes. We do not want to fall into old habits of comparing ourselves to others and wishing that we are someone who we are not.

So how do we do this? How do we embrace our qualities?

First of all, we must learn to recognize what our qualities are. We can do this by writing things down about ourselves and reading what we have written back to ourselves daily. We can ask friends and loved ones, "What are my good qualities?" Chances are they will tell us things we haven't ever thought about. We can ask ourselves, *What makes us happy?* More often than not, we are happy when we are doing something that involves our positive qualities. Now is the time to start doing things that make us happy rather than trying to please everyone else.

## Helping Others

Before we were diagnosed with BPD and discovered what it is that we suffer with, we probably went through life feeling very alone and misunderstood. There are still millions of people in the world who are feeling just like that: alone and misunderstood. When we come into recovery and are finally freed from the life we have lived for so long, we have the rare opportunity to reach out and help others who are in the same situation that we once were.

By helping others like ourselves, we are able to share our knowledge and experience and offer them hope. We can remember just how hopeless we once felt, and now we have the chance to help prevent others from feeling that there is no way out. We can show them that there is light at the end of the tunnel before they are able to see it for themselves.

The way in which we help others can vary, and it is up to us to decide what we are comfortable doing. Volunteering, writing a blog, creating a YouTube channel, writing a book, speaking on the radio, and participating in online BPD forums are all ways in which we can reach out and help those less fortunate than ourselves. We must always remember that we are no different or any better than them; we are simply farther along in our recovery. They too can be where we are by working at their recovery and being guided by us.

While we are not necessarily medically trained, we are trained in experience and therefore have much to offer the still suffering. Whether we are a week into our recovery or multiple years does not matter. If we have a story to tell and share, then we can make a difference. Each of our stories carries a message. Our story may be that we relapsed multiple times and struggled with recovery, and this is okay. For all those out there who keep relapsing, this story shows them that they are not alone and they are not a failure because they find recovery difficult. Not everyone with BPD will relate to everyone else with BPD—our journeys are all so different —which is why it is important that we share our experience with others. There will be someone out there who *can* identify with our personal story and gain hope from hearing it.

## Avoiding Complacency

There are those of us who have been in recovery from BPD for multiple years, and, while this is wonderful, we must never forget where we came from and the struggle that we fought to overcome. There is no cure for BPD, and, although it can be managed, we are wise to acknowledge that it is still there, lying dormant in us, thanks to the hard work that we have put in.

We should never become complacent when it comes to our recovery, for if we do, we may begin to see some of the traits reappearing in our life, seemingly completely out of the blue.

Luckily for the majority of us, once we have learned the skills needed to manage the BPD, we eventually use those skills subconsciously, without even having to think about it. This happens for us after practicing the skills daily until we finally see them working in our lives. The more we practice them now, the less we have to think about doing so in the future.

We should be aware of old behaviors surfacing; if and when we see them arising, we must deal with them immediately. Taking daily inventory is beneficial, as it opens our eyes to any behaviors that may have resurfaced before they get out of control.

At the end of each day we should consider these questions:
- Have I reacted to something without considering the consequences?
- Have I behaved in a way that is reckless or self-destructive?
- Have I viewed any situation or person in black or white?
- How have my relationships been today?
- Have I put off doing something today that I should have? If yes, why?
- Have I been grateful today?
- Have I been dishonest today?

- Am I worried about anything?
- Have I been kind today?

These are the types of questions we need to ask ourselves every day if we want to stay happy and content. It sounds like hard work, and yet, once we have been doing it for a few months, it comes naturally to us; we automatically start to ask ourselves these questions throughout the day without having to sit and think about it. If we have been dishonest, we notice it straightaway; if we are worried about something, we pick up on it quite early on. Once we are able to do this, we can then change our behavior when needed. Taking daily inventory does not mean that every single day we need to be apologizing to people. We take daily inventory to keep check on ourselves; if we are behaving in a way that we shouldn't, we can take immediate action to prevent our behaviors from spiraling out of control. The actions we take depend very much on what behaviors we are trying to change. By this point, we should have enough knowledge of the skills to know which ones we need to start putting in place.

There are times when we need to ask ourselves numerous questions to discover what is going on with us. For example, if I had been dishonest today, I might ask myself, *What caused me to be dishonest?* The answer may be that "my partner annoyed me yesterday." I then would ask, *Why did they annoy me?* The answer could be that "I don't really know, but they just annoyed me." We can then question whether perhaps it is our black-and-white thinking resurfacing. Once we know this, we can take steps to stop it. So from looking at the fact that we have been dishonest about something and questioning it, we are able to uncover the behaviors that come prior to it. If we do find that some of our old behaviors are surfacing, it is vital that we then question *why* they are resurfacing, because if we do not do this, we are not tackling the root cause.

**Reasons for our behaviors resurfacing tend to be:**
- Something stressful is going on in our lives and we are not dealing with it. Maybe we are trying to ignore it and hoping it will

disappear, when in fact all we have done is suppress it—and it *will* resurface in one way or another.

- We've stopped practicing any of the skills that can help us daily: a routine, balance, being grateful, and so forth.

- Isolating—maybe we are busy with work and don't make time to do anything else (no balance). Isolating can have a very negative effect on us, as can swinging the other way and socializing so often that we have no time to clear our heads.

- A big event, such as a death, a breakup, or losing our job. These are all things that can have a huge impact on us; although we *can* deal with them and get through them without resorting to old behaviors, we often get so caught up in the emotional pain that we do not deal with them in the new and healthy ways that we have learned.

We find that by helping others, we are constantly reminded of how life used to be for us, and this reminder keeps us on our toes and stops us from becoming complacent. Helping others benefits both those who we help and ourselves in equal proportions; it is the power of one borderline helping another.

Chapter 27

# COPING IN DIFFICULT TIMES

*"Life is like riding a bicycle.*
*To keep your balance, you must keep moving."*
—Albert Einstein

It is easy for us to make the presumption that once we start learning to manage our BPD symptoms and we are seeming to recover life will be easier. While this holds some truth—life is less painful on a daily basis—it does not mean that life will be uncomplicated and painless. Life happens and we have absolutely no way of predicting the future or controlling everything in it. To say that life will run smoothly from now on is preposterous. What recovery does give us, however, are the tools to face life head on, without having to hide from it and without succumbing to our old destructive coping mechanisms.

Within this chapter we will look at some major life events that can happen to any one of us, at any given time, and look at ways to help us get through them in one piece.

**Breakups and Divorce—When Our Partner Ends the Relationship**

Having our heart broken by someone we love is possibly one of the most painful and agonizing things anyone can experience—let alone when those who suffer with unregulated and extremely intense emotions.

When our heart breaks, we can feel as if our world has ended, and the pain we feel is so much more than just emotional—we feel as if we are physically hurting, as if our heart is actually breaking into pieces, like we are going to die.

The tidal wave of emotions we experience at times like this are numerous: hurt, anger, guilt, embarrassment, relief, and confusion may all sweep through us one after another and back again. We feel as if we are drowning, unable to catch our breath. We have lived so long fearing that someone we love will leave us, and yet when it happens we are no more prepared for it. We spend weeks, months, going over the scenario in our head, again and again, replaying it in our minds, and each time we feel as if we are reliving it, it is so intense and fresh. We often wonder if life will ever be the same again, because at this moment in time we cannot see how it ever will be.

It is during times like this when we desperately do what we can to stop the pain: drinking, using drugs, self-harming, recklessly having sex with anyone, shopping, or attempting suicide. Yet nothing seems to work—in fact, we always end up feeling even worse.

There are those of us who react by bottling up our feelings and pretending as if we don't care. Our feelings are still there, but they are being suppressed, building and building until they start resurfacing in different ways.

How often do we try to control the situation? Relentlessly sending messages to our ex, sometimes friendly ones and sometimes vile ones. Our thinking toward our ex flips from idealizing them and remembering all the good times, to absolutely hating everything about them, completely unable to see the gray area.

So what can we do to get us through?

## Things We Can Do

### Allow ourselves to have time to grieve and heal

When a relationship ends it is important that we allow ourselves time to grieve. We have suffered a loss and need to understand that we shouldn't expect to be feeling amazing a few days later. If we want to cry, then we should cry; by suppressing our feelings we are preventing ourselves from healing.

### Distract

There are times when our feelings are simply too intense and we

COPING IN DIFFICULT TIMES

are left feeling completely helpless. When this happens, we need to do something that momentarily gives us some time away from the intense feelings. By distracting, we are able to give ourselves time to (a) calm down and (b) prevent us from reacting without considering the consequences.

## Acceptance

So often we spend time fighting against what has happened and refusing to accept the reality of the situation. Rather than stopping the pain, this only prolongs our suffering. We therefore need to accept it. Accepting does not mean we are happy about it, but it does mean that we acknowledge it has happened and that we accept that we cannot change it.

## Self-care

Most of us can relate to the "heartbreak diet," either going off our food completely or eating to comfort ourselves. It is not just our eating habits that can be affected following a breakup. We may find that we can't sleep or we don't want to get out of bed at all. It is vital that we take care of ourselves physically, however, for if we do not, we will only cause ourselves further pain emotionally. We know that our physical and mental well-being are linked, so it is imperative that we take care of both—which includes avoiding alcohol and other mind-altering substances that make things worse for us.

## Surround ourselves with understanding and supportive people

We may not feel like facing people in the aftermath of a breakup, but it is so beneficial to be around those who want to support us, be a shoulder to cry on, and listen to us rant. Talking is essential, as it allows us to process what has happened and seek advice from others. By communicating our feelings with others, we are also preventing ourselves from suppressing them.

## Be kind to ourselves

We feel very low, unwanted, and unloved when a relationship breaks down, and we can easily get consumed with self-pity. Now is the time to treat ourselves with kindness and love. We could enjoy a pamper day, enjoy a night watching a movie, or buy ourselves a small gift. Although this does not change what has happened, it can certainly lift our mood.

## Things We Should Not Do

### Isolate

We may feel like shutting ourselves away from the outside world to try and cope with our feelings on our own. Some alone time can be beneficial, but we should never cut all contact with those who love us. We need them right now even if we do not feel as if we do. Isolation can lead to us slipping into a depression and developing social anxiety, which essentially cause us more pain.

### Try to find a replacement

Many of us have the belief that by jumping into a new relationship our pain will disappear. In trying to find a "replacement" for our ex, all that we are doing is trying to fix our feelings. We are trying to forget the current situation and distract ourselves from what has happened. Initially it may even seem to work, however, we mustn't fool ourselves into believing that we have dealt with the situation. Those feelings have merely been suppressed and they will resurface at some point. We bring all of the hurt and anger into our new relationship, not only causing ourselves pain but also harming another person. We start to compare our new partner with our ex, thinking in black and white again, only this time we think of our ex in white and our new partner in black. So often we hurt new partners because of this. When a relationship ends, we *must* allow ourselves time to grieve and heal completely, or we risk harming ourselves and others.

### Make any major life changes

Making life-changing decisions when we are so vulnerable and emotional is never a wise idea. Yet again, we may try to fool ourselves into thinking that if we make a massive change in our life, whether it be moving our home or quitting our job, we will feel happy again. Whatever we do will only temporarily mask our feelings, and eventually we may cause all kinds of destruction in our lives through our erratic choices. We must understand that when we are making decisions while in this emotional state, the chances are high that we are not thinking rationally or logically. We need to allow ourselves time to heal before making any rash decisions.

### Try to stay friends with our ex

In a perfect world, remaining friends with our ex is a possibility, and even those of us with BPD may eventually find that we can rebuild a friendship with an ex-partner. As for trying to remain friends immediately succeeding the breakup? This is nearly always a recipe for disaster. We will be highly emotional, extremely vulnerable, and desperate to fix things. We may try and convince ourselves that remaining friends with our ex will help us move on gradually and enable us to have closure. We find that when we try to do this, our relationship with our ex will alternate between being friendly and being antagonistic and disagreeable, with the latter often leading to outrage and arguments. We are left feeling resentful and hurt all over again. The truth is that we want to remain friends, because at the back of our minds we believe we can win them back and everything will go back to being the way it was. What happens is that we drive our ex farther away from us and prolong our pain, our suffering. Instead we need to cut all ties and allow ourselves time to heal. There are those of us who, a year or so down the road, find that we can restore the friendship with our ex, but this can only happen if we (1) have truly healed from the breakup and (2) we no longer have romantic feelings toward them.

### Breakups/Divorce—When We End the Relationship

Not all of the breakups we experience are due to our partner leaving us. Surprisingly, there are some of us who decide that we need to end a relationship. While this may not seem as though it would cause us as much pain as if it were the other way around, the pain we can feel is still immense.

Unfortunately, many of us have seemed to just walk away from a partner without looking back or without caring in the slightest. While it certainly can seem this way due to our behaviors, it is never as simple as that for us. Our seeming disregard is often a mechanism that we use in order to protect ourselves from our own feelings.

There are those of us who end one relationship only to jump straight into another one, leaving our ex-partner devastated and believing that we must never have loved them in the first place. When we look at it in this way, it is unsurprising that they would feel this way; if it were the other way around we too would be devastated.

The fact is, there are multiple reasons why we might end a relationship. Some include:

- We are not happy
- We're depressed
- We don't feel that a partner treats us right
- We think our partner is too good for us and we will hurt them eventually
- We are having a manic episode
- We don't even know why we want to break up, we just do

There are times when we may be perfectly happy in a relationship, have a blazing row, and walk out never to return. Other times we might be thinking in black and white, and although yesterday our partner was the best living thing in the world, today we despise them and we end it. There are even those of us who fear abandonment so much that we abandon our partner before they get the chance to abandon us first.

Most times when we end a relationship, it is done in the height of an emotional outburst. There is no planning or thought that goes into it, we just find that we are rowing one minute and ending the relationship the next. We have ended things using our emotional mind and absolutely no rational thinking has taken place.

## Tips to Get Us Through

### Don't make a final decision when in an emotional state

When we are in the height of an episode, we must remind ourselves, no matter how much we believe we are thinking rationally, the chances are we are not. The more we learn about BPD and the more we become self-aware, the easier it becomes to do this. With self-awareness comes the ability to recognize traits in ourselves as they are happening. Of course, most of us start off completely unaware of our behaviors and thought patterns. We can, however, remind ourselves daily that if we have a highly emotional episode we should not make any final decisions.

### Our fear of abandonment does not mean we will be abandoned

This truth is extremely important for us to recognize. When we throw away a perfectly good relationship because of our unsubstantiated fear of them leaving us first, we hurt ourselves and our partner. To make matters worse, we will have not truly dealt with the real issue, meaning that it will only follow us into future relationships.

### Be Aware of Guilt, Blame, and Shame

These are all feelings we may go through either preceding or following a breakup. Guilt and shame should never be reasons to drag a relationship out that has clearly run its course. Feeling guilty about hurting our partner and therefore staying in the relationship is dishonest, and we will only grow resentful as the time goes on. If we do decide to end the relationship, we should not throw all the blame at our partner and neither should we carry all the blame. It takes two to make a relationship, and it is good for us to accept our part in why it went wrong.

### Let Go of Regrets

Having regrets about leaving an ex-partner can be common, considering the way we can swiftly leave one relationship and move on to another. The reason for this stems from the fact that we left them without thinking things through rationally. Regret, therefore, can be a feeling that many of us can experience. It is not, however, a positive emotion to live with; we must learn to let go of it while also learning from our experiences. If we make a mistake and learn from it, we can ensure it doesn't happen again.

### Make Amends

For those of us who have hurt someone through our actions, the act of making amends to that person is something we should consider. If doing so would only cause the person further harms, we should refrain from it. If, however, we believe that it may help the person understand why we acted the way we did and will help them understand that it was not their fault, then we should. We may write them a letter, send them a message, or call them. If we are to do this, we should never point fingers or try to pass the blame on to them in any way—we are simply apologizing for the hurt that we caused to them. When doing this, we must ensure that we do not have another motive behind this action. Apologizing in the hope that they will take us back is not advised, nor is apologizing when they have happily moved on to another relationship, as this can cause harm to their new partner.

**An Unfaithful Partner**

One of the most painful experiences we can go through is discovering that the person we love so dearly has betrayed us. As we already suffer with a fear of abandonment and low self-esteem, being betrayed exacerbates all these symptoms. Although many of us fear our partner leaving or cheating on us, it does not make it any less painful or any less of a surprise when it happens. If our loved one who has betrayed us also knows about our BPD and understands our insecurities, it seems to make it so much worse. For this person, who means the world to us and who knows that we struggle with our self-esteem, to be able to hurt us in one of the worst ways imaginable seems incredibly cruel.

The nonstop stream of agonizing emotions that surges through us causes us to act out; we scream, we cry, we self-harm, we attack, not knowing what to do with ourselves and lacking any self-control. We feel wounded and want everything to stop, want it to be a bad dream, for we do not feel strong enough to face the reality of the situation. The hurt is then transformed into pure rage, where we feel nothing except a deep loathing and absolute disgust at our partner. Yet the hatred does not last, and once again we feel like an injured child, desperate for someone to come and make it all better.

There was betrayal in my own relationships that caused me great turmoil. When I discovered that my then-husband had been phoning my best friend every day for the past year, my whole world was turned upside down. I had spent many years with this man, and we had built up a trust, or so I thought. The discovery that this trust had been broken absolutely floored me.

In the immediate aftermath I screamed and I cried, desperate for answers. Why? For how long? What did you do? I wanted to know every single detail, and if I wasn't given them, then I would make them up in my head.

All the times he had walked her home from the pub when I had been at home getting our daughter to bed—what happened then? He told me nothing happened except that they walked and talked, yet how was I to know this was true? I started making up scenarios in my head: them kissing, them laughing at me behind my back, them having sex. Of course, I had no proof of any of these scenarios, except for the fact that he had gone behind my back and admitted to calling her every day for the past year. Sometimes this was even worse than them having sex—they had built up an emotional attachment to each other. Why would he need to do this when he had me? Did I really mean that little to him?

The months and months that followed did so in a blur. I drank, used drugs, self-harmed, and attempted suicide, all while trying to make my marriage work. My marriage was never going to work again, though, because so long as I was with him my mind would constantly remind me of what I knew he had done—and even what he hadn't done but what I convinced myself was true. If there was any moment in the day when I was alone—in the shower, cleaning the house, or walking the dog—my mind would torment me. Daily tasks that I once found pleasant became things that terrified me. I couldn't be on my own, for when I was, I felt as if I was going crazy.

Ending my marriage was bittersweet. I was finally able to live my life free from my intrusive thoughts over what he did, yet I had lost my best friend and the family that I shared with him.

When we have been betrayed, we find it extremely difficult to recover from it, no matter how much we want to. Although we desperately want to go back to how things once were, our minds constantly replay what has happened back to us, again and again, and each time it is replayed in our minds, the same feelings we experienced when it first happened flood us once more. If we decide to stay with a partner and try to work through things, we typically find that we constantly remind them of what they did. We want them to hurt as we hurt, feel how we feel. There are those of us who are able to overcome the obstacles and manage to rebuild both the trust and the relationship, although it takes time and is by no means easy.

## What We Can Do

### Keep safe following the initial aftermath

Immediately after discovering that we have been betrayed, we are devastated beyond words and, unless we are in recovery, are highly likely to react impulsively without a second thought. Even those of us in recovery can find that a situation like this can cause us to behave in a completely uncontrolled manner. Our minds are taken up with what has happened, and to think rationally seems an impossibility. The most important thing we can do right now is keep safe.

We need to use distress tolerance skills immediately, as by doing this we can give ourselves time for the initial shock to sink in and prevent us from lashing out. It is also important that we are around people who can support us, rather than being alone, which is unsafe at this time. Phone a loved one and let them know (a) what has happened and (b) where you are and where you are going (to meet them if possible or someone else). Although we are desperate for answers, now is not the time to be asking for or receiving them.

### Discuss what has happened

This conversation needs to be had after we have calmed down, no matter how much we want to have it straightaway. Once we have had some time to digest what has happened, although the pain won't have lessened, we will have allowed ourselves adequate time to let our rational mind join our emotional mind. This enables us to think before reacting.

We should try and prepare ourselves mentally as much as possible prior to the conversation. We should consider what questions we will ask and what questions we won't ask. Our questions should be directed at trying to determine the facts, for example, "How long has the affair been going on?" Questions such as "Are they better in bed than me?" or "Are they better looking than me?" are not helpful. We must be aware that the conversation is going to be painful but necessary, so that we can then consider our options and decide what to do next.

If we feel safe enough, we can have this conversation with our partner in a private place. If we are unsure of how we are going to react, we should consider having someone sit in as a mediator—ideally a relationship counselor or a member of our mental health team—who can help guide the conversation. If a professional is not available to us, a supportive family member or friend can take on this role.

During the conversation we should try and listen to what our partner has to say, despite how much we want to hurl abuse at them. We should also have time to speak and explain how we feel, and to ask questions.

Once the conversation is over, we need to leave and go somewhere quiet to process everything. At the same time, it is important that we are not completely alone; we could go to a parent or friend's house and sit in a bedroom. When we feel ready, we can then talk with a supportive friend or loved one. Talking helps, as it prevents us from bottling everything up.

### Make a decision

When making a decision, it is vital that we do not do so at the height of our emotions. Decision making must come after we have calmed down, had a conversation with our partner, and then taken time to process everything. For some of us, this can take place within twenty-four hours of discovering the betrayal, for others it may take much longer.

We have two options at this point: stay and make the relationship work or walk away. Neither decision is an easy one, and the pros and cons of both need to be considered.

When making a decision we should consider the following:

1. Are there children involved?
2. If I stay, will my partner allow me access to their phone, email, social media, and so on for at least the next three to six months? This is important if trust is to be rebuilt. If they have nothing to hide, they will not mind agreeing to this.
3. If I stay, will I be able to truly forgive? The relationship will never work if in every argument that we have we bring up the betrayal.
4. Has our partner truly apologized, accepted responsibility, and vowed that it will never happen again?
5. An affair typically happens due to another root problem—will we be able to work on what that root problem is? Relationship counseling can help with this. Is our partner willing to engage in therapy?
6. We may have other questions that are important to us that we can also ask ourselves.

Write down a list of pros and cons for staying and a list of pros and cons for leaving.

### Self-care

We are particularly vulnerable following such an event, and it is vital that we look after ourselves. We should ensure that we attend any therapy sessions, practice our skills for BPD, and look after our physical health. Although this does not change what has happened, it leaves us in a stronger position and can help limit our suffering.

If we make the decision to leave, we can also follow the advice in chapter 27 for "Breakups—When Our Partner Ends the Relationship." Although it was our decision to end the relationship, it was their behavior that led to its demise.

## The Death of a Loved One

Losing someone we love dearly can devastate us and can seriously impact our BPD symptoms due to the intensity of the emotions that we feel. Unfortunately, death is part of life, and losing a loved one is something most of us will experience within our lifetime.

The overwhelming feelings of loss, loneliness, anger, and frustration, although painful, are all part of the grieving process. There are different stages to the grieving process, from denial and anger to eventually accepting what has happened. The nature of the death can also impact our feelings following it. If someone dies suddenly, commits suicide, or is murdered, the recovery process is typically far more complicated and takes a much longer time. If we have lost a loved one in this way, it is important that we seek professional help immediately rather than trying to cope with it on our own.

## Tips for How to Cope

*Allow ourselves to grieve*

Crying and feeling mixed emotions are all normal after the death of a loved one, and we should not try to fight them. It is okay to cry. We cannot put a time limit on how long we should grieve, as everyone is different. Some of us can take years to recover from the death of a loved one, and some of us never truly get over it but learn to live and cope with the pain.

*Expect good days and bad days*

There will be days when we wake up and feel as if we are finally healing, followed by days when we feel just as raw as when it first happened. This is normal and so we shouldn't feel as if we are going backward if this happens.

*Keep busy*

Keeping busy keeps our mind occupied and gives us something else to focus on. We shouldn't use this tactic to completely avoid our feelings but more to avoid just sitting with our feelings all of the time.

## *Make a memorial*

We can create a special place where we can go and either "talk" to our deceased loved one or sit and think of them. We may create an area with photos and candles, or we might prefer to go and sit somewhere we used to spend time with our loved one. Some of us might find solace in a place of worship, whereas others may find it alone in their bedroom.

## *Seek professional help*

If we feel as if we are not coping very well, we should seek professional help as soon as possible. Talking with either a bereavement counselor or our mental health team is important. We must understand that anyone can struggle with losing a loved one and even more so when we have BPD. We do not have to suffer alone and should ask for support when we are struggling.

## The Death of a Pet

Many of us find that we are closer to our pets than we are to people. Our pets love us unconditionally and are always there for a cuddle when we need one. A pet is like family to us; therefore, losing a pet can have as big an impact on us as if it had been a family member.

Unfortunately, not all people understand this, and there are some people who just assume we should "get over it." If we lose a family member, people rally around us for support—this doesn't often happen with the death of a pet.

Those of us with BPD go through life feeling very misunderstood by everyone; the relationship that we have with our pet is probably the most uncomplicated one we've ever had. So it's not surprising then that losing our "closest friend" can leave us feeling helpless, lost, and distraught.

Our grieving process will be the same as if we have lost a loved one. We must allow ourselves to grieve, expect good and bad days, keep busy, create a memorial, and seek professional help. Just because it is an animal we have lost does not make our feelings any less valid.

## Family Gatherings

Most of us can relate to the feeling of dread we have when we know there is an upcoming family gathering, be it a wedding, christening, birthday, or Christmas. There are various reasons for our trepidation in seeing our family members. For a start, many of us feel as if we are the black sheep of the family, the odd one out, misunderstood and judged. We often fear the look that we receive from our family members. The look may be one of fear, pity, or outright disgust at them having to be in our presence.

We should understand that sometimes they have a valid reason for the way they feel toward us. Perhaps our nearest and dearest have told other family members about our "episodes." While those closest to us can see past our negative behaviors, it is more difficult for more distant relatives to do so. There may have been times when we have actually had an episode in front of these family members. We know that to outsiders our outbursts can be absolutely terrifying, so surely their look of fear and apprehension when they see us is justified, as much as we hate it. The same goes for the looks of disgust. Most people can't see past our behaviors, having no idea that both our thoughts and feelings are what drive our behaviors. Rather than being offended, we need to recognize that these people are not educated when it comes to the disorder and, therefore, have no way of understanding why we behave the way that we do.

## Ways to Handle Family Gatherings

### Preempt

Prior to any family event, we should prepare ourselves mentally for it and make decisions on what we will do in certain situations. By preempting different scenarios, we can make conscious decisions before they happen, thus hopefully preventing us from acting impulsively should such a scenario occur.

### Steer the conversation

People like to talk about themselves, and we do good to bear this in mind. At any point during a gathering, if we feel we are being put on the spot and asked too many or too personal questions, we should guide the conversation back toward the person talking to us. By asking them questions about themselves, we can avoid feeling as if the pressure is on us to give answers that we do not want to give. We do not need to disclose anything to anyone if we are not comfortable doing so.

*Take a time-out*

If during a family event we experience strong emotions of any kind—be they anxiety, anger, fear, or anything else—we should excuse ourselves and go for a walk on our own in order to calm down. Perhaps someone has said something rude to us or is ignoring us completely, causing our emotions to skyrocket. By taking ourselves out of the situation we can give ourselves time to recover from the intense emotions before we return. Doing this can prevent us from acting out impulsively.

*Do not attend or only attend for a short time*

There is nothing wrong with only attending the gathering for a short amount of time. If we feel as if it is all too much, we should make our excuses and leave. There is no point in us staying on when it is causing us such distress. Nor should we even attend if we feel it will be detrimental to our mental health. There will be other family gatherings in the future when, hopefully, we will be stronger emotionally and therefore able to attend.

## Christmas

Christmas is often a time when our family gathers together, so all of the above advice is also applicable here. However, Christmas has many other difficulties that come with it as well and should therefore be discussed separately.

Christmastime has never been more commercialized than it is nowadays, and this merely adds to the pressure already associated with this time of year. Many people have fears regarding Christmas, so those of us with BPD are not alone in our feelings, although the intensity of our fears differs to that of the general population.

## Considerations Around the Holidays

### Money

Half of the world's wealth is in the hands of a mere 1 percent of the population. Most of us, however, are in the 99 percent bracket, meaning money is an issue for us. Christmas is a time of buying presents, decorations, food, and socializing, and it certainly doesn't come cheap. While there are a few people who start their Christmas shopping in January and spread it out over the year, the majority of us leave it until the months or weeks (or days!) in the run-up to the big day. We feel an immense pressure to have the "perfect" Christmas, and yet most of us cannot afford to have the Christmas that we imagine. Rather than getting ourselves into debt, we should change our expectations. We should ask ourselves, *What would my perfect day really look like?* We usually base our "perfect Christmas" on what we have seen in films or adverts, but this is just not realistic for most of us to achieve. Would our perfect day actually include beans on toast and a day lying on the sofa watching films? If this is the case, then this is what we should be aiming for, not the unrealistic vision that we see commercially.

How many of us feel the need to give the best presents even though we simply cannot afford to do so? Chances are, our family and friends feel the same way but are too embarrassed to say so. We should have this discussion with them months beforehand, telling them we cannot afford to buy everyone presents this year and for them not to buy us anything either. This will immediately reduce some of the pressure on us. If we still wish to give presents, there are plenty of ways to give meaningful yet cost-effective presents—all we have to do is look online for inspiration.

Whether it is presents, food, or socializing, we shouldn't put so much pressure on ourselves that we end up financially worse off, as this will only cause us further problems down the line.

### Feeling happy

Everyone seems to be so happy and joyous at this time of year, but sometimes we are just not feeling it, preferring to curl up in a ball and hibernate until it is all over. When feeling like this, we need to ask ourselves, *Why should I feel happy just because other people are?* We don't *have* to feel anything. If we don't want to celebrate, we do not have to. Also, recognizing the fact that we are not the only ones who feel this way can be a comfort to us.

### Drugs and alcohol

There are those of us who use drugs or alcohol to try and make ourselves feel better, and Christmastime is no exception. In fact, due to the Christmas parties, the pressure, and fear of this time of year, many of us find that we drink or use drugs more than at any other time of the year as a coping mechanism to get us through. Abusing drugs and alcohol to help us cope only ever causes us numerous other problems, and we should remind ourselves of this constantly and instead try to use healthier coping skills, such as those described in this book. If we find that everywhere we go alcohol is present and the temptation is too great, we should avoid these places when possible.

### Giving back

Often at Christmastime we can get so wrapped up in ourselves that it is easy to forget those less fortunate than ourselves. There are homeless people, elderly people with no family, and severely sick children who spend Christmas in the hospital. Although we may not feel like it, we should try, if we can, to give back where possible. We may volunteer to work in a homeless shelter during the holidays, visit the elderly who have no other company, or put together a small box of gifts to deliver to a children's hospital. There are so many different ways in which we can do something kind for someone else, and, once we have done so, we feel much better about ourselves also. We realize that so many people on our planet have their own daily struggles and that we are not alone. We start to appreciate that we can be a help to others and, in doing so, we also distract ourselves from our own daily struggles.

PART VI

# OTHER
# PERSPECTIVES

Chapter 28

# FOR FAMILIES
# AND LOVED ONES

*"When you can't look on the bright side,*
*I will sit with you in the dark."*
—From Alice In Wonderland

To My Loved Ones:
    I am writing this letter to help you understand what those of us with borderline personality disorder (BPD) go through. It is a severe mental illness, and yet describing it is often very difficult to put into words.

Studies have shown that people diagnosed with BPD actually have brains that differ from that of the general population. The part of our brain that deals with emotional responses is overactive, meaning that we are highly sensitive and our emotions are extremely intense and unstable. The prefrontal cortex is the part of the brain that is responsible for reasoning and logic. It is this part of the brain that will stop people from behaving in a certain way due to consequences. In those of us with BPD, this part of our brain is underactive—meaning we are unable to think rationally and often act out without thinking of the consequences.

I feel this is important to tell you, as so many people are misinformed regarding this disorder, with a few questioning whether BPD is even a thing, due to the fact that you cannot "see" our mental health. If you were to see inside our brain, however, you would realize that BPD is there.

I know you are probably fed up with hearing my apologies and sick and tired of the emotional roller coaster that I always seem to be on, often dragging you along for the ride, but there are a few things I need you to know.

I hate the way that I am as much as you do. For all the pain that I cause you, I am suffering ten times as much. I struggle daily with the fear that those I love are going to leave me, often desperately attempting to avoid the inevitable abandonment. I know that you think my fear is irrational—and maybe it is—but it feels so real to me.

Every day I wake up never knowing what sort of day I will have. Just like you, I wish I could live a happy life, free from the chaos that seems to follow me wherever I go. The chaos that I feel is best described as like having a beast that lives inside of me. Sometimes the beast is sleeping and it is easy to forget he is there. Even I can begin to fool myself that maybe the beast has disappeared. I never know when my beast is going to awaken, ready to wreak havoc on myself and everyone I hold dear to me—all I know is that he will awaken. Just like you, I feel as if I am walking on eggshells most of the time—except that you are walking on them as you fear me, and I walk on them as I fear my beast.

When my beast does rear its ugly head, my world is turned upside down and I lose control. I may self-harm, jump into a relationship, fight, drink, or use any of the other coping mechanisms that I have taught myself over the years. You see, to you my behaviors are simply destructive, but to me they are survival skills that I use when I don't know how to cope anymore.

To the outside world, I behave in a way that is completely unacceptable. I understand why people have this view—except that nobody knows what is going through my head or how I feel, yet these are the driving forces behind my behavior. Yes, I am highly emotional and no, I do not consider the consequences of my actions, but I know no other way to be right now. This is who I am. This is me.

When I scream at you that I hate you, it is only because I am being torn apart inside and unable to deal with the immense pain. I know

I am not a child, and yet that is exactly how I feel—as if I am a child trapped in an adult's body, being expected to live a normal "adult" life but feeling as if I am a lost and frightened child who desperately needs to be looked after and protected. But because I am not a child it is easier to walk away from me, leaving me to fend for myself.

There is help out there for people like myself with BPD. There is no cure but it can be managed. I need recovery as much as you need me to recover, but it will be much easier for me if I know that I have your love and support.

I must also tell you that recovery takes time, and there will be times when you feel as if I am going backward—I am not, it is just part of the journey. I hope there will come a time when together we can look back on the way that I was as a distant memory. I know that we can get through this and come out the other side stronger—all I ask is that you have understanding and patience. I know that my behaviors are damaging, but please know that I am not a bad person, I'm a person struggling with a disorder that I never chose to have but am choosing to learn to live with.

Lots of love,
Your Loved One with BPD

• • • • •

Family members and those who we love are often the ones who feel the full force of our intense emotions and unpredictable behavior. It seems unfair that we can so easily hurt those closest to us, smashing apart relationships to the point of seemingly no repair, and all while acting as if we don't even care. We seem cold, detached, spiteful, hurtful, manipulative, selfish, destructive, callous, and the list goes on. It is not a pretty list, and from the outside it seems to portray us perfectly accurately. Unfortunately, or perhaps fortunately, it is not as simple as "our behaviors."

Anyone who has a loved one with BPD is advised to read through at least chapters 5 through 13. These chapters look in depth at the nine traits of BPD that are listed in the DSM-IV-TR. In each of these chapters, the thoughts, feelings, and behaviors prevalent among those of us with BPD are discussed. Learning about these traits is important for family members because it helps them to understand *why* we behave the way that we do. It is not a case of "he or she behaves like that, so they must be a bad person." Loved ones need to have an understanding of the thoughts and feelings that drive the behaviors.

Many of us with BPD have driven away our loved ones and are left alone to pick up the pieces of the destruction that this disorder has left behind. If you are a loved one reading this, then we must thank you. Thank you for taking the time out to understand your loved one and to look for answers rather than walking away when the times get hard.

Within this chapter, there is advice for you on how best to live a life with a borderline loved one. The next chapter includes questions and answers that you may find useful.

## Setting Healthy Boundaries

We all have boundaries in place within our lives, often ones that are so ingrained that we do not even have to think twice about them. Boundaries could include: I don't share my toothbrush, I would not allow my next-door neighbor to come around to my house and strip naked, I would not be okay with a shop assistant coming over and grabbing my boobs. Boundaries are like rules that we have put in place for ourselves, and everyone's boundaries may differ. Perhaps Josie wouldn't mind letting the assistant grab her boobs, Rosie likes her neighbors walking around naked, and perhaps Jack just loves sharing his toothbrush ... but if we don't, then we must put certain boundaries in place. If someone crosses one of our boundaries, we react and take action to prevent it happening again.

How many family members would have boundaries such as "I will not tolerate violence" or "I will not have someone come in and smash up my home"? Now ask yourself: *How many times have I let my borderline loved one cross those boundaries? Do I not react, for fear of making the situation worse?* Maybe you don't want to react because you love the person

342

and you feel genuinely bad for them, or maybe you are scared that you will drive them away.

The problem with not having boundaries in place when it comes to those of us with BPD is that we can fall into a pattern of behaving a certain way—and when we get away with it, we feel we can do it again. When we have no consequences for our actions, there is no way for us to learn from them. This may sound confusing, as I have said previously that we do not think of the consequences before we react, and that is also true. However, if given the same consequence repeatedly, we can learn from it. It doesn't happen overnight and it may take time, but eventually it works. Not only does it work, it is actually good for us and good for you. Just as children thrive on boundaries so too can we.

If you often feel angry or resentful at your BPD loved one, chances are you haven't put boundaries in place. It is never too late to start though and the sooner you start, the quicker you will notice the positive effects.

## How to Put Boundaries in Place

How you put boundaries in place will determine how successful they will be. You need to be assertive and understand that by putting a boundary in place you are not being selfish; in fact, you are being kind to yourself and your loved one.

There are dos and don'ts when it comes to establishing boundaries:

### Do's

- Be assertive
- Discuss the boundaries with your borderline loved one at a time of calm
- Explain clearly what the boundaries are, which may include:
    1. I will not tolerate verbal or physical abuse.
    2. I will not give you money.
    3. I will not allow you to treat my home like a hotel and live here rent free.
    4. I will not be blackmailed by you.

- Stick to your boundaries

*Don'ts*
- Feel guilty about setting boundaries
- Be unclear about what the boundaries are
- Be nervous when trying to explain your boundaries or when implementing them
- Implement them some times and not at others
- Allow yourself to be persuaded to change your mind
- Be either too flexible or too rigid

When my partner first put boundaries in place, he discussed it with me at a time when I was calm. The last thing you want to do is decide on putting a boundary in place when we are in the middle of a crisis, as we will not understand why you are doing it, and we will likely see it as a form of rejection.

Here's how boundary setting worked for my partner and me. He and I had been going through a tough time, with me screaming abuse and physically attacking him on a regular basis. In these instances, he would walk out, as he did not know how to deal with me when I was like this. I would take his walking out as a sign of abandonment. I would phone him continuously, and when he didn't answer I would start sending vile, abusive text messages. I would then internalize my rage, punch walls, and self-harm. When my partner returned, either later that night or the next morning, he would walk into a scene you would expect to see in a horror movie. The flat had been trashed, blood was everywhere, and I was a heap on the floor.

This was not a one-off occurrence but a weekly one, and it got to the point where my partner did not know how much more he could take; he didn't think he could stay in a relationship with me and yet he still loved me. He felt torn and he was at the end of his tether. A few days after one of my many outbursts, when we were sitting on the sofa and watching television together, he explained to me that in order for our relationship to work he had to put some boundaries in place. I was calm at the time but can remember all of a sudden feeling as if I was on high alert, my heart rate increased and my leg started shaking, but I listened.

*"I love you and I want our relationship to work,"* he began.

If you are a family member, by telling your loved one that you love them before you start explaining what boundaries you are putting in place, you are preventing them from feeling attacked and vilified.

*"When you start throwing accusations at me I find it really difficult to stay calm, and I am likely to say something I don't mean in retaliation."*

It is important that you explain *why* you are putting the boundaries in place. You may explain it is for their well-being as well as your own.

*"I think it is important that we have some boundaries."*

By saying "we" have some boundaries, as opposed to "I" have some boundaries for "you," your loved one will not feel as if they are being attacked.

*"Next time you start accusing me of something, I am going to tell you that I love you but I need a time-out. I will then leave. When I leave, it is not me breaking up with you or me abandoning you in any way. I will come back. I just need some space, and I think it will be good for both of us in the long term."*

By explaining it in this way you are not pointing fingers or blaming your loved one in any way, and you are making it clear that you love them and are not leaving them.

Then comes the action. Next time your loved one starts behaving in a way that you find difficult, simply tell them you love them and you need some space and will be back later. Then leave.

When my partner first did exactly as he said he would do, I did not accept it at all, even though we had discussed it beforehand and I had told him I understood. Discussing boundaries and having a boundary implemented are very different. I kicked, I screamed, and I threw every single toy out of my pram. I chased after him hurling abuse, and then I came back in the house and started text messaging him, telling him he had better get home now or he would regret it. He did not respond. I was absolutely furious, even though he had said that he loved me and would be back. It must be remembered that my prefrontal cortex was not working at this point—I was unable to think rationally. An hour later, I had calmed down and was able to process what had happened. Half an hour later my partner came home, and although I was calmer I still chose to not talk to him as punishment. I am sure he was relieved, as previously I would still have been raging when he returned.

The next time I started an argument and he could see where it was heading, he did exactly the same thing and left. Yet again I was angry and I hurled some abuse at him, but this time I didn't chase him all the way to the car. I still messaged him, but not as many times as I would do usually. When he returned, I was calm and my sulking did not go on for as long as the previous time.

My partner implemented this boundary every time he felt the need, and each time he did it the easier it became for me. It got to the point where I no longer hurled abuse or sent messages. I think the change happened as I learned that he would return; I no longer had the fear that he wouldn't. I was also able to calm down a lot more quickly, as I no longer had him there to feed my anger.

Another thing to consider when setting boundaries is discussing them with other close family members. There are times when you may want to set a boundary but another close family member doesn't agree with it. The problem arises if your BPD loved one crosses the boundary and is allowed to get away with it by the other family member.

For example, take a couple who has a son with BPD who keeps stealing money from them. The dad decides enough is enough, and the next time it happens the son will have to leave; but the mom does not agree, and when the son next steals money she lets him stay. The boundary has proven to be pointless. If the mom and dad first had a discussion together about certain boundaries and consequences, they may come to a decision beforehand that they both agree with.

## When Your Loved One Keeps Crossing Boundaries

It is borderline personality disorder we are talking about here—and boundaries are bound to be crossed. When this happens, you get to decide the consequences, and there needs to be consequences if you wish to protect yourself.

As tough as it may sound, there may come a time when you have to distance yourself from your loved one. While this is not an outcome that is wanted by either side, it may be the necessary course of action. You may explain to your loved one that although you love them, you can no longer tolerate their behavior, and, therefore, you need to distance yourself from them until changes are made. Although this may seem cruel, you are, in fact, being assertive and protecting yourself; you are not enabling them to continue as they are, and this could be the push your loved one needs to seek help.

## Verbal and Physical Abuse

When we think of "abuse" we often imagine someone screaming and shouting or physically attacking another person. Abuse can come in many forms, however, and not one of them is acceptable or should be tolerated.

Due to the nature of BPD, we can often behave in an abusive way. Whether we do it on purpose or do not truly mean to do it, it is still unacceptable.

Types of abuse that you may experience at the hands of your loved one include:

*Psychological*
1. Intimidation
2. Blaming
3. Humiliation
4. Controlling
5. Threats (this can be threats to you or threats to ourselves)
6. Coercion
7. Harassment

*Financial*
1. Theft
2. Misuse of your possessions

3. Damage to your property
4. Fraud

*Physical*

1. Physically restraining you to stop you from leaving, calling for help, and so on
2. Slapping, hitting, punching, kicking, biting, and the like
3. Assault

Sometimes abuse is blatantly obvious and at other times is it subtle, but either way abuse is abuse and must be stopped.

It is true that those of us with BPD do not intentionally mean to manipulate or cause the amount of pain that we do. Internally we are suffering and are so overwhelmed by our feelings that we lash out impulsively, often hurting our nearest and dearest. The fact that we do hurt those close to us often causes us even more pain. We do not like how we behave, and the guilt and shame that we carry around following an outburst is intense, causing us further suffering. Until we learn how to manage our emotions, to tolerate distress, and implement new coping strategies, it is highly likely that we will continue to cause harms along the way.

While you as a family member may try desperately to tell yourself, *It is the illness causing them to behave like this*, unless something is done to stop their behaviors, you will continue to get hurt. Although it is important to recognize that it is the disorder that is behind our behaviors, it cannot be an excuse for the behaviors to continue unchallenged.

You may find that you are walking on eggshells around your loved one, which is certainly no way for anyone to live their life. If you are suffering any form of abuse, it is vital that you take action to stop it. Putting boundaries in place is imperative to help achieve this. Of course, there may still be some of us who either continue to push boundaries or outright cross them, and when this happens you need to continue to enforce the consequences. The type of abuse you are suffering will determine your course of action. If you are being violently attacked or you fear for your safety, call the police. No, we will not appreciate it, but neither should you put up with this treatment.

## Do Not Blame Yourself

When reading about borderline personality disorder, you will discover that a high percentage of those with it have suffered some form of abuse, loss, or neglect at some point in their lives. It is very easy for family members to start asking themselves, *Is this my fault? Where did I go wrong?*

You must understand that while BPD can be caused by certain events in a person's life, there are those of us with BPD who never suffered in our childhood and some of us who suffered "perceived" trauma. For example, maybe a parent needed to work away from home a lot in order to pay the bills. The child may have perceived that as abandonment because they were too young to comprehend the complexity of the situation.

Divorce and death are two more types of trauma that a child may experience that can bring on BPD, so experiencing trauma isn't as simple as a parent outright causing harm or damage to their child. Of course, there are some of us who have suffered abuse or neglect at the hands of our caregivers, but the issue can be more complex that it first seems. Perhaps a caregiver suffered with their own mental health, maybe they never realized that their actions were causing harm, or they may have been unaware that the child was being abused by someone else and was unable to protect them.

It is believed that multiple factors are involved in someone developing BPD. While environmental factors are included, so are genetics, brain chemicals, and brain development.

If you are a family member who is reading this, chances are you are doing so because you want to understand and help your BPD loved one. The fact that you are reading this is proof that you care. There is no point in constantly beating yourself up about the past, blaming yourself, questioning everything, or feeling guilty. These things cannot change the fact that your loved one has BPD, nor will it help yourself or them to hold on to these feelings. You very much need to focus on the present moment and leave the past where it is—behind you. Guilt, shame, and regret serve no purpose, and they need to be let go. These feelings can actually prevent you from:

1.  Accepting that your loved one has BPD—you may not want to accept it, perhaps because you believe it is your fault
2.  Meeting with professionals, because you think they will blame you and you are embarrassed
3.  Having a close relationship with your loved one, as you feel too guilty or embarrassed about their diagnosis

Understand that you are not alone in your feelings. There are many family members out there questioning the disorder is their fault, and most never find out what the actual cause is. Not even scientists can tell you for sure what the cause is, so stop blaming yourself and instead invest that energy into looking after yourself and being there for your BPD loved one.

**Looking After Yourself**

Borderline personality disorder affects the whole family, but so often everyone concentrates solely on the person with the diagnosis, and they forget to take care of themselves.

Many family members neglect themselves completely. They feel so embarrassed and ashamed of their loved one's behaviors that they cut themselves off from other people—you do not want to hear anyone speaking badly of them. Although you may hate your loved one's behaviors, you still love them. Maybe you fear others will judge you for standing by your loved one and so you decide to isolate instead.

Family members can spend years worrying that one day they will get a call saying their loved one has committed suicide, self-harmed, or drove drunk and been arrested. The list of consequences for our behaviors is long, and family members can live in fear of them, more than we do ourselves. We are too caught up in emotions to consider the consequences of our actions, but for a loved one watching us our behaviors are terrifying.

I don't think my own mother had a good night's sleep or ate properly in more than ten years due to worry. Lack of sleep, food, and the company of others is a recipe for disaster, making everything feel a million times harder. Self-care is vital. You need to remain as physically and mentally well as possible, as this will ensure that your inner strength will get you through the dark times.

When considering self-care, you may ask yourself the following questions:

### Do I have a support network?

Having a loved one with BPD can make life extremely stressful, and it is easy for family members to think that they have to deal with the stress all on their own. The truth is, by trying to cope with absolutely no support you are leaving yourself vulnerable and actually making things harder for yourself. It is important that you see friends or family regularly; although you may not want to discuss your circumstances with everyone, you should have at least one person with whom you can talk openly and honestly.

Family members often get forgotten when borderline personality disorder is in the picture, and they can feel as if they have nobody to turn to. Just like those of us with BPD, you too are not alone. There are so many loved ones out there, struggling just as you are, feeling just as you are.

A support network does not only need to be people who are already in your circle of friends. Finding others in a similar situation to yourself online is also helpful. There are online communities for family members that you can join. The site www.bpdtribe.com has a section that is specifically for family members and loved ones, offering you not only the chance to be part of a safe community but also online courses that focus on the healing of yourself, rather than your BPD loved one, who has their own separate section and courses.

Having someone with BPD in your life can also cause problems such as depression or anxiety. Loved ones often think it is only the

351

person with BPD who needs professional help when, in fact, you may benefit from having some professional counseling; you too can benefit from discussing your feelings and receiving some nonjudgmental advice.

### Do I eat regular and healthy meals?

When we are stressed, it is so easy to just not eat, or to comfort eat, both of which can have an impact on our physical and mental well-being. The type of food you eat will also have an effect on you, so it is worth having a look at your diet and eat as healthily as you can.

### Do I get enough sleep?

Lack of sleep can make everything seem ten times worse than it is. When we are tired, we simply cannot function properly. Family members often struggle with their sleep due to stress and worry. If you are one of those who struggles to sleep, there are a few things you can do:

1. Wind down before bed: have a warm drink (not one with caffeine in it), try and not look at your phone for at least thirty minutes before bed, read a book, and relax.
2. If you lie in bed unable to fall asleep, rather than just lying there and trying unsuccessfully to fall asleep, get up and go through your bedtime wind-down routine again for half an hour, and then get back into bed.
3. Put a lavender scent on your pillow, which has a relaxing effect.
4. If you are still struggling it may be worth speaking with your doctor, as sleeping pills may be a short-term answer to help you get back into a good sleeping pattern.

### If I am ill, do I make time to see a doctor if necessary?

You may find that you concentrate so much on your BPD loved one, that you completely neglect your own health. If you are feeling poorly, see a doctor. Your health is as important as your loved one's.

### Do I have boundaries in place?

If you have yet to put boundaries in place, you may find that you struggle with a range of emotions, from fear and anxiety to resentment and rage. When putting boundaries into place it is you who decides what those boundaries are. Only you know how much you can take and what you are willing or not willing to put up with.

### *Do I get time to myself to switch off or do things I enjoy?*

Many of us can relate to just "getting through the day," with no fun, no laughter, and no time for ourselves. Family members can often find that they spend all of their time either working to pay bills, running around after (or tiptoeing around) their loved one, or dealing with a personal crisis. Life becomes worse than dull—it becomes positively painful.

Bills need to be paid and your loved one may need support, but where does that leave you? Where do you come on your list of priorities? Are you right at the bottom of that list, or aren't you on it at all?

For your own mental well-being, it is vital that you take time for yourself. This could include seeing friends, taking up a hobby, relaxing on your own, or having a short break away. Not only should you make sure you get time for yourself, but you should also not feel guilty about doing so. You deserve to be happy, and you can still be supportive while being kind to yourself at the same time. Having time out and taking time to breathe enables you to come back feeling emotionally stronger and less drained.

If your loved one tries to make you feel guilty, kindly explain to them that although you love them dearly, you also need a break to look after yourself. Explain that you will be returning and you are not leaving them forever. Those of us with BPD have a strong fear of abandonment, and having a loved one leave the house can cause us to panic. This does not mean that you should therefore stay in—quite the contrary. By "leaving" us and then returning regularly, over time we can adjust and learn that just because you go out somewhere does not mean that you are abandoning us.

### *Am I able to stay on top of things—work, paying bills, and the like?*

If your BPD loved one struggles to function on a day-to-day basis, chances are your days are also affected. Perhaps you can't work as often as you like or your life becomes chaotic and unorganized. Financial worries can hugely impact your mental health, causing anxiety, stress, or depression. It is therefore important that you do what you can to stay on top of your finances, including opening bills that come through the door and dealing with them, working if possible, not lending your BPD loved one large amounts of money, and, if you live in an area that offers some type of caregivers' allowance, looking into it and seeing if you are entitled to anything.

*Could I do with some professional help?*

There may come a point when you feel as if you are struggling to cope, and if you do find yourself in this position, please know that you are not alone. While your BPD loved one may be able to access help from their mental health team, family members can feel as if they have no support. Due to the fact that they are not the ones with a psychological disorder, family members can be under the impression that help is not available for them. Depending on where you live, you may have a word with your doctor and ask if they can refer you for some counseling. If you live in an area where the cost of counseling is too high, you should consider joining an online community of family members in the same situation as yourself. The bpd tribe (www.bpdtribe.com) has a section especially for people like yourself. You can connect with others in a similar position and sign up for online courses aimed specifically at family members and partners. Also see the Resource section at the end of this book.

*Am I neglecting other close relationships?*

It is understandable that you love your BPD family member, but this should not compromise your other relationships. This can have a detrimental effect on the whole family, with others growing resentful and angry. Family members need to come together and support one another, rather than cutting each other out. It is important that you make time for the other relationships in your life and let them grow and thrive, as opposed to neglecting them. Not only will your other family members and friends be grateful and happy, you will too—and you will not have to suffer the guilt of not giving them enough time.

## Dealing with a Crisis

Being witness to one of our "episodes" can be scary and leave you feeling helpless, angry, frightened, and a whole host of other feelings. How you deal with the crisis can make all the difference in the outcome of the situation.

### *Notice the Warning Signs*

In an ideal world, you would be able to spot the warning signs prior to a crisis and be able to avoid it altogether. By paying close attention to your loved one, you may start to notice changes in their behavior. Changes may include:

1. Isolating
2. Change in eating habits
3. Drinking, using drugs, or other reckless behaviors
4. Self-harming
5. Threatening to commit suicide

All these behaviors are our way of trying to cope with our intense emotions. If we are "acting out" in these ways, it suggests that something is going on for us that we are unable to verbalize. If you notice any of these behaviors, there are a couple of things you can do:

1. Talk to your loved one. Often, those with BPD do not know how to communicate feelings in a healthy way. Some family members feel too nervous to bring up the topic in case it pushes their loved one over the edge, when in fact it can have the opposite effect. We struggle to verbalize how we are feeling, and this is what leads to our destructive behaviors. If you ask your BPD loved one questions and talk to them about how they are feeling, they may feel better able to express those feelings.

2. Talk with your loved one's doctor or therapist. If your loved one is over the age of eighteen, then all of their medical records are private, unless they have given their consent for you to access

them. You can, however, phone their doctor or therapist and talk about any concerns that you have.

### Stay Calm

Staying calm is extremely important, especially when your loved one is anything but calm. The fact that they are having a crisis means that their emotions are running extremely high, and the rational part of their brain has shut down. If you are to scream and shout at them, the problem will only escalate to magnitude proportions.

### Don't Take It Personally

Your loved one with BPD may hurl abuse at you and blame you for things that are simply not reality. When this happens, the immediate reaction would be for you to become defensive, which is completely un-derstandable. The problem with this is that, when you become defensive, your loved one takes it to mean that you are questioning whether their feelings are valid. Now, the truth more often than not is that they are wrong, they have taken something the wrong way, and they are being completely irrational, but now is not the time to tell them this. Rather than focusing on what they are saying, try instead to focus on the feel-ings that they are trying to express. Remember that their emotions are so intense that they are often unable to verbalize them in a constructive way.

### Listen and Show Empathy

Trust that your loved is as frustrated at themselves as you are of them. As their emotions flood through them, they feel desperate to let them out, often in a huge dramatic outburst. If you argue back with them, they are unable to feel that they are being heard, and this can make the situation worse. The louder you get, the louder they will get. It is important that you let your loved one express their feelings, no matter how irrational the words are that are coming out of their mouth. If they are unable to express themself with their words, the chances are high that they will act on them instead. To ensure that they feel both heard and validated, you need to listen to what they say. You may nod along to show them that you are listening or say things such as, "I understand what you are saying." Saying that you understand does not mean you agree with what they are saying—because more often than not you won't—but, as mentioned before, now is not the time for your loved one with BPD to hear that.

### Distract

Distraction techniques are skills that those of us with BPD should learn to help us in times of distress. Not all of us have yet had treatment, however, and those of us who have may still not be completely capable of putting the skills into action when we need them. Learning these skills to the point that they become ingrained in us takes time and practice. Family members can help their loved one use distraction as a way of calming themself when they are having an episode. You may ask your loved one to go for a walk, have a cup of tea, go shopping, do some gardening, or put away some washing, among other things. By distracting them, you are buying them time during which their intense emotions can start to lessen, and they can begin to think more clearly and behave less recklessly.

### Walk Away

If you feel that you have tried all of the above and your loved one is still not calming down, you can walk away—only you know how much you are willing to take. If you do this, you should let your person know that you will talk to them when they are calm. This way, they are not left feeling that you have walked away, never to return, which is what their mind will tell them due to their fear of abandonment.

## Living with Someone with BPD

Once those of us with BPD can accept that we have borderline personality disorder and that the problems in our relationships are caused due to our intense emotions and our perception of the world around us, we can accept that it must be extremely difficult to live with us. It probably won't make you feel any better, but we find living with ourselves difficult too.

There is certainly no magic wand that you can wave to make life with your BPD person easier, but there are certain things you can do that will help.

### Educate Yourself About BPD

The more you learn about this disorder, the more you will understand your loved one. Those of us with BPD spend our whole lives feeling misunderstood, and the reason that we feel this way is because we are. It isn't just our loved ones who don't understand us; until we learn about the disorder, we too do not understand why we behave the way that we do. When you understand the underlying causes of your loved one's behaviors, you can begin to see them not as bad people but people who are fighting an internal battle.

### Communicate

More often than not your loved one is unable to put their feelings into words. By talking with them regularly you can assist them in trying to verbalize their feelings. Likewise, if you also discuss your feelings with them, you are demonstrating that it is okay for people to talk about their feelings. It is also good for your loved one to be able to listen to someone else's problems and try to be of service to them; it is a distraction from their own problems, and helping others is a way of building their self-esteem rather than feeling worthless and of no use to anyone.

### Know That It's Not All About the BPD

Those of us with BPD can often feel as if our whole life revolves around the disorder, especially when we are going through less-functioning times or we are newly into recovery. Although discussing our BPD symptoms, how we are feeling, and our recovery is a positive thing, it is important to not make it the only thing that everyone focuses on. We have to live with our brains 24/7, and sometimes we just need a break.

Having conversations that have absolutely nothing to do with BPD is a must. Talk to your loved one about your day, plans for the weekend, or a funny story you've been told. Try to spend some quality time with them having fun. Watching a movie, taking a shopping trip, going for a coffee, or spending a day at an amusement park are all fun activities that can keep us distracted and allow us time to laugh rather than being left alone with our thoughts.

If your BPD loved one has a favorite hobby, then maybe you could make time to enjoy doing it with them. Not only are these fun things to do, but they can also help you bond and enable your relationship to grow.

### Get Involved in Your Loved One's Recovery

Recovery takes time and effort; it is certainly no walk in the park. Having your loved one with BPD have their loved ones supporting them during the process makes recovery feel much less daunting and more achievable.

So many of us have absolutely no support during the recovery process, and while it is still possible to recover, it is likely that we will have more ups and downs along the way. The whole process will take longer for us to get to where we want to be without support.

If you have a loved one with BPD, please support them as best as you can. Supporting them can include a whole host of things, including the things mentioned above, such as communication, learning about the disorder, and watching for warning signs. There are also other ways that you can help.

### Understand the Recovery Process

There will be times when you think you are helping your BPD person, such as telling them how amazing they are doing and that they can now start planning their wonderful future. You may even suggest things for them to do, such as sign up for a college course or apply for the job they have always wanted. Of course, when you say such things, your best intentions are meant; however, these are the types of comments that can backfire. You must remember that one of the core BPD traits is fear of abandonment.

When we start recovering, while it is a wonderful thing, it is also very daunting. Having family members encouraging us can almost feel as if we are being pushed into an independence that we just are not ready for. When we feel this way, the fear may cause us to "relapse"— just so we can feel that we have our loved ones rallying around us again.

None of us want to spend time in a mental health ward; yet, so often this is where we can end up after we were seemingly doing so well. To be looked after again and have our family members reminded that we are ill can be a comfort to us, especially when we feel that they have "forgotten" that we have BPD. When family members push us to better ourselves, this can lead to us thinking that they are trying to "abandon" us, so that they do not have to look after us anymore. Of course, this is not the case at all, but, unfortunately, the BPD mind sees things differently than other people's.

Recovery must be taken at your loved one's own pace, step by step. Big life changes, such as starting a college course or a new job, is not advised, as those with BPD are often are just setting themselves up for failure and can be left feeling worse than they did before. If your BPD loved one suggests doing such a thing, you should explain that, while it is a great idea and something they should consider in the future, for the meantime they should just take each day as it comes and focus on their recovery.

There will be times when your loved one seems to be doing so well, only for them to relapse back to their old ways. You can be left feeling as if they are back where they started; while it can appear that way, it is certainly not the case. Steps backward are a part of the recovery process. It must be understood that many of your loved one's unhelpful and destructive behaviors have been their way of surviving for years. These old behaviors are so deeply ingrained in them that they do them unconsciously a lot of the time.

Recovery involves learning new, helpful coping skills to replace the old behaviors, but it doesn't happen overnight. The more your BPD person practices new skills, the more likely they will be used in a time of crisis.

As explained in chapter 2 in the section titled "Neural Pathways," every time any of us do something new, a new neural pathway is formed. The more we repeat that action the stronger the neural pathway becomes. Previously, if every time your loved one felt a strong emotion they self-harmed, they built a neural pathway connecting that strong emotion and behavior. Next time they have a strong emotion they will automatically self-harm. Recovery involves learning new skills and thus growing new neural pathways. Keep in mind that, for a while, the old neural pathway is going to be a lot stronger than the new one. It takes time and practice for the new neural pathway to grow stronger and the old one to weaken and finally disappear.

### Discuss Therapy

You can take an interest in what your loved one is learning in their therapy group. If you are able to discuss with your loved one what they have learned, it helps to instill the lesson. You may encourage your loved one to explain the new skills they have learned; ask them which ones they believe will be helpful.

Once you know the types of skills they are learning, you may encourage them to actively practice some. You might suggest going for a walk or having a relaxing bath.

Mindfulness is a core skill taught in DBT, but it isn't necessarily the easiest skill to learn. Many struggle with it to begin with, not really understanding how to do it or simply not being able to quieten the mind enough to be able to do it. You can help by having conversations with your BPD person about mindfulness. Perhaps you and your loved one could try a mindfulness activity together and then each discuss your experiences afterward. Remember, the more they practice it, the easier it becomes—but it takes time and patience. Mindfulness is a useful skill for anyone to have, so you too will learn something beneficial from practicing it.

It must be added that any of the new skills your loved one learns can benefit you as well. Even if you do not necessarily struggle with intense and dysregulated emotions, everyone struggles at times. Wouldn't it be lovely if we all had a tool box full of coping mechanisms for times of stress or upset? Family members know all about stress and upset, so it wouldn't hurt for you too to arm yourself with some of the skills mentioned in this book—you might just find that you use them a lot more than you thought you would.

Chapter 29

# QUESTIONS
# AND ANSWERS

*"Happiness can be found,*
*even in the darkest of times,*
*if one only remembers to turn on the light."*
—Albus Dumbledore

Here are some questions commonly asked about BPD—plus my answers.

### Questions from Family Members

Q. My girlfriend, who has BPD, and I have been together for four years. Her BPD is untreated and we had been rowing recently. One day I came home from work and she had left. I texted her and she replied that she is seeing someone else now. I am devastated. Did she ever love me at all?

A. It is impossible for me to give you a definitive answer, as I cannot speak on behalf of your girlfriend. I personally would say that, yes, of course, she loved you. Just because our emotions are so intense and unstable it does not mean that we are incapable of love. It sounds as if she was struggling emotionally, causing arguments between you. Those of us with BPD have a fear of abandonment, and perhaps she felt that you were going to abandon her due to the fact that you had been arguing; therefore, she decided to leave first. By jumping into a new relationship she is trying to "fix" herself and distract herself from the pain she is feeling. Unfortunately, unless the BPD is treated these behaviors are likely to continue.

Q. My daughter has BPD and she has cut me out her life. She used to live here with her three-year-old son, but tensions have been growing between us, and last week she hooked up with some man (who is recently out of prison) and taken my grandson to live with him. She has cut off all contact from me, and I am so worried about them I don't know what to do.

A. Those of us with BPD can behave in a reckless fashion, jumping into relationships and cutting people out of our lives if they have upset us in any way. What you can do very much depends on the circumstances. Mainly, do you think your daughter is a danger to herself or your grandson? Or do you think this new man is a danger to either of them? If you believe that yes, they are in danger, then you must take action. Your daughter may not appreciate it, but you can call social services and explain the situation to them and get some advice. Of course, the problem with doing this is that your daughter may not speak to you again, but your number-one priority must be your grandson and doing what is best for him. You did not mention what this man was in prison for, and therefore it is hard to know whether he poses a risk. Another option, if you do not believe them to be at risk, is to write her a letter explaining that you love her and are worried about her and that you will be there for her when she needs you. She may or may not respond, but at least you have reached out to her.

Q. My twenty-five-year-old son has BPD and lives at home. He lives here rent-free, treats myself and his dad like dirt, and refuses to go to the doctor to get help. He was diagnosed when he was nineteen, and the years before and after his diagnosis have been a living hell. He steals money off us, comes and goes as he pleases, sometimes not coming home for days and leaving us desperate with worry. Then he turns back up at home without any explanation for his disappearance. I love my son but am sick and tired of living like this. Any advice?

A. I can hear both your resentment and anger through your letter, as well as the fact that you feel torn—you love your son but you hate his behaviors. I think it is time you and your husband have a discussion about boundaries. Start thinking about what you are no longer willing to put up with. Stealing? Not coming home after a certain time? This is your home and you must remember that. You have every right to feel safe in your own home. Your son needs to have consequences for his actions. You should sit down and explain to him the specific things you are no longer willing to tolerate. It might be that you decide if he continues to behave in this way then he must move out. If you decide this is the consequence, you must stick with it, otherwise he will then know you do not follow through with your threats. If you sit back and do nothing, you are actually enabling your son to carry on as he is. He needs to learn to take responsibility for his actions, and it is you who can teach him this valuable lesson. Hopefully, as life is made more difficult for him to carry on as he has, he may decide to seek professional help.

Q. I think my sister has BPD. I have read up on the disorder and she literally has every trait. She makes both my life and my mum's life a misery. Nobody else in the family wants to know her, and if we try to talk to them about her they tell us we should just cut her out of our lives. We are getting to the point where we just don't know what to do anymore. I mentioned to her that she might have BPD and she went mental on me, and I haven't been able to talk to her since. How can we persuade her to see a doctor?

A. Unfortunately, unless she is a danger to either herself or others, there is very little you can do. If the next time she is with you or your mum, and you believe that she is a threat to either of you or herself, you may call an ambulance. If she does have BPD, life will get continually more painful for her. Often it takes for us to hit rock bottom before we realize that we need help. If we are at a point of denial and believe that it is everyone else who is the problem, rather than ourselves, we are unlikely to take kindly to people telling us that we may have a mental health illness. The chances are high that we will take this as an insult on our character and lash out.

Q. My best-friend has BPD and I never know what mood she will be in when I see her. We've been best friends since school. I love her dearly but can't deal with her biting my head off for any little thing. All of our other friends refuse to hang around with her anymore, so she only has me. She wants to spend every single day together, and if I tell her I'm busy she stops talking to me for days. I feel like ending the friendship but am scared of what she will do, as she doesn't have anyone else.

A. I would suggest you learn as much as you can about BPD in order to understand your friend a bit more. Up and down moods are common, as is taking what people say personally and interpreting things the wrong way. The fact that she has nobody else is the reason she has become so clingy with you. It sounds as if she is going through a stage of idealizing you and then devaluing you. I think you need to sit and talk with her about your feelings at a time when she is calm. Explain that she means a lot to you but sometimes you need to do other things—and that it doesn't mean that you are abandoning her. You shouldn't be made to feel as if you are walking on eggshells around her. If you feel that she is in one of her bad moods, you could perhaps talk to her about how she is feeling. If she is able to verbalize her feelings, her mood may lift. If she is not willing to talk, there is very little you can do except look after yourself. That might mean having some time apart so that you can focus on yourself.

Q. My wife and I have been together for more than twenty-five years and have three teenage children together. She has untreated BPD (she refuses treatment). She left me last weekend for another man (this isn't the first time she has done this, and she always comes back). I don't know what to tell the kids or whether I should let her come back when she eventually decides to. What should I do?

A. The problem is that, every time she has done this, you have allowed her to come back home. There have been no consequences for her actions. If you allow her home this time, I am pretty sure it will happen again. You need to focus on your own well-being and that of your children. This is not teaching them how a healthy relationship should be. The fact that your wife refuses help means that nothing is likely to change for the better. You need to be strong now for the sake of your kids. Perhaps by giving your wife consequences for her actions she may actually realize she needs to get help. If she does this then maybe one day in the future you could consider rebuilding your relationship, but, until then, you first need to heal from the hurt that you have been put through.

Q. The mother of my child has BPD, and she has made false accusations against me to prevent me from seeing my son. Is this a BPD thing?

A. I wouldn't necessarily say it is a BPD thing, although it certainly could be. Those of us with BPD can find ourselves lashing out at those around us due to a number of our traits, including low self-esteem, intense rage and fear of abandonment. Until she becomes self-aware I doubt this behavior will stop. To be honest, she probably doesn't even think she is doing anything wrong. It always makes me sad when mothers try to stop their children from seeing their dad—especially when the dad is a loving one who has done nothing wrong. I have a friend who has twin daughters, and their mother also did this many years ago. She not only made up allegations against the dad but brainwashed the girls into believing all these awful things about him. The poor guy hasn't seen his daughters in years; it is such a shame because he is the nicest man, and those girls have missed out on having a wonderful father in their lives who loves them so much. Hopefully one day they will learn the truth about their mother. I suggest you fight the allegations as much as you can to prove your innocence, and I hope your son gets reunited with you very soon.

Q. My girlfriend always makes me out to be the worst partner in the world when she talks to her friends. Why does she do this when she then comes home and acts as if nothing is wrong?

A. I would say this is her thinking in black and white. When we do this, we only see things as all good or all bad. You can do one thing wrong and become the world's worst person, unfortunately. It isn't until those of us with BPD begin to recover that we can start questioning our black-and-white thinking and recognizing the gray area.

## Questions from Those of Us with BPD

Q. I have never been able to hold down a job and have gotten to the point where it is really getting me down. Will I ever be able to work? Can people with BPD have a good career?

A. Of course, we can have a wonderful career—eventually. When our BPD is unmanaged, life in general is difficult for us, especially when it comes to work. With the right treatment, however, we can learn to manage the BPD and go on to have a successful career. If you have the option of being able to focus solely on your recovery for now, it is worth doing so. If it is not an option, then still try to fit in recovery whenever you can.

Q. None of my friends want to know me. They think I am too clingy and argumentative, and they have all cut me out their lives. What shall I do?

A. Sometimes it is good for us to put ourselves in other people's shoes. It sounds as if your friends have gotten to a point where they have had enough. They have distanced themselves as a way of protecting themselves from being hurt. You haven't mentioned if they know you have BPD or if they understand BPD. For now, it is probably wise to give them some time and space; you should focus on your recovery. You could, at a later date, write them a letter explaining how you feel and say you are sorry that they feel the way that they do. If you do this, please bear in mind that they may not respond. Sometimes people are too hurt, and we must accept this.

Q. My children live with my mum. She doesn't want me to see them, as she says it is too upsetting for them. But they are *my* children. What should I do?

A. I feel for you, but I would say your mum is probably only trying to protect your children at this time. Use this time to focus on yourself and on getting well. And be thankful that your children are being well looked after. I think in time, when your mum sees you making an effort with your recovery, she will be more than happy to welcome you back into her house to be with your children. Just give it time and patience.

Q. I broke up with my boyfriend a year ago but still can't stop thinking about him, even though I am with someone else now. Should I make contact with my ex?

A. It sounds as if you are looking back on your old relationship and seeing it as "perfect," but there was a time when you didn't see it this way or you wouldn't have ended it. This could be you thinking in black and white. I don't think that any good can come from contacting your ex. Chances are, he has long dealt with the breakup and has moved on. You too are now in a relationship, and to contact your ex would only cause harm to your new partner. Rather than focusing on the past or looking into the future, try to focus on the here and now—and your recovery.

Q. I do not get on with my therapist. She talks to me, and then my mum comes in the room, and my therapist makes up things that I have said and twists my words to make me look like a bad person. What should I do?

A. Having a good relationship with your therapist is important, and it certainly sounds as if you do not feel happy with the relationship. If it were me, I would ask my therapist, "Why do you do this?" When she explains it, you may realize that you have perceived what she said to be different to what was actually said. If you still find you are struggling to build trust with her, you could always change therapists. But maybe you just need to start again with this one and hopefully your trust in her will grow.

Q. I do not agree with taking medication—do you think spiritual healing could help me?

A. I personally think there is a lot to be said for spirituality and alternative medicines. I suppose, like with everything, it is trial and error—it doesn't hurt to try it, so long as it is safe. Worst-case scenario is that it doesn't work, then you are no worse off.

Q. I have vague recollections of some kind of abuse when I was younger, but then I think maybe I am making it up in my head. What do you think?

A. The brain is an amazing mechanism—and, yes, it can "forget" traumatic events. I personally have struggled with this. Perhaps my mind is trying desperately trying to "fill in the blanks," even if the "memories" are in fact a figment of my imagination. I have found it so much easier to stop "trying" to remember stuff and instead to focus on the present moment. Some people have "regression" to help them remember things from their past. This was something I was all set to do, but when my daughter came along, I decided I would rather focus on her than open up possible old wounds.

Q. Why do lots of women with BPD tend to get with men who are narcissists?

A. I think this is very much because each of the disorders can feed off each other. BPD women are often vulnerable, and this can make a male narcissist feel powerful. A BPD woman can see a narcissist male as strong and someone who can protect them. This could also stem from unhealthy attachments formed in childhood.

Q. Where I live there is absolutely no therapy for people with BPD. No DBT, nothing. What can I do?

A. It is a sad fact that treatment for BPD isn't widely available everywhere. Luckily, we do live in the age of the Internet, and there is so much information readily available on there. A colleague and I have started the website www.bpdtribe.com. On there we are building a community of people who suffer with BPD and also a community for our family members. The site offers videos and online courses. Just because there is no therapy where you are does not mean you cannot recover.

Q. I am sure I have BPD, but I was assessed and diagnosed with depression. What can I do now?

A. Unfortunately, a lot of people are misdiagnosed, at least to start with. Chances are, you do have depression, but you can also have BPD.

I would suggest going back to your mental health team and asking them why they do not believe you have BPD. You may then explain your reasons for believing that you do have it. Only through communication will you get some answers.

Q. I can't stop picking my skin to bits until it bleeds. Is this a BPD trait?

A. No, this isn't a BPD trait, but I have come across a lot of people with BPD who suffer with this, myself included. I believe the name is trichotillomania, an anxiety disorder that involves picking skin, hair, scalp, and the like. If you think you suffer with this, it's worth speaking with your mental health team about it. You may be able to take part in a group that teaches skills for overcoming anxiety.

Q. When should I tell a new partner about my BPD?

A. There is no right or wrong answer here, but I would suggest not too soon and don't leave it too late. Maybe after a week? For some people that sounds very soon, but those of us with BPD move quickly, and we do not want to leave it until it rears its ugly head, without us explaining beforehand.

Q. I think I have BPD—what should I do?

A. Go to your GP (family doctor) and ask to be referred to a mental health team for an assessment. A GP cannot usually diagnose BPD—a specialist does that.

Q. Can we become addicted to our illness?

A. I would personally say no, but we can get so used to the chaos in our lives and the attention we can receive due to the BPD that, when we start to recover, we actually self-sabotage just so we are back again in the chaos and receiving attention. It's partly due to our fear of abandonment and partly due to the fact that this is the only life we know—anything that seems different can at first seem scary. In time we can learn to let go of the chaos, however, and embrace the peace and calm.

Q. Can cannabis help with my BPD?

A. I personally say no. It is another mind-altering substance, so all we would be doing is swapping one unhealthy coping mechanism for another. Instead, we need to learn healthy coping skills rather than trying to mask our feelings.

Q. Myself and my partner both have BPD. Can our relationship work?

A. Yes, it can, but only if you are both trying to treat your BPD. If one of you is in therapy and the other isn't, there are going to be lots of problems along the way. You both need to be focused on your recovery—and you both need to focus on your *own* recovery—not each other's. Chances are, you will still have your ups and downs, but the positive is that you will understand one another.

Q. What is the difference between a healthy crush and an obsession?

A. A crush tends to not last a really long time, whereas an obsession does. With a crush, you may think about the other person a bit too much, but it won't affect our day-to-day life. An obsession takes over our mind and we are consumed with thoughts of this person—it interferes with our life. With a crush, we may have a fantasy about them in our head—but we are able to distinguish between this and reality. With an obsession, we can lose sight of reality and start living in the fantasy world. If we have a crush on someone and we "turn up" somewhere hoping to bump into them, this is quite normal. If we start turning up everywhere that this person goes, this is obsessive.

Chapter 30

# THEN AND NOW

*"You can't go back and change the beginning, but you can start where*
*you are and change the ending."*
—C. S. Lewis

For this chapter, I invited people who know me well to reflect on
my recovery. I hope that these additional perspectives give us all
confidence that we, too, can recover. The final story is my own.

**Esther Rooney, My Mother**

I contemplate Shehrina's journey in wonder and bewilderment.
Fifteen to twenty years ago our lives, my life, were so torn apart and
shattered to smithereens from seeing my beautiful, clever, warm, caring,
and compassionate daughter going from being all of these things to
something which would not have looked out of place in an adaptation
of *The Exorcist*—and I don't say that whimsically. Shehrina had become
nothing short of what could only be described as someone possessed by
the most wretched of demons, with crippling consequences.

Looking back, I think it was as if it had insidiously crept upon us
gradually and almost imperceptibly before our very eyes, with certainly
myself just accepting that this was so ghastly and horrible but also just
normal explosive teenage behavior, and that Shehrina and all of us were
only at the mercy of her raging hormones, coupled with a personality
tending toward and prone to extreme emotion, nothing more, nothing
less. But the teenage years went by and Shehrina was now in her twenties, and the BPD had hold of her with a vengeance, crushing everyone
and everything around and about her, not least and more harrowingly
herself!!

I say "wonder and bewilderment" because today our lives have taken a 360-degree rotation from nothing but bleakness, despair, horror, and uncertainty with what was to come next, so out of control was Shehrina's life, to a life of joy and happiness, tranquility, and freedom to hope and dream.

The demon has been banished and left behind that beautiful, clever, warm, compassionate, and, might I say, truly amazing woman...my daughter.

To see how she manages to not only be ebulliently happy, fulfilled, and always smiling—yes, now really smiling, no longer a smile with a thinly veiled deep sadness and emptiness, but truly beaming—but to also bring joy and laughter and so much hope to so very many who are suffering the desperation and hopelessness of the debilitating curse of BPD and to give them the belief and knowledge that they too can have what Shehrina now has: contentment and belief in oneself.

Welcome back, Shehrina.

### Yolanda Williams, My Mental Health Therapist, 2003–2008

Shehrina arrived like a shooting star from the skies and landed with an explosion into our Anger Management group.

In the time that followed, we shared her sadness, her fears, her chaos, her pain, her joys, her depression, her anxiety, her low self-esteem, her dreams, her dreads, her exhaustion, her drive, her creativity, her numbness, her hopes, and her hopelessness.

I shared these times with Shehrina, her lovely mum, Esther, and her then-boyfriend. Together we worked at singing from the same song sheet, learning with Shehrina what was working and wasn't working—we shared the frightening times of suicidal high risk and other times when she would have glimpses of hope break through the darkness.

I think that the best achievement for me was watching Shehrina learn to believe and trust in the therapeutic relationship, something she was able to build again with other professionals during her journey to recovery, the ability to move from a position of deep mistrust to trust.

After getting married and having her first adorable baby, we had to abandon the idea of her exploring past trauma, in the second stage of DBT and the psychotherapy that she'd needed, for another time. But she left with some skills to build on, a better understanding of herself and her condition, and I hope a knowledge of how hugely proud I was to have walked those first rocky steps with her and her family and to later see her hard work over many years result in the wise, confident, inspiring, creative, and beautiful woman she has become.

## Sarah Irwin, Care Coordinator/Registered Mental Health Nurse, 2014-2016

I met Shehrina when she was pregnant with her third child. She had been unable to get an appointment with the mental health team for some time, due to thresholds for admissions. This was frustrating for her.

However, she turned up in the pouring rain and described a journey to Bournemouth that was littered with difficult and challenging situations.

I heard a story of a woman who had experienced abuse and hurt herself. Over time, we explored how she had used these experiences to grow rather than fade away. She was also realistic about pacing herself to get to the next part of her journey. She was clear about what she needed to do: get to the place she wanted to go and figure out what she needed to avoid.

She told me that the theory from the Big Book of AA and other educational sessions, such as counseling, had informed her internal dialogue.

It was very memorable, her sense of empowerment about her own responsibility and ability to take control. She believed in the possibility of a different life. She had hope for her future.

She continued to have challenges, such as being separated from her two children. During her pregnancy, she was tormented with intrusive thoughts that could have derailed her from her goals. So it wasn't easy— it wasn't a straight line from A to B.

She made the situation she was in work for her and continued to battle her own demons.

After a while, Shehrina no longer needed a community care nurse, and her vlog, Recovery Mum, and her active life were keeping her busy. I asked her to come to the university with me to talk to student nurses about her diagnosis and journey. Sharing her experience of her own recovery journey was very brave. She is very inspiring—her attitude inspires hope that change is possible.

I love the way she is open about her diagnosis in a society where mental health issues are so hidden.

## Cathrine Appleton, Best Friend Since 2000

Shehrina and I have been friends for more years than not. Back then I always knew Shehrina was destined for great things. She had the most amazing charm about her, was so kind and made me laugh until I cried. But I also knew how difficult life was for her, because I often had the same fears and feelings and we were able to share them with one another.

So many people didn't understand us and more often than not we were gossiped about and judged. We were fortunate that we had a friendship based on acceptance and were able to laugh, even briefly, at the predicaments we got ourselves in and were able to empower one another.

Being part of Shehrina's life and watching her stick two fingers up at the world who didn't believe in her has inspired myself and so many others. I couldn't be prouder to call her my best friend.

I love this lady, she has been to hell and back more times than I need to mention, but when she went through those awful, painful times, she came back stronger and wiser. She survived and I am so grateful that she did because now she is showing the world her success, she is sharing her methods with people who suffer with their own mental health illness and addictions, and is proving that recovery is possible!

## Carl Rooney, My Brother

My memories of ever having a good relationship with my sister when we were younger are non-existent. She would spend her time screaming, shouting and running away from home or stealing money from me and our Mum.

In her teenage years, living with her was hell and things did not improve as she went in to her twenties, only now I had the choice to move away from the chaos at home. I knew at this point she was addicted to cocaine as she had told me so. I knew our Mum would lend money to her from time to time and tried to advise her against this as I knew what it was being spent on, but I don't think our Mum wanted to face up to this harsh reality at this point. My relationship with my sister only continued to worsen until it was non-existent.

Whilst working abroad I would sometimes hear stories from my family about how Shehrina really wasn't doing very well. It saddened me but I knew I couldn't be the one to save her and so I purposefully blocked her from my mind.

My Mum continued to have problems with my sister, finding her passed out in the road, violent attacks against herself where she would smash her head into the wall, numerous suicide attempts, punching me in the face, attacking our Mum, being admitted to a mental health ward, the list is endless. And then I heard the news that she was pregnant. All I could think was "but she can't even take care of herself—what a moron!" The birth of her first child came and then her second and about a year later she finally started to realize she had a problem. It was a very emotional time for her as she had hit rock bottom, but now there was only one way for her to go—up!

She went to rehab and spent seven months there before deciding to relocate somewhere a few hours from home. I think this is where her miracle started to happen. She fell in love and went on to have two more children. I personally think that her children saved her as she loves them all so much.

I strongly believe that anything is possible. Wherever you are in the world right now, I want you to know that if my sister can change, then anyone can.

As the months and then the years go by my sister is continuing to improve and become a nicer person, far nicer than ever before. She is a wonderful Mum now and my relationship with her has finally healed, with us communicating weekly with one another. Our relationship used to feel as if we were on a rollercoaster, but nowadays we are very close and finally have a wonderful brotherly-sisterly love.

## A Message From My Doctor, Dr. Menzies Schrader, Associate Specialist Psychiatrist, 2014-Current

As a clinician, and a human being, it can be very rewarding helping people to achieve the improvements that they want to make in moving towards a better quality of life. At the start of this journey, it is often not easy, as the individual patient might not yet recognize or consider what journey it is that they are undertaking. It can be very difficult to hear about a 'personality disorder', the stigma, the misunderstanding, the confusion and the disbelief in relation to this. Yet, it can also make sense of some of the difficulties that have been occurring up to the point of considering this. Many people get hung up on a 'diagnosis' or 'label'. These are often just ways for us, the professionals, to consider what the best evidenced based pathway is that will provide the best assistance and improvement.

Once we are on that path, and are in a place to consider options available, we see our patients begin to make a difference in their lives. For most individuals, this is a psychological intervention that enables development and improvement in life management skills. Sometimes, medications can be helpful but these are not always easy to tolerate, and we should not consider these as the answer. We know this is not an easy process, we understand the difficulties that many will face in taking these steps, but the eventual outcome can be a very positive life-affirming change.

I have been engaged in a therapeutic alliance alongside Miss Rooney for several years. I have seen the journey that she has taken, the ups and the downs and commitment being tested at times. She has stayed the path despite these challenges and draw-backs to the old default ways of attempting to address things. Even though those testing times arose, she persevered and has continued to manage her life with her skill processes every day.

The message is clear: it will be difficult at times, it will appear impossible at others, we might hear things we do not want to hear or accept, and we might not even believe that things can be different. But, if you persevere, take advice and use it even when it is hard to consider, you will achieve the change you want to make.

**Shehrina**

Looking back on the person I once was, I hardly recognize myself. I look back and see a child who was very lost and helpless, unable to see the light at the end of the tunnel and believing that nothing positive lay ahead.

Relationships saturated with abuse, self-harming to help me cope, using drugs and alcohol just to survive, vomiting daily—I believed that these would make me more likable. I pushed anyone who truly cared about me as far away as possible.

I spent years feeling not only as if I had hit rock bottom but that I was stuck there, sinking ever deeper and deeper into the ground. I didn't believe that there was any way out, and therefore I didn't see any point in trying to muster up the energy to even try to escape. I desperately jumped from one relationship to another, under the illusion that someone else had the power to save me. In fact, I always believed that recovery would come if only I could discover the external solution. Not for a moment did I consider the possibility that the solution didn't consist of other people, places, or things; it was internal—it lay within me.

For anyone who says that recovery is easy, it is not. Having had to put down the drink and the drugs, I had nothing to numb my extreme emotions. I was "feeling" for the first time in years and it was painful. I could have quite easily reverted back to my old ways, the ways that came naturally to me and gave me instant relief from how I felt. I suppose what stopped me from doing this was the realization that my "old behaviors" inevitably produced a whole load of other problems. Imagine a boiled egg that is still in its shell but has been dropped on the floor repeatedly. That was me—cracked and damaged all over. Using drugs and drinking alcohol were akin to sticking plasters on the cracked egg—they may have covered the cracks temporarily, but the cracks were still there, and eventually the plaster started peeling off, revealing the damage underneath.

Rather than plastering over the problems in my life, I finally had to face them head on—or continue as I was, living a life of pain and suffering. I was sick and tired of feeling sick and tired.

Today, when I wake up in the morning, I don't necessarily bounce out of bed shouting that I am thankful to be alive. But the truth is, I *am* happy to be alive today. It is strange, but all the things that your average person would take for granted are the things that mean so much to me. Sitting on the floor and playing games with my kids, walking into a shop, chatting with the mums at the school, falling asleep with ease, communicating how I feel without it turning into the most humongous argument, not hating myself, being assertive, having meaningful and healthy relationships, being able to recognize when I am wrong and do something about it, and laughing—not a fake laugh or a laugh to fit in with others but a real laugh, a laugh that causes my belly to ache because I feel so wonderful inside. I no longer live in fear of my emotions. That's not to say I don't get emotional, but they no longer have the power to consume me, they no longer control me.

Today I can be myself, and, although I'm not perfect, I am okay with that because I am real. I no longer spend my days worrying about what others think of me or trying desperately to fit in somewhere that I may not belong.

I no longer waste my time living in the past or fearing for my future. I can enjoy the present moment. I am happy, content, and free. If someone had told me this is how I would one day feel, all those years ago, I may have laughed in their face. I didn't ever believe it was a possibility for me. But here I am and I want to make it my mission to let you know that there *is* light at the end of the tunnel and you too can live a happy, contented life, a life free from BPD.

# REFERENCES

Gunderson JG: Borderline Personality Disorder: A Clinical Guide. Washington, DC, American Psychiatric Press, 2001.

Jogems-Kosterman, B. J. M., D. W. W. de Knijff, R. Kusters, J. J. M. van Hoof. 2008. "Basal Cortisol and DHEA Levels in Women with Borderline Personality Disorder." *Journal of Psychiatric Research* 41 (12): 1,019-26. DOI: 10.1016/j.jpsychires.2006.07.019.

Redmayne, K. 2015. "It's All In Your Head: Borderline Personality Disorder and the Brain" *Medium* May 23. https://medium.com/@KevinRedmayne/its-all-in-your-head-borderline-personality-disorder-and-the-brain-c14b66eb0966.

Ruocco, A. C., S. Amirthavasagam, L. W. Choi-Kain, S. F. McMain. 2013. "Neural Correlates of Negative Emotionality in Borderline Personality Disorder: An Activation-Likelihood-Estimation Meta-Analysis." Biological Psychiatry 73 (2): 153–160. DOI: https://doi.org/10.1016/j.biopsych.2012.07.014.

Weill Cornell Medicine. 2007. "Scientists Identify Brain Abnormalities Underlying Key Element of Borderline Personality Disorder." Newsroom, Weill Cornell Medicine, Office of External Affairs. https://news.weill.cornell.edu/news/2007/12/scientists-identify-brain-abnormalities-underlying-key-element-of-borderline-personality-disorder.

McGlashan TH, Grilo CM, Skodol AE, et al. The Collaborative Longitudinal Personality Disorders Study: baseline Axis I/II and II/II diagnostic co-occurrence. Acta Psychiatr Scand. 2000; 102:256-264.

National Health Service. "Mental health problems and pregnancy." Accessed September 24, 2018. https://www.nhs.uk/conditions/pregnancy-and-baby/mental-health-problems-pregnant/.

# ACKNOWLEDGEMENTS

Sitting down and writing the acknowledgments for this book has proven more difficult than writing the book itself. For it is not only those who were around whilst I wrote the book that I need to thank, but also everyone who got me to the point in which I was able to write a book. If it had not been for these people, who knows where I would be now—certainly not in recovery.

First and foremost I need to thank my Mum, my real life hero, who stuck by me through the darkest of times, never allowing herself to be influenced by others that I was a hopeless case. Mum, I know I dragged you through hell and back and I am so grateful that you never once let go of my hand, holding on to me and showing me the true meaning of a Mother's love. I love you to the moon and back and then some and am eternally grateful that I was blessed with you as my Mum.

Lee, my amazing step-dad. I hate to call you a 'step-dad' because you are so much more than that to me. I thank you for everything you do for me and the children and most importantly for being there as a rock for Mum. You have been a tower of strength for all of us and we are so lucky to have you.

My little brother Carl, thank you for being you. Your positivity and sense of humour abounds and you truly are an inspiration.

My darling children, thank you for making me smile, for my cuddles and for the various ways in which you all amaze me. Thank you for the never-ending laughs, from telling your teachers that 'Mummy makes adult films on YouTube' to asking me "Is it the BPD?' when I've had a bad day. You make my recovery so worthwhile and I love you with all my heart.

My partner, Darren, for teaching me patience and tolerance! Thank you for always saying just the right thing when I feel down, for boosting my confidence when I'm doubting myself and for all the loves. Thank you, thank you, thank you.

My Dad, Ann and Daniel. Thank you for always being there and loving me even when I was at my most horrid. I love you higher than the sky.

Megan Hunter, my publisher, my business partner and more importantly, my dear friend. Thank you for having faith in me and for allowing me to be me. You are a ray of sunshine that has come in to my life and I am so very glad that you did—we all need a bit of sunshine!

Ann Stavrou, thank you for all the times you were there for me, a shoulder to cry on and someone to confide in. Thank you for being there for my Mum and helping her through the difficult times. We love you so much.

Cat, my partner in crime and one that has shown me the utmost love and loyalty throughout our years of friendship. Thank you for 'getting me' when many didn't. Probably the quote that best describes us is "So you think I'm crazy? You should see me with my best friend"! Thank you for the years of love, laughter and tears—may they long continue!

Joanne Lynch and Eve Davidson, my recovery friends who helped me through the difficult early stages and whom both inspire me to this day. You both came into my life at a time when I needed some friends the most. All three of us distrusted other women to the max and yet we somehow overcame this distrust and the most beautiful friendships developed. I love you girlies—thank you for being in my life.

My mental health team, Yolanda Williams, Sarah Irwin and Dr Schrader. I am so fortunate to have had such amazing people responsible for my care. You have all shown me both compassion and guidance when I needed it most and for that I can never thank you enough.

Ann Brown and Nicole, thank you for doing everything you could to get me in to rehab when I so desperately needed it and for your continued support throughout my time there.

The Sunshine Team, the specialist midwives who helped me through my last two pregnancies and the wonderful student midwife, Kathryn Mercer, who not only held my hand through the pregnancy but also through the birth! Thank you so much.

Thank you, all the staff at Clouds House and Quinton House, where my recovery from addiction all began. Thank you Lorraine Parry and a very special thank you to Sue Russell and Maria Laderia for helping me through my time at Quinton House. Without these amazing women, my time there would have been so much more painful. Thank you for supporting me, always being an ear to listen and always there to offer me guidance, even if I didn't always take it! Thank you.

My family —my wonderful Nan, aunts, uncles and cousins. There are simply too many of you to name individually but you all know who you are! Thank you for all you do. I love you all so much.

Mỹ Tran, thank you for listening to me go on and on and on about the book every single week and thank you for never judging me on my past and for being a truly wonderful friend. You are a beautiful person inside and out my dear.

Jeff Trace, thank you for all your wisdom, kind words and for always being so excited for me—friends like you are hard to come by.

To all the staff at both my children's nursery and my children's' school. You have never judged me as a Mother due to my history, but instead have offered me support and kindness. Every day I am happy to drop my children off to you knowing that they are in the safest hands. Thank you so much for all you do.

Chambers Solicitors—thank you for allowing my Mum to take a year off work to look after my children so that I could recover. Not all workplaces would have been as understanding and I want you to know that I am so grateful for your kindness.

Thank you to my editors, Jess Been and Marisa Solis, for all your hard work and wonderful advice.

Thank you to the designers who made my book pretty! Julian Leon at The Missive and Jeffrey Fuller at Shelfish—thank you.

A huge thank you to all the wonderful Mummies at the school, not only do you make the school drop off and pick up so much more fun, you have also all been so wonderfully supportive and non-judgemental. You are all so amazing.

Thank you to the Children's Centre, particularly Talene Radja-bi-Pittwood. Talene, thank you for all the support in the early days of my recovery and for not giving up on me, even when I was rubbish at answering my phone!

Tim Judge, thank you for taking my photos and not leaving until I was happy! You are a star!

My fellow YouTuber, Cory. Thank you for taking the time to read through my manuscript and for being there as a friend that I can talk to. You rock!

Thank you to all those who have played a part in my recovery within the 12 step meetings and recovery workshops at CMHT. Being amongst others that understood me and never judged me was freeing and enabled me to be myself. Thank you all.

And last but by no means least—thank you to my super-duper, amazingly wonderful, strong and loyal subscribers. Thank you all for not only watching my videos but for sharing your stories with me. You guys help me more than you will ever know and for that I thank you with all my heart. I love you guys!

# RESOURCES

BPDtribe.com (for those with BPD and their families) (UK & US)

EmotionsMatterBPD.org (US)

Hopeforbpd.com (US)

PDAN.org (Personality Disorder Awareness Network) (US)

BPDfoundation.org.au (Australia)

Mind for better mental health: https://bit.ly/2q3mqEb (UK)

BPDfamily.com (US)

Behavioraltech.org/resources/find-a-therapist/

Nyp.org

Borderlinepersonalitydisorder.com

Suicide.org/international-suicide-hotlines.html

BPDcentral.com

# ABOUT THE AUTHOR

Shehrina Rooney founded the YouTube channel Recovery Mum in 2015, which has grown to more than 10,000 subscribers in 3 years, and co-founded The BPD Tribe website in 2018. She was diagnosed with borderline personality disorder (BPD) at age 21, after struggling for more than half her life with fear of abandonment, self-hatred, anger, and eventually addiction. Although dialectical behavior therapy helped, her "dark years" continued into motherhood and through a divorce. Attending 12-step meetings, she realized peer support could work for BPD, too. Today, she dedicates her life to encouraging and teaching others who face the same struggles. She is grateful to have the skills to calm her emotions and be a wonderful mum.

Shehrina's websites are:

bpdtribe.com

recoverymum.com

YouTube: Recovery Mum

# More Books by Unhooked Books

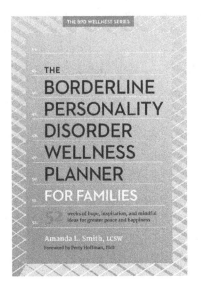

## UNHOOKED BOOKS
An Imprint of High Conflict Institute Press
Scottsdale, Arizona

9 781936 268610